BENJAMIN FRANKLIN

An American Man of Letters

BENJAMIN FRANKLIN

An American Man of Letters

By

BRUCE INGHAM GRANGER

Department of English, University of Oklahoma

UNIVERSITY OF OKLAHOMA PRESS : NORMAN

By Bruce Ingham Granger

Political Satire in the American Revolution, 1763–1783
   (Ithaca, 1960; New York, 1971)
Benjamin Franklin: An American Man of Letters (Ithaca,
   1964; Norman, 1976)

To

PERK AND ADAM

Preface

BENJAMIN FRANKLIN is an important American man of letters. If such a statement does not seem a sufficiently bold thesis, we should remember how often and vigorously it has been denied. To be sure, the critical majority from the time of David Hume have placed him high in the world of English letters, but a significant minority have assigned him to a low station or excluded him altogether. In 1889 Paul Leicester Ford, to name one of the most formidable of the dissenters, stated flatly that Franklin "never was a literary man in the true common meaning of the term." Like many other critics before and since, Ford is here guilty of applying the wrong yardstick, of measuring Franklin the writer against a definition of literature that does not accord with what we now know about colonial culture.

Because the canon of Franklin's writings has been greatly expanded and revised since John Bach McMaster published *Benjamin Franklin as a Man of Letters* in 1887, a new study is needed. And the fact that a definitive edition, *The Papers of Benjamin Franklin,* is in process makes one timely. Because the present volume undertakes to examine and assess Franklin's achievement in the world of letters, the focus throughout is on those writings that have belletristic qualities, not on scientific and official papers except as they are treated incidentally. Since to divorce Franklin the writer from his times would be to misrepresent his achievement, these works are studied in the historical and biographical context that called them forth. The organization by chapter is loosely generic and chronological.

Of the many who have contributed to the making of this volume I am particularly grateful to Dennis Baumwoll, Whitfield J. Bell, Jr., Willis Bowen, David P. French, Jack Grigsby, and Leonard W. Labaree; to the staffs of the American Philosophical Society Library, the Historical Society of Pennsylvania, and the Yale University Library; to the American Philosophical Society for a grant-in-aid in the summer of 1958; and to the Faculty Research Committee of the University of Oklahoma for largely defraying travel and clerical expenses. I am grateful also to the editors of *American Heritage* for granting permission to use material from my article, "'We Shall Eat Apples of Paradise,'" which appeared in the June 1959 issue.

BRUCE INGHAM GRANGER

Norman, Oklahoma
February 1964

Contents

BENJAMIN FRANKLIN

An American Man of Letters

I

Literary Background

"AMERICA has sent us many good things," Hume assured Franklin in 1762, "gold, silver, sugar, tobacco, indigo, &c.; but you are the first philosopher, and indeed the first great man of letters for whom we are beholden to her."[1] There was ample warrant for the high praise this Scottish man of letters bestowed on the American Doctor who had met him in Edinburgh three years before. Already Franklin had distinguished himself in such popular types as the periodical essay, the almanac, and the personal letter; ahead lay most of his letters to the press, his familiar letters and bagatelles, and the *Autobiography*. Wherever his curiosity and genius led him, throughout a seventy-year career he conceived of himself first and always as "B. Franklin, Printer," in which capacity the written word spoke louder than the deed.

[1] *The Writings of Benjamin Franklin*, ed. Albert H. Smyth (New York and London, 1905–1907), IV, 154; referred to hereafter as Smyth. Priority will be given to the texts in *The Papers of Benjamin Franklin*, ed. Leonard W. Labaree and Others, I–VII (New Haven, 1959–1963); referred to hereafter as Labaree.

I

The literary environment at home and abroad in which Franklin's genius grew and flourished was predominantly neoclassical. Fundamental to the theory, if not always the practice, of neoclassicism was an insistence on what Arthur Lovejoy calls "aesthetic uniformitarianism," requiring that literature appeal to that reason which is fixed and universal in human nature.[2] The bulk of Franklin's writings, especially his pamphleteering and letters to the press at Philadelphia, London, and Paris, confidently appeal to human reason. This appeal imposed on the neoclassical writer a sense of social responsibility. "I shall venture to lay it down as a Maxim," writes Franklin early in his career, *"That no Piece can properly be called good, and well written, which is void of any Tendency to benefit the Reader, either by improving his Virtue or his Knowledge."*[3] Ahead of even the art of writing Franklin set the art of living virtuously. In essential agreement with Bunyan, Defoe, Addison, and Cotton Mather, whose work he early admired, he sought in all his most belletristic writings, down to the most whimsical of his letters and bagatelles, to educate the mind and conscience of his age.

Although American literature would not experience a neoclassical flowering until the time of the Revolution, the New England of Franklin's boyhood (1706–1723) was already feeling the impact of English neoclassicism. In spite of the desperate efforts of the Mather party to maintain the *status quo* in Massachusetts, the Puritan oligarchy was being seriously challenged by popular forces from

[2]*Mod. Phil.*, XXIX (1932), 291–292.

[3]*Pennsylvania Gazette*, Aug. 2, 1733; reprinted in Labaree, I, 331.

within and without its ranks. As the intellectual climate grew more and more worldly, members of both the Mather and anti-Mather factions began to realize "that greater attention must be paid to elegance, grace, and ease."[4] The immediate popularity of the English periodical essay in America and early efforts to emulate it are striking testimony that late seventeenth-century plain style was becoming more richly varied and urbane in the early eighteenth century. In 1726, the year he launched his almanac at Boston, Nathaniel Ames informed his readers that he was exposing himself for their sake "to the dangerous & sharp Teeth of envious Detractors, which is a great Hazard especially in this polish'd Age, among so many fine & curious Wits, who scarcely can approve of anything, tho' never so Judiciously Composed."[5] This same year Cotton Mather, who had himself attained variety and sophistication of expression long ago, urged candidates for the ministry to adopt a tolerant attitude toward literary style: "I wonder what ails People, that they can't let *Cicero* write in the *Style* of *Cicero,* and *Seneca* write in the (much other!) *Style* of *Seneca;* and own that *Both* may please in their *several* Ways."[6] At least as early as his sixteenth year Franklin's instinct for plain and even coarse expression was confronted by the urbanity of Addison, which tension gave rise in time to a range of styles far wider than Mather's.[7]

[4]Perry Miller, *The New England Mind: From Colony to Province* (Cambridge, Mass., 1953), p. 395.

[5]*The Essays, Humor, and Poems of Nathaniel Ames,* ed. Samuel Briggs (Cleveland, 1891), p. 50.

[6]*Manuductio ad Ministerium* (Boston, 1726), p. 46.

[7]H. M. Jones, *Hunt. Lib. Bul.,* VI (1934), tracing the direction in

In such an atmosphere Boston-born Franklin grew up and first took literary flight. It is fortunate that Josiah Franklin did not carry out his intention of seeing this tithe of his sons trained for the ministry, for assuredly "the Harvard of that day would have choked or expelled him."[8] More important by far than the scant two years of formal schooling he did receive was the plan of self-education on which he early embarked. In the course of these eclectic studies, in his father's and Matthew Adams' libraries and at his brother's newspaper office, young Benjamin's theory of literary expression was shaped largely by the Port-Royalists and Locke and his practice, by the prose of Bunyan, Defoe, Addison, and Swift.

The boy not only read widely, he tried his hand at writing verse. Uncle Benjamin, who encouraged his namesake in these efforts, early prophesied,

> This Forward Spring Foretells a plentious crop,
> For if the bud bear Graine what will the Top?[9]

When in after years a French critic observed that he wrote poetry, Franklin is said to have replied: "Not poetry. I have written verse all my life only for one reason—because it crystallizes my prose."[10] The reply, if apocryphal, is

---

which American prose style moved between 1700 and 1770, over-simplifies Franklin's stylistic development when he writes, "I shall assume that the movement of progress is the movement in the direction of plainness and lucidity—in the direction which Franklin represents" (p. 118).

[8] James Parton, *Life and Times of Benjamin Franklin* (Boston and New York, 1864), II, 641.

[9] Labaree, I, 5.

[10] Willis Steell, *Benjamin Franklin of Paris* (New York, 1928), pp. 196–197.

certainly true in spirit. Conscious of how much he had learned from such exercises, he recommended for fifth-year students at the English School in Philadelphia the writing of verse, "for this Reason, that nothing acquaints a Lad so speedily with Variety of Expression, as the Necessity of finding such Words and Phrases as will suit with the Measure, Sound and Rhime of Verse, and at the same Time well express the Sentiment." When he first ventured into prose, the discipline gained from writing verse had so far matured his manner of expression that his brother James and the other Couranteers supposed the author of the *Dogood* papers to be a man "of some Character among us for Learning & Ingenuity."[11]

II

Before examining Franklin's views on what he called *"Writing well* in his Mother Tongue,"[12] a word about those books on logic, rhetoric, and grammar which seem to have influenced him most powerfully and those authors by whose example he profited. Arnauld and Nicole's *Port-Royal Logic* (Paris, 1662), by setting reason above authority as the court of highest appeal,[13] helped free his mind from the Calvinist conviction that the ultimate purpose of logic is (in the words of Alexander Richardson) "to direct

[11]*Benjamin Franklin's Memoirs. Parallel Text Edition,* ed. Max Farrand (Berkeley and Los Angeles, 1949), p. 46; referred to hereafter as *Par. Text Ed.* Except toward the end of Chapter VIII (and then for reasons explained in the Appendix), I shall give the manuscript reading when quoting the *Autobiography.*

[12]Labaree, I, 328.

[13]Wilbur Samuel Howell, *Logic and Rhetoric in England, 1500– 1700* (Princeton, 1956), p. 360.

5

man to see the wisdom of God."[14] Logic they define less
dogmatically than the Calvinists as "the Art of directing
reason aright, in obtaining the knowledge of things, for
the instruction both of ourselves and others."[15] The empiri-
cal young Franklin, who was reared "piously in the Dis-
senting Way," must have welcomed with enthusiasm this
"modern" method of approaching truth. In its general
syllogistic form, for example, his London pamphlet, *A
Dissertation on Liberty and Necessity* (1725), observes the
eight rules set forth at the end of *The Port-Royal Logic*.[16]
Symbolic of the distance separating him from the scholarly
community at Boston is the fact that well into the eighteenth century the theses delivered annually at nearby
Harvard College continued to observe the older, more
authoritarian method.

In addition to John Locke's *Essay concerning Human
Understanding* (1690), which Franklin read at an early
age, it seems probable that he was acquainted with Bernard
Lamy's popular rhetoric, *The Art of Speaking* (Paris,
1675); at least, it is listed in 1722 as being on sale at his
brother's newspaper office. "Great care is to be taken,"
warns Lamy, in a passage foreshadowing Locke, "that we
use no Tropes, but where we must express our selves im-
perfectly without them; and when we are obliged to use
them, they must have two qualities; one is, they must be
clear, and contribute to the understanding of what we
intend, seeing the only use of them is to make us more

[14]Quoted in Perry Miller, *The New England Mind: The Seventeenth Century* (New York, 1939), p. 160.

[15]*The Port-Royal Logic,* trans. T. S. Baynes (2d ed.; Edinburgh
and London, 1851), p. 25.

[16]See *The Port-Royal Logic,* pp. 346–347, and Labaree, I, 58.

intelligible; the other is, that they hold proportion with the Idea we design to delineate."[17] In a fundamental and comprehensive sense Locke, who foresaw the main course that rhetoric would take in the eighteenth century, was one of Franklin's most important teachers. Proceeding on an assumption the Port-Royalists had made a generation earlier, that "words, in their primary or immediate signification, stand for nothing but *the ideas in the mind of him that uses them*," Locke emphasizes the importance of using language in a responsible fashion at all times: "If we would speak of things as they are, we must allow that all the art of rhetoric, besides order and clearness; all the artificial and figurative applications of words eloquence hath invented, are for nothing else but to insinuate wrong ideas, move the passions, and thereby mislead the judgment; and so indeed are perfect cheats."[18] Such a view of rhetoric was favorably received by the majority of neoclassical writers, whose final appeal was ever to reason. "I shall not attempt to amuse you with Flourishes of Rhetorick," promises the young Franklin. "I intend to offer you nothing but plain Reasoning, devoid of Art and Ornament; unsupported by the Authority of any Books or Men how sacred soever; because I know that no Authority is more convincing to Men of Reason than the Authority of Reason itself."[19] Sharing in the general Protestant distrust of the whole realm of sense, he confined himself

[17]*The Art of Speaking* (2d ed.; London, 1708), p. 65.

[18]*An Essay concerning Human Understanding*, ed. A. C. Fraser (Oxford, 1894), II, 9, 146.

[19]"On the Providence of God in the Government of the World," Commonplace Book, [1731–1732?], Hist. Soc. Pa. MS, p. 64; printed in Labaree, I, 264, 265.

just as rigorously as his great American contemporary, Jonathan Edwards, to such easily controlled tropes and rhetorical figures as metaphor, simile, analogy, illustration, and example.

In the Preface to *An Essay towards a Practical English Grammar* (1711), a handbook Franklin recalled having read as a boy, James Greenwood deplores the fact that youth are taught "Grammar in Latin, before they have learned any thing of it in English," and urges that English grammar be taught first in the schools. Within a few years Hugh Jones, author of the first English grammar written in America, was stressing the importance of learning to read, write, and talk "proper English [meaning London English]; without which no Englishman, of what condition soever he be, can make any tolerable figure."[20] In 1749 Franklin proposed that at the College of Philadelphia "the English Language might be taught by Grammar; in which some of our best Writers, as Tillotson, Addison, Pope, Algernon Sidney, Cato's Letters, &c. should be Classicks: The *Stiles* principally to be cultivated, being the *clear* and the *concise*." Forty years later he was so vexed to see how the Latin School of Philadelphia had prospered at the expense of the English School that he dubbed Latin and Greek "the *Chapeau bras* of modern Literature," that is, a still prevailing custom no longer serving any useful end. Again, Franklin's concern for instruction in the vernacular and composition in English stands opposed to that of the Harvard scholars, who came around to this view only slowly.[21]

[20]*The Present State of Virginia* (London, 1724), ed. Richard L. Morton (Chapel Hill, 1956), p. 18.

[21]Porter G. Perrin, "The Teaching of Rhetoric in the American

Bunyan, Defoe, Addison, and Swift are the writers who figure most prominently in the development of Franklin's prose style. "Honest John" Bunyan he describes as "the first that I know of who mix'd Narration & Dialogue, a Method of Writing very engaging to the Reader, who in the most interesting Parts finds himself as it were brought into the Company, & present at the Discourse."[22] Franklin frequently employed Bunyan's semidramatic method, in his periodical essays, almanac writings, letters public and private, bagatelles, and autobiographical writings. In a statement at the end of *An Essay on Projects,* one that defines the main stream of Franklin's prose as well, Defoe explains that he has chosen rather to write in a language "free and familiar, according to the nature of essays, than to strain at a perfection of language which I rather wish for than pretend to be master of." It should be noted here that James Franklin, from whose caustic manner in the *New-England Courant* young Benjamin learned much, had long held Defoe's journalistic writings in high esteem. Forty years before Hugh Blair, in his *Lectures on Rhetoric and Belles Lettres* advised those who wished to acquire "a proper style" to possess fully the thoughts on "a page of one of Mr. Addison's papers," rewrite the passage from memory, and then compare the two (Lecture XIX), Franklin engaged in similar exercises. Like Samuel Johnson he admired Addison's "middle style," though his own was never so urbane. Although Franklin nowhere expresses his indebtedness to Swift so explicitly as he does to Addison, Swift's influence was at work early. By 1722 the *Courant*

Colleges before 1750" (unpublished dissertation, Univ. of Chicago, 1936), pp. 56–57.

[22]*Par. Text Ed.* p. 54.

library had in its possession *A Tale of a Tub,* and it is clear that before his twenty-eighth year Franklin had encountered *A Proposal for Correcting, Improving, and Ascertaining the English Tongue* and *A Letter to a Young Gentleman, Lately enter'd into Holy Orders.*[23] What Martin Price has said applies equally well to Franklin, that the rhetorical end Swift "typically sets himself is teaching men to distinguish their true interest from plausible deception."[24] Cherishing virtue as dearly as the Dean, Franklin, without ever abandoning the urbanity acquired from the example of Addison, attacks academic and literary dullness, the tyranny of church and state, astrology, British mercantilism.

III

John Hughes's "Of Style" (1698), often cited as a manifesto of neoclassicism, clearly prefigures Franklin's literary theory:

All the Qualifications of a good Style I think may be reduced under these four Heads, *Propriety, Perspicuity, Elegance,* and *Cadence:* And each of these, except the last, has some relation to the Thoughts, as well as to the Words. Propriety of Thoughts is two-fold; the first is when the Thoughts are proper in themselves, and so it is opposed to Nonsense; and the other when they are proper to the Occasion, and so it is opposed to Impertinence. Propriety of Words, the first Qualification of a good Style, is when the Words do justly and exactly represent, or signify, the Thoughts which they stand for.... There is another Particular which I shall mention here, because I think it differs but little from *Propriety,* and that is *Purity,* which I take

[23]See Labaree, I, 329.
[24]*Swift's Rhetorical Art* (New Haven, 1953), p. 66.

10

more particularly to respect the Language, as it is now spoke
or written.... Little need be said of the second Qualification, *viz. Perspicuity.* If your Thoughts be not clear, 'tis
impossible your Words shou'd, and consequently you can't
be understood.... *Elegance* of *Thought* is what we com-
monly call *Wit,* which adds to Propriety, Beauty, and pleases
our Fancy, while Propriety entertains our Judgment....
The last Qualification I mention'd is *Cadence....* It con-
sists in a Disposing of the Words in such Order, and with
such Variation of Periods, as may strike the Ear with a sort
of musical Delight, which is a considerable Part of Eloquence.[25]

Franklin's views on writing well reveal a continuing concern for propriety, purity, and perspicuity, ideals he practiced from the outset of his career. Elegance and cadence he
practiced too, but about these he seldom theorized.

"If the Author does not intend his Piece for general
Reading," writes Franklin, "he must exactly suit his Stile
and Manner to the particular Taste of those he proposes
for his Readers."[26] Agreeing with Swift that "proper words,
in proper places, make the true definition of a style,"[27] he
suited his expression to the particular audience and
occasion. At one extreme lies the homespun wisdom
addressed to leather-apron men at Boston and Philadelphia,
and at the other his epistolary love-making in France. His
indigenous plain style, far from wholly yielding to Addisonian urbanity, in time acquired greater range than that
of his early teacher.

[25]*Critical Essays of the Eighteenth Century,* ed. W. H. Durham
(New Haven, 1915), pp. 80–83 *passim.*

[26]Labaree, I, 330–331.

[27]*The Works of Jonathan Swift,* ed. Sir Walter Scott (London,
1883), VIII, 199.

Many eighteenth-century English writers favored purifying and "fixing" the language. In *An Essay on Projects* Defoe proposed that a society be founded "to encourage polite learning, to polish and refine the English tongue, and advance the so much neglected faculty of correct language, to establish purity and propriety of style, and to purge it from all the irregular additions that ignorance and affectation have introduced."[28] "What I have most at heart," declares Swift, "is, that some method should be thought on for ascertaining and fixing our language for ever, after such alterations are made in it as shall be thought requisite. For I am of opinion, it is better a language should not be wholly perfect, than that it should be perpetually changing; and we must give over at one time, or at length infallibly change for the worse."[29] Addison went so far as to call for "an academy, that by the best authorities and rules drawn from the analogy of languages shall settle all controversies between grammar and idiom" (*Spectator* 135). Franklin, whose linguistic habits became increasingly conservative in later years, participated in the century's effort to purify the language by proposing, in his unfinished *Scheme for a New Alphabet and Reformed Mode of Spelling* (1768), to regularize and standardize orthography and pronunciation.

Late in the century George Campbell called that English pure which is reputable, national, and present. By

[28]*The Earlier Life and the Chief Earlier Works of Daniel Defoe*, ed. Henry Morley (London, 1889), p. 126.

[29]*A Proposal for Correcting, Improving, and Ascertaining the English Tongue*, in *Works of Swift*, IX, 147. See also *Tatler* 230 and *A Letter to a Young Gentleman, Lately enter'd into Holy Orders*.

reputable he meant the English used by *"a great number, if not the majority, of celebrated authors,"* and by present, that which is current. His interpretation of national is more elaborate.

> I consider [it] in a two fold view, as it stands opposed both to *provincial* and *foreign....* The introduction of extraneous words and idioms from other languages and foreign nations cannot be a smaller transgression against the established custom of the English tongue, than the introduction of words and idioms peculiar to some precincts of England, or, at least, somewhere current within the British pale. The only material difference between them is, that the one is more commonly the error of the learned, the other of the vulgar.[30]

While Franklin did not apply so absolute a yardstick as Campbell, increasingly he opposed provincialisms, foreign words, and neologisms and sought to rid his own style of such impurities.[31] "I hope with you," he told Hume in 1760, "that we shall always in America make the best English of this Island [Britain] our standard." So it is that he disapproves of using the word "improvement" in the sense of "employment" because this meaning is "peculiar to New England,"[32] and thinks "spell" (in the sense of "season") "a Vulgar English Word, therefore improper."[33] In 1751 he was convinced that German immigrants to

[30]*The Philosophy of Rhetoric* (New York, 1871), pp. 168–169.

[31]Lois MacLaurin, *Franklin's Vocabulary* (Garden City, N.Y., 1928), pp. 133–136, lists nineteen Americanisms which Franklin used down to 1751. After that time the number steadily declined.

[32]Labaree, IV, 265. Franklin was apparently ignorant of the long history of this meaning of the word; see *The Beginnings of American English*, ed. M. M. Mathews (Chicago, 1931), p. 55.

[33]Smyth, V, 464.

Pennsylvania "will shortly be so numerous as to German-
ize us instead of our Anglifying them, and will never adopt
our Language or Customs, any more than they can acquire
our Complexion." Two years later, however, he sounded
a more hopeful note: "All that seems to be necessary is,
to distribute [the Germans] more equally, mix them with
the English, establish English Schools where they are now
too thick settled."[34] At the end of his life, in a well-known
letter to Noah Webster, he stigmatized the verbs "notice,"
"advocate," "progress," and "oppose" as unfortunate inno-
vations introduced into the language during his sojourn
in France.

Under the heading of perspicuity Franklin placed plainness, economy, precision, and method. He was largely of
a mind with Thomas Sprat, who had announced in 1667
that the Royal Society of London, decrying "this vicious
abundance of *Phrase,* this trick of *Metaphors,* this volu-
bility of *Tongue,* which make so great a noise in the
World," would require of all its members "a close, naked,
natural way of speaking; positive expressions; clear senses;
a native easiness: bringing all things as near the Mathematical plainness, as they can, and preferring the language
of Artizans, Countrymen, and Merchants, before that, of
Wits, or Scholars."[35] Throughout his literary career Franklin, a tallow chandler's son in whose veins the Puritan
blood ran deeper than he knew, strongly favored the plain
artisan prose that was native to him. For example, he revised the letter from Alice Addertongue at two points in
the direction of greater plainness: "But, Thanks be praised,

[34]Labaree, IV, 234, 485.
[35]*History of the Royal Society* (London, 1667), pp. 112, 113.

[thank Providence] no such Misfortune has befel me these Dozen Years"; "one of the gravest of Mama's [my Mother's] Company."[36] And to the original draft of the letter from Celia Single he added the second and third aphorisms in the following sentence in order to underline Mr. Careless' plain thrift: "Well, but my Dear, *says he,* you know a penny sav'd is a penny got, a pin a day is a groat a year, every little makes a mickle, and there is neither Sin nor Shame in Knitting a pair of Stockins; why should you express such a mighty Aversion to it?"[37]

In composition Franklin let himself be guided by the golden mean he approved in conversation: talk neither overmuch nor too little; do not tell long, insipid, trifling stories simply for the sake of talking.[38] "Tho' a multitude of Words obscure the Sense," he cautions, "yet a Writer should take especial Care on the other Hand, that his Brevity doth not hurt his Perspicuity."[39] Irritated by the habit of "Amplification, or the Art of saying *Little in Much*," he once went so far as to publish a mock-legal petition exposing the prolixity of lawyers.[40] Sometimes he

[36]Commonplace Book, Hist. Soc. Pa. MS, pp. 47, 49, and Labaree, I, 244, 245–246. In this and subsequent examples in this chapter the original wording appears in brackets.

[37]Commonplace Book, Hist. Soc. Pa. MS, p. 41, and Labaree, I, 241–242.

[38]*Pennsylvania Gazette,* Oct. 15, 1730, excerpted from *The Universal Spectator* (London), Oct. 11, 1729; reprinted in Labaree, I, 178–181.

[39]Labaree, I, 330.

[40]*Pennsylvania Gazette,* June 17, 1736; reprinted in Labaree, II, 146–149. Since the appearance of this volume Leonard Labaree has informed me that while Franklin certainly wrote the preliminary

strives for greater economy in his own work; he revises a passage in the letter from Celia Single to read, "I hate to be thought a Scandalizer of my Neighbours, and therefore forbear [shall say nothing about 'em]."[41] Conversely, he saw the danger of too great brevity. Once he confided to Strahan, "When any thing of mine is abridged in the papers or magazines, I conceit that the abridger has left out the very best and brightest parts";[42] he complained that the editor of his *Causes of the American Discontents before 1768* had "drawn the teeth and pared the nails of my paper, so that it can neither scratch nor bite. It seems only to paw and mumble."[43] Among all his writings the familiar letters and bagatelles addressed to Mme Brillon are perhaps the most eloquent testimony to how far he succeeded in realizing the golden mean.

Precision, a stylistic habit acquired in part from the discipline of writing verse, was a point of the greatest importance with Franklin. Frequently he revised his own work in the direction of greater precision. In "The Handsome and Deformed Leg," for example, there occurs this change: "In every Face they may discover fine Features [Beauties] & Defects, good & bad Qualities";[44] and in the letter from Celia Single, this one: "Mrs. Careless was just then at the Glass, dressing her Head [self]."[45] In "Remarks Concerning the Savages of North America" he adds the

---

paragraphs, he probably reprinted the petition itself from some British source.

[41]Commonplace Book, Hist. Soc. Pa. MS, p. 43, and Labaree, I, 243.
[42]Smyth, IV, 259.
[43]*Ibid.*, V, 90.
[44]J. G. Rosengarten, *Proc. APS*, XL (1901), 89.
[45]Commonplace Book, Hist. Soc. Pa. MS, p. 41, and Labaree, I, 241.

word "acquired" to sharpen the meaning of the following sentence: "Having frequent Occasions to hold public Councils, they have acquired great Order and Decency in conducting them."[46]

In 1789 Franklin told the London editor Benjamin Vaughan, whose language and sentiments he admired, that his style wanted perspicuity, "owing principally to a neglect of method."

> What I would therefore recommend to you is, that, before you sit down to write on any subject, you would spend some days in considering it, putting down at the same time, in short hints, every thought which occurs to you as proper to make a part of your intended piece. When you have thus obtained a collection of the thoughts, examine them carefully with this view, to find which of them is properest to be presented *first* to the mind of the reader, that he, being possessed of that, may the more easily understand it, and be better disposed to receive what you intend for the *second;* and thus I would have you put a figure before each thought, to mark its future place in your composition.

The letter from Alice Addertongue, fashioned from "Hints for Paper on Scandal," is proof that for over half a century Franklin had been following his own advice. While most of these hints are retained in the essay that went to press, they are carefully shaped and reordered. Of the ten paragraphs that comprise the printed essay only the last five, as set down in "Hints," even approximate the final order; the material that went into the first and third, for example, appears at two widely separated points. In reordering the parts Franklin seems to have been guided throughout by the desire to build steadily toward the climactic moment

[46]Undated Lib. Cong. MS, p. 3, and Smyth, X, 99.

when the Gazetteer asks to be excused from printing the inventory of scandal Alice has sent him, *"such Things being in Reality* no News at all."[47]

When Franklin recalled, "Prose Writing has been of great Use to me in the Course of my Life, and was a principal Means of my Advancement,"[48] he was voicing a general colonial attitude. In prose and poetry, secular as well as religious, *utile* mattered far more than *dulce.* The critic approaching colonial literature must be ever mindful that author and audience alike judged a work successful or not insofar as it finally served a utilitarian, not an aesthetic, end; mindful, too, that the overwhelming majority of these works were not belletristic, in the restricted sense in which we apply that term to lyric poetry, fiction, and drama. Bearing these facts in mind, I propose to demonstrate how Franklin, while being guided by neoclassic precept, achieved distinctiveness and vitality through a wide range of popular nonfiction prose types and thus deserves to stand in company with his early teachers, Addison and Swift, as an important eighteenth-century man of letters.

[47]Commonplace Book, Hist. Soc. Pa. MS, pp. 49–50, and Labaree, I, 243–248. Forty years later Franklin prepared a topical outline before beginning to write the *Autobiography.*

[48]*Par. Text Ed.,* p. 32.

II

The Periodical Essay

"I HOLD it very indecent," writes Shaftesbury, "that a man should publish his meditations or solitary thoughts. These are the froth and scum of writing, which should be unburdened in private and consigned to oblivion, before the writer comes before the world as good company."[1] This neoclassical insistence, that the writer address himself to the social rather than the individual consciousness in man, helps account for the rise of the periodical essay at the turn of the eighteenth century. Conversely, Montaigne says in the Preface to his *Essais* (March 1, 1580): "I want to be seen here in my simple, natural, ordinary fashion, without pose or artifice; for it is myself that I portray.... I am myself the matter of my book"—thus setting the tone and suggesting the topical range of the familiar essay. Because they shared Shaftesbury's belief that such familiarity is indecorous, eighteenth-century English

[1] Quoted in F. O. Matthiessen, *American Renaissance* (New York, 1941), p. 67. Matthiessen, who may have been trusting his memory, seems to have had in mind passages in *Characteristicks of Men, Manners, Opinions, Times* (London, 1732), notably two in vol. I, 163–164.

writers who might otherwise have worked in the tradition launched by Montaigne initiated a new one instead: the periodical essay. For all its apparent intimacy of tone, this genre was less personal than the familiar essay and correspondingly more dramatic.[2] The new tradition can be dated from January 1692, the month in which Peter Motteux undertook the *Gentleman's Journal*.[3] In less than a generation it came to flower with the *Tatler, Spectator,* and *Guardian* papers.

The English periodical essay is moral in purpose and social in point of view. "The general purpose of this Paper," explains Steele in the Dedication to the *Tatler,* "is to expose the false arts of life, to pull off the disguises of cunning, vanity, and affectation, and to recommend a general simplicity in our dress, our discourse, and our behaviour." So far did he and his associates succeed that John Gay declared shortly, "Bickerstaff ventur'd to tell the Town, that they were a parcel of Fops, Fools, and vain Cocquets; but in such a manner, as even pleased them, and made them more than half enclin'd to believe that he spoke Truth."[4] The Spectator promises in the first number, "I never espoused any Party with Violence, and am resolved to observe an exact Neutrality between the Whigs and Tories, unless I shall be forced to declare myself by the Hostilities of either Side." Indeed, not only Addison

[2]Melvin R. Watson, *Magazine Serials and the Essay Tradition, 1746–1820* (Baton Rouge, 1956), p. 69.

[3]Walter Graham, *English Literary Periodicals* (New York, 1930), p. 57.

[4]*The Present State of Wit* (1711), intr. Donald Bond (Augustan Reprint Society: Ann Arbor, 1947), p. 3.

but all the early periodical essayists adopted and, for the most part, maintained a nonpartisan, social point of view.

The presence of a rising middle class helped determine the manner and matter of these essays. Addison in particular cultivated a gentlemanly style that fell between the ornateness of the scholar and the plainness of the artisan. "His prose is the model of the middle style," writes Johnson; "on grave subjects not formal, on light occasions not groveling; pure without scrupulosity, and exact without apparent elaboration; always equable, and always easy, without glowing words or pointed sentences.... His sentences have neither studied amplitude, nor affected brevity; his periods, though not diligently rounded, are voluble and easy."[5] The rhetorical conventions that came to be associated with the tradition were dictated in large part by a genteel, coffeehouse audience of merchants and professional men, and included dream vision, moral dialogue, beast fable, genealogy and adventures, transformation, mock-advertisement, aptronym, and (later in the century) foreign visitor and oriental tale. The matter ranged widely through manners and morality, philosophical reflection, character, humor, and criticism.[6]

Precisely because it was addressed in the first instance to a middle-class public, the tradition quickly caught hold

[5]*The Lives of the Most Eminent English Poets* (London, 1896), II, 103–104. Jan Lannering's detailed analysis, *Studies in the Prose Style of Joseph Addison* (Upsala, 1951), substantiates Johnson's well-known judgment.

[6]Ernest Claude Coleman, "The Influence of the Addisonian Essay in America before 1810" (unpublished dissertation, Univ. of Illinois, 1936), p. 16.

in America. Not content with merely reading the chief English periodical collections that could be found on the bookstalls and in private libraries, Americans soon began working in the tradition themselves. Between September 9 and November 1, 1721, thirteen numbers of the "Telltale," a student periodical, circulated in manuscript at Harvard.[7] In the same year the colonial newspaper started carrying periodical essays in its columns; these at once became a regular feature and enjoyed a vogue down to the time of the Revolution and even beyond.

I

But for circumstance and growing class consciousness at Boston, the *New-England Courant,* a weekly newspaper established by Benjamin Franklin's older brother James on August 7, 1721, might have observed as strict a neutrality as the *Tatler* and *Spectator*. The *Courant* did in fact profess such a policy in the second number: "The Undertaker promiseth, that nothing shall here be inserted, reflecting on the Clergy (as such) of whatever Denomination, nor relating to the Affairs of Government, and no Trespass against Decency or good Manners." But in view of the smallpox epidemic then raging and the fact that the Mathers, anxious to strengthen the provincial oligarchy, had sided with Dr. Zabdiel Boylston who favored inoculation, James Franklin was soon forced by the belligerent tone of certain of his contributors to show his hand and the *Courant* was quickly identified in the public mind with the cause of anti-inoculation. "The *Courant* was never design'd for a Party Paper," he admitted shortly.

[7]See W. C. Lane, *Pub. Col. Soc. Mass.,* XII (1909), 220–231.

"Yet the Envy of some Men has represented me as a Tool to the Anti-Inoculators."[8]

This envy arose among the Mathers themselves, three generations of them. As early as December 9, 1721, Cotton Mather privately fulminated, "Warnings are to be given unto the wicked Printer, and his Accomplices, who every week publish a vile Paper to lessen and blacken the Ministers of the Town, and render their Ministry ineffectual."[9] The following month Cotton's son Samuel dubbed James Franklin and his associates "the *Hell-Fire Club of Boston*."[10] The attack was now so firmly mounted that it could no longer be safely ignored, and James countered:

> That the *Courants* are carry'd on by a *Hell-Fire Club* with a *Nonjuror* at the Head of them, has been asserted by a certain Clergyman [Cotton Mather] in his common Conversation, with as much Zeal as ever he discover'd in the Application of a Sermon on the most awakening Subject.... There has been nothing in the *Courants* against Law.... Notwithstanding which a young scribbling Collegian, who has just Learning enough to make a Fool of himself, has taken it in his Head to *put a Stop to this Wickedness* (as he calls it) by a letter in the last Week's *Gazette*.... The young Wretch, when he calls those who write the Several Pieces in the Courant, *The Hell-Fire Club of Boston*,...little thinks what a cruel Reflection he throws on his Reverend Grandfather, who was then, and for some time before, a *Subscriber* for the Paper.[11]

Within a week this same grandfather, Increase Mather, announced in the *Boston Gazette* that he was cancelling

[8]*New-England Courant,* Dec. 4, 1721.

[9]*Diary of Cotton Mather* (New York, [1957]), II, 663.

[10]*Boston Gazette,* Jan. 15, 1722.

[11]*New-England Courant,* Jan. 22, 1722.

23

his subscription to the *Courant* and urged others to do the same.

This battle of words, into which young Benjamin entered shortly, dragged on through the spring. Then suddenly matters came to a head. On June 11, 1722, James Franklin slyly insinuated that the provincial government was slow to act against pirates operating in Massachusetts waters. The next day the General Court ordered him jailed for the balance of the session and on July 6 resolved that the *Courant* not "be hereafter Printed or Published without the same be first perused and allowed by the Secretary, as has been usual."[12] Upon making apology James was released. In spite of Silence Dogood's spirited defense of freedom of the press and her portrait of "hypocritical Pretenders to Religion" and Dic. Burlesque's Hudibrastics on a painter (James Franklin) arraigned for circulating black-and-white likenesses of rogues and knaves,[13] the year ended without further incident.

Then on January 14, 1723, the *Courant* carried three articles offensive to church and state, notably an "Essay against Hypocrites," apparently written by James Franklin. Again the General Court imposed censorship and, when James defied the order, had him arrested for contempt. Andrew Bradford in far-off Philadelphia, learning of this action, indignantly declared, "An indifferent Person would judge by this vote against Couranto, That the Assembly of the Province of Massachusetts Bay are made up of Oppressors and Bigots, who make Religion the only Engine

[12]*Journals of the House of Representatives of Massachusetts* (Boston, 1923), IV, 23, 72.

[13]*New-England Courant,* July 9, 23, Sept. 17, 1722.

of Destruction to the People."[14] Before the charge against James Franklin was dropped, the *Courant,* victorious in this round of the struggle for a free press in colonial America, saw fit to characterize the Anti-Couranteers as "a sort of *Precisians,* who mistaking Religion for the peculiar Whims of their own distemper'd Brain, are for cutting or stretching all Men to their own Standard of Thinking."[15]

In spite of the partisan stance the *Courant* was forced to assume, it was the first colonial newspaper to feature the periodical essay. "To expose the Vices and Follies of Persons of all Ranks and Degrees, under feign'd Names," announced James Franklin, setting forth his purpose and point of view, "is what no honest Man will object against; and this the Publisher (by the Assistance of his Correspondents) is resolv'd to pursue, without Fear of, or Affection to any Man: And as the Paper will contain Variety of Speculations, every Subscriber will often find a Subject to please him, and, 'tis presum'd, nothing that shall give any just Cause of Offence."[16] To this end the *Courant* solicited "short Pieces, Serious; Sarcastick, Ludicrous, or otherways amusing; or sometimes professedly Dull."[17] James introduced his contributors as a "most generous Clan of Honest *Wags,*" bachelors all, well versed in the theory if not the practice of love,[18] and entertained his

[14]*American Weekly Mercury,* Feb. 26, 1723, quoted in W. G. Bleyer, *Main Currents in the History of American Journalism* (Boston and New York, 1927), p. 62.

[15]*New-England Courant,* Apr. 15, 1723.

[16]*Ibid.,* Jan. 29, 1722.

[17]*Ibid.,* Aug. 14, 1721.

[18]*Ibid.,* Sept. 4, 1721.

readers with a series of exchanges, in prose and verse, between aptronymous bachelors and maids on such conventional topics as love and marriage. To lend a greater
air of fiction to these informal debates he himself and certain other of the Couranteers frequently wrote under the
guise of "Couranto," "an *old rusty Bachelor*...short
Neck'd, stubbed Shank'd, rusty Hair'd."[19] In the earliest
of many attacks on this persona, Reverend Thomas Walter,
nephew to Cotton Mather, reviles him as

> the miserable and dull *Couranto*, who, had he a true Sight
> of himself, and what a wretched Figure he makes in writing,
> would quarrel with all Mankind for having more Wit than
> himself.... Your Works declare, your *Guts are in your
> Brains*.... Go on, Monsieur *Courant*, and prosper; Fear
> not to please your stupid Admirers, which will be an easy
> Task, if you will but consult your own heavy *Genius*, and
> write in your native Stile, of which you have been so sharp
> and discerning as to give us the apt and proper Character,
> VERY, VERY DULL!"[20]

The clan of Couranteers over whom James Franklin
informally presided included John Checkley, whose pro-
Anglican bias he would disavow within a month; Dr. William Douglass, vehement in his attacks on inoculation; and
(though James was not at first aware of the fact) his own

[19]*Ibid.*, Jan. 29, Mar. 5, 1722. "Timothy Turnstone" (see Apr.
9, 1722, issue) and "Janus" (see June 18, 1722) are extensions of this
original persona.

[20]*The Little-Compton Scourge*, Aug. 10, 1721; reproduced in
facsimile in *The New-England Courant: A Selection of Certain Issues
Containing Writings of Benjamin Franklin or Published by Him
during His Brother's Imprisonment*, ed. Perry Miller (Boston, 1956).
In this instance Walter's attack was directed at John Checkley, who
wrote the opening essay in the first number of the *Courant*.

26

brother Benjamin.[21] Notwithstanding the charge hurled
by the Mathers, the Couranteers never constituted themselves a formal club. They did, however, speak for the
tradesman class at Boston in opposition to the gentry, who
frequently set forth their views in the *Gazette*. So earnestly
did the Couranteers take Checkley's advice: "Speak to the
Hearts of Men in a very easie and familiar manner, so that
the meanest Plough-man, the very meanest of God's People
may understand them," that a *Gazette* critic, intending no
compliment, called their style "low & phlegmatic, and insipid."[22] Even so, Harold Dean is probably right in thinking that "they caught the literary standards of the neo-
classicists better than any of their contemporaries in
Boston."[23]

II

The apprenticed Benjamin, whose fourteen *Dogood*
papers appeared anonymously in the *Courant* between
April 2 and October 8, 1722, learned much from the manner and matter of the aggressive Couranteers. For all their
apparent good humor and urbanity, these essays are openly
critical of Harvard College, the suppression of free speech,
religious hypocrisy, and blind zeal; and in the "Couranto"
Benjamin had at hand a precedent and partial model for

[21]See W. C. Ford, *Proc. Mass. Hist. Soc.*, LVII (1924), 350–353,
wherein these Couranteers and twelve others are identified by name
in Benjamin's marked file of the first 43 numbers of the *Courant*.

[22]John Checkley, Preface to *Choice Dialogues* (Boston, 1720);
Boston Gazette, Feb. 5, 1722. Both sources are quoted in George F.
Horner, *Stud. Phil.*, XXXVII (1940), 508.

[23]Harold Lester Dean, *"The New-England Courant,* 1721–1726:
A Chapter in the History of American Culture" (unpublished dissertation, Brown Univ., 1943), p. 300.

his earliest persona, Silence Dogood. A mock-advertisement on January 29, 1722, wherein several gentlemen express a willingness "to dispose of themselves in Marriage" to "old Virgins" and "old or young Widows" of sufficient fortune, lies behind Silence's proposals to alleviate the distressing condition of widows and spinsters. And an anonymous letter on April 9, describing "a certain young Lady in Town who seldom makes her Appearance abroad in the Day Time; but between the Hours of Twelve and One at Night, is often called up by one or other Debauchee of the Town with a Hem," anticipates her animadversions on certain of the nightwalkers she encounters on Boston Common.

A comparison of two essays on the same general topic, *Dogood* 9 and the "Essay against Hypocrites," will make it clear, however, that Benjamin's style differed from that of the other Couranteers. There is more restraint and less rhetorical color in his essay. Only once does he resort to invective, calling him a "Monster" who *"leaves the Gospel for the sake of the Law"*;[24] in fact, the force of this essay depends finally on the excerpt from *Cato's Letters* which brings it to a close. On the other hand, the author of the more vituperative "Essay against Hypocrites" make extensive use of Biblical allusion and invective. At one point he declares:

[24]Labaree, I, 31. The editors identify the "Monster" as probably Governor Joseph Dudley. Thomas Gordon and John Trenchard began a series of letters signed "Cato" in the *London Journal* in Nov., 1720; the letter here quoted appeared in the issue of May 27, 1721. Eventually these letters were published in four volumes as *Cato's Letters* (London, 1724), the title by which Franklin referred to them.

This sort of *Saints,* If they do but perform a few Duties to GOD Almighty, in a Hypocritical manner, they fondly think it will serve to sanctify their Villany, and give them a Licence to cut their Neighbour's Throat, *i.e.* to cheat him as often as they have opportunity: And no doubt, had they the Advantage in their Hands, they would, like *Judas,* sell their Lord and Master for 30 pieces of Silver, if not for half that value.... Moral Honesty, tho' it will not of it self carry a Man to Heaven, yet, I am sure there is no going thither *without it:* And however such men, of whom I have been speaking may palliate their wickedness, they will find, *that Publicans & Harlots will enter into the Kingdom of Heaven before themselves.*

He follows this with an apostrophe: "But, are there such Men as these in THEE *O New-England!* Heaven forbid there should be any: But alas! it is to be fear'd the Number is not small."[25] In short, the second essay calls to mind, much more forcefully than the first, the angrier rhetoric of the previous century.

It is inevitable, especially in view of Franklin's familiar account of how he disciplined himself to write prose, that the *Dogood* papers should be compared with the *Spectator.* I cannot agree with those critics who call Franklin's manner and matter imitative of Addison's, though I grant that some of Addison's urbanity rubbed off on his style and that the vision of Public Credit (*Spectator* 3) and the paper on hoop petticoats (*Spectator* 127) offer probable analogues for two of Silence's papers. The most dramatic evidence that Franklin, even at this impressionable age, had

[25]*New-England Courant,* Jan. 14, 1723. Perry Miller, who reprints this essay in his facsimile edition, thinks that it was aimed first of all at Cotton Mather.

overcome his dependence on his teacher is to be seen in the matter of point of view. Whereas the Spectator claims never to have "espoused any Party with Violence," Silence swears mortal enmity "to arbitrary Government and unlimited Power." In a statement that defines the middle-class point of view common to all of Franklin's American personae, she observes "that the Generality of People, now a days, are unwilling either to commend or dispraise what they read, until they are in some measure informed who or what the Author of it is, whether he be *poor* or *rich, old* or *young*, a *Schollar* or a *Leather Apron Man*."[26] The words *poor, young, Leather Apron Man* tell us where Silence's sympathies lie and distinguish her sharply from that university man, Mr. Spectator.

Frugal, industrious, prosaic, even slangy at times, Silence characterizes herself as "an Enemy to Vice, and a Friend to Vertue...one of an extensive Charity, and a great Forgiver of *private* Injuries: A hearty Lover of the Clergy and all good Men, and a mortal Enemy to arbitrary Government and unlimited Power.... I have likewise a natural Inclination to observe and reprove the Faults of others, at which I have an excellent Faculty.... To be brief; I am courteous and affable, good humour'd (unless I am first provok'd,) and handsome, and sometimes witty."[27] By her own account she was born during the passage from London, on the day her father was swept overboard. Eventually she was apprenticed to a country minister near Boston, "a pious good-natur'd young Man, and a Batchelor," who took pains to instruct her "in all that

[26]Labaree, I, 9.
[27]*Ibid.*, I, 12–13.

Knowledge and Learning which is necessary for our Sex."
At a proper time they were married. "We lived happily
together in the Heighth of conjugal Love and mutual
Endearments, for near Seven Years, in which Time we
added Two likely Girls and a Boy to the Family of the
Dogoods." Then of a sudden he died. "I have now remained in a State of Widowhood for several Years, but it
is a State I never much admir'd, and I am apt to fancy
that I could be easily perswaded to marry again, provided
I was sure of a good-humour'd, sober, agreeable Companion: But one, even with these few good Qualities, being
hard to find, I have lately relinquish'd all Thoughts of
that Nature." She now proposes to communicate her
small stock of knowledge "by Peacemeal to the Publick."
Shortly she comes to Boston "in order to compleat her
Observations of the present reigning Vices of the Town."[28]
Although Silence several times attacks the local aristocracy
of church and state, she devotes more space to less libelous
topics like pride of dress, funeral elegies, the distressing
condition of widows and spinsters, drunkenness, and nightwalking.

The most fully developed of these essays is the fourth,
Silence's dream vision of Harvard College. Its full sig-
nificance only breaks upon the reader when it is viewed
in the larger perspective of the Couranteers' running battle
with the Mather party; for as artisans and scholars parted
company on the question of inoculation, so too on the
importance of a classical education and training for the
ministry. On March 12, 1722, James Franklin, perhaps
recalling the outburst of that scribbling young collegian,

[28]*Ibid.*, I, 9–21 *passim.*

Samuel Mather, published John Williams' letter on the abuses of logic, written in the *"Mundungian Language . . .* for the Benefit of those *Sons of Harvard,* who strive in vain or are too lazy to learn the other *learned Tongues."* The letter reads in part:

> Ould it not be of equll Benefet to the Poblecke, if whilt thay are theching the Arth of Lojeche, they could infuese Onesti in to their Pupels to youse it onestly, that thar may be no more fals erecketed *Hiphotices,* with a desine to delude the Pepole, wich they noes is a Lye before God, to dra Conclucenes ethar to gaine the Point of Inockelacion or any other thing wich their secret Iche shuld put them upon?

Dogood 4 appeared two months later.

Ruminating on what her boarder Clericus has said about sending her son William to college, Silence falls asleep in the orchard and dreams that "a great Company of Youths from all Parts of the Country" are traveling to the Temple of Learning: Riches and Poverty guard the gate, and only those who gain favor with the former are admitted by the latter. "However, as a Spectator I gain'd Admittance, and with the rest entred directly into the Temple." Here Learning sits enthroned, "apparelled wholly in Black, and surrounded almost on every Side with innumerable Volumes in all Languages," busily employed "preparing a Paper, call'd, *The New-England Courant.* On her Right Hand sat *English,* with a pleasant smiling Countenance, and handsomely attir'd; and on her left were seated several *Antique Figures* with their Faces vail'd. I was considerably puzzl'd to guess who they were, until one informed me, (who stood beside me,) that those Figures on her left Hand were *Latin, Greek, Hebrew,* &c. and that they were very much reserv'd, and seldom or never unvail'd their Faces here, and then to few or none, tho' most of those who have in this Place acquir'd so much Learning as to distinguish them from *English,* pretended to an intimate Acquaintance with them." The whole tribe began to climb the throne, "but the Work proving troublesome and difficult to most of them, they withdrew their Hands from the Plow, and contented themselves to sit at the Foot, with Madam *Idleness* and her Maid *Ignorance....* But the Time drawing nigh in which they could no way avoid ascending, they were fain to crave the Assistance of those [the tutors] who had got up before them, and who, for the Reward perhaps of a *Pint of Milk,* or a *Piece of Plumb-Cake,* lent the Lubbers a helping Hand, and sat them in the Eye of the World, upon a Level with themselves." At commencement time "every Beetle-Scull seem'd well satisfy'd with his own Portion of Learning, tho' perhaps he was *e'en just* as ignorant as ever." Most of those who go forth beat a path to the Temple of Theology, attracted thither by Pecunia. As she travels homeward Silence reflects "on the extream Folly of those Parents, who, blind to their Childrens Dulness, and insensible of the Solidity of their Skulls, because they think their Purses can afford it, will needs send them to the Temple of Learning...from whence they return, after Abundance of Trouble and Charge, as great Blockheads as ever, only more proud and self-conceited." Clericus, walking by, accidentally awakes her and, hearing her dream, explains that *"it was a lively Representation of* HARVARD COLLEGE, *Etcetera."*

Although this essay resembles Addison's vision of Public Credit in that the scene is a great hall in the midst of which the allegorical figure of a woman sits on a throne, it is no mere imitation. In fact, Franklin manages certain of the

33

conventions in a far less perfunctory manner than Addison, rendering the setting in which Silence falls asleep more fully and motivating her dream more naturally. He saves the dream allegory itself from slipping into sterile abstraction by infusing such homely details as the students rewarding their tutors with milk or plum cake. Dream vision affords Franklin the artistic distance necessary to objectify and give point to his rising anger with the Harvard community and proves as efficient a vehicle, if a modest one, for exposing the ineffectualness of collegiate education in colonial America as the Hudibrastics John Trumbull employed in *The Progress of Dulness* half a century later.

A fortnight after Silence had her vision a member of the Mather party, supposing James Franklin to be the author, sneered: "Is not Couranto a fine Rhetorician and a correct writer when he says in his last but one...'they withdrew their Hands from the Plow.' Friend, who ever heard of ent'ring a Temple and ascending the Magnificent Steps of a Throne with a Plough in his hand! O rare Allegory! Well done, Rustic Couranto! This may cause matter of speculation."[29] What is here significant is the implied criticism of Benjamin's plainer artisan prose. One of the Couranteers, by way of rebuttal, reinforced Silence's views and concluded with a pious hope:

> Long have the weaker Sons of Harvard strove
> To move our Rev'rence and command our Love,
> By means, how sordid, 'tis not hard to say,
> When all their Merit lies in M. and A.
> The knowing Sons of Harvard we revere,

[29]*Boston Gazette,* May 28, 1722, quoted in Bernard Faÿ, *Franklin, the Apostle of Modern Times* (Boston, 1929), p. 48. The author, who signed himself "John Harvard," was probably Samuel Mather.

And in their just defence will still appear;
But every idel Fop who there commences,
Shall never claim Dominion o'er our Senses.
We judge not of their Knowledge by their Air,
Nor think the wisest Heads have curled Hair.
　　May Parents, Madam, your Reflections mind,
And be no more to Childrens Dulness Blind.
May your sharp Satyrs mend the lazy Drone,
Who by anothers Help ascends the Throne.
And not by any Merit of his own.
Then will both Church and State be truly blest
With Men whose Worth will be by both confest.[30]

Writing with natural vigor and rhetorical point, the young Franklin strove to impose his own idiom on this series of essays. In *Dogood* 12, though much too mechanically, Silence trots out a list of euphemisms to describe the condition of drunkards: "They are seldom known to be *drunk,* tho' they are very often *boozey, cogey, tipsey, fox'd, merry, mellow, fuddl'd, groatable, Confoundedly cut, See two Moons,* are *Among the Philistines, In a very good Humour, See the Sun,* or, *The Sun has shone upon them;* they *Clip the King's English,* are *Almost froze, Feavourish, In their Altitudes, Pretty well enter'd,* &c." Elsewhere, giving an account of a night walk in Boston, she introduces nautical diction, this time more imaginatively:

I met a Crowd of *Tarpolins* and their Doxies, link'd to each other by the Arms, who ran (by their own Account) after the Rate of *Six Knots an Hour,* and bent their Course towards the Common. Their eager and amorous Emotions of Body, occasion'd by taking their Mistresses *in Tow,* they call'd *wild Steerage:* And as a Pair of them happen'd to trip and

[30]*New-England Courant,* June 4, 1722.

come to the Ground, the Company were call'd upon to *bring to,* for that Jack and Betty were *founder'd.*

Even at this early age Franklin recognized that tropes are useful only insofar as they clarify a writer's meaning and render it vivid. Employing a military simile that must have delighted the women and frightened the men of Boston, Silence describes hoop petticoats as "monstrous topsy-turvy *Mortar-Pieces,*" which if "well mounted on Noddles-Island...would look more like Engines of War for bombarding the Town, than Ornaments of the Fair Sex." More ambitious and effective still is the conceit with which she seeks to explain the different effects of liquor: "Some shrink in the Wetting, and others swell to such an unusual Bulk in their Imaginations, that they can in an Instant understand all Arts and Sciences, by the liberal Education of a little vivifying *Punch,* or a sufficient Quantity of other exhilerating Liquor." As a final example, the essay on nightwalkers is brought to a resounding close with this anecdote: "I have heard of a *Shoemaker,* who being ask'd by a noted Rambler, *Whether he could tell how long her Shoes would last;* very prettily answer'd, *That he knew how many Days she might wear them, but not how many Nights; because they were then put to a more violent and irregular Service than when she employ'd her self in the common Affairs of the House.*"

Two months after the last of these papers appeared an anonymous correspondent asked Mrs. Dogood why she had kept silent so long: "Can you *observe* no faults in others (or your self) to *reprove?* Or are you married and remov'd to some distant Clime, that we hear nothing from you? Are you (as the Prophet supposed *Baal* that sottish

Deity) *asleep,* or *on a Journey,* and cannot write? Or has the Sleep of *inexorable unrelenting Death* procur'd your *Silence?*"[31] Silent she remained; as Franklin later explained, "My small Fund of Sense for such Performances was pretty well exhausted."[32] Even so, in this his first ambitious literary venture he had created a vital, indigenous character, one that is in retrospect more fully realized than his other women characters, Celia Single, Alice Addertongue, Bridget Saunders, Polly Baker. In manner and matter these essays owe less to the example of Addison and the Couranteers than they do to Franklin's own sense of invention. The perceptive criticism in the essay on funeral elegies (by one who had tried his hand at verse and found it was not his forte); the colloquial vigor of the essays on drunkenness and nightwalking; his skill in handling the traditional conventions; above all, the controlled prose itself—in these respects the *Dogood* papers achieve a large measure of originality.

In January 1723, on the occasion of his second arrest, James Franklin was ordered to stop publishing the *Courant* over his name, an order he circumvented by having it published henceforth over Benjamin's. Temporary editor while James was in prison, Benjamin, aware that the Boston press had long "groaned in bringing forth an hateful, but numerous Brood of Party Pamphlets, malicious Scribbles, and Billingsgate Ribaldry," promised "to entertain the Town with the most comical and diverting Incidents of Humane Life";[33] and for the time being, the *Courant* bore the impress of his greater urbanity. It seems

[31]*Ibid.,* Dec. 3, 1722.
[32]*Par. Text Ed.,* p. 46.
[33]Labaree, I, 49.

probable that before his departure for Philadelphia in
September he composed at least six additional essays for
the *Courant*.[34] A "fresh Difference" arising between the
brothers, Benjamin committed "one of the first Errata" of
his life by breaking his secret indenture with James. On
September 30, 1723, the *Courant* carried what is surely
the most famous such advertisement in American history:
"James Franklin, Printer in Queen-Street, wants a likely
lad for an Apprentice."

III

An anonymous poem in Titan Leeds' almanac for 1730
foretold the greatness of his native city:

'Tis here Apollo does erect his throne;
This his Parnassus, this his Helicon.
Here solid sense does every bosom warm;
Here noise and nonsense have forgot to charm.
Thy seers how cautious, and how gravely wise!
Thy hopeful youth in emulation rise;
Who, if the wishing muse inspired does sing,
Shall liberal arts to such perfection bring,
Europe shall mourn her ancient fame declined,
And Philadelphia be the Athens of mankind.[35]

The Philadelphia to which Franklin came in 1723 was in
fact on the threshold of a cultural flowering that would

[34]"On Titles of Honor," *New-England Courant*, Feb. 18, 1723;
"High Tide in Boston," Mar. 4; "Tatlers and Tale Bearers," Mar. 18;
"Timothy Wagstaff," Apr. 15; "Abigail Twitterfield," July 8; and
"On Lecture-Day Visiting," Aug. 19. See Labaree, I, 51–53, wherein
only the first of these essays is attributed to Benjamin Franklin with
certainty.

[35]Quoted in Moses Coit Tyler, *A History of American Literature,
1607–1765* (New York, 1878), II, 239.

make it "the Seat of the American Muses"[36] in the second half of the century. This flowering was by no means so wholly of Franklin's making as it has often been represented.[37] In such company as John Bartram, Thomas Godfrey, and James Logan he stands forth as only one virtuoso among many, a fact he readily acknowledged in his proposal of 1743 for the establishment of the American Philosophical Society. Culture in the Quaker city rested on a broader base than at Boston. "The poorest labourer upon the shore of *Delaware*," wrote Jacob Duché in Revolutionary times, "thinks himself entitled to deliver his sentiments in matters of religion or politicks with as much freedom as the gentleman or the scholar.... Such is the prevailing taste for books of every kind, that almost every man is a reader; and by pronouncing sentence, right or wrong, upon the various publications that come in his way, puts himself upon a level, in point of knowledge, with their several authors."[38] Moreover, such culture was predominantly utilitarian, its vital literature "a literature of action, integrated with contemporary life in all its aspects—religious, economic, social and political."[39] Francis Daniel Pastorius' wry observation, "Never have meta-

[36]Labaree, II, 405.

[37]Among those who have corrected this false representation are M. Katherine Jackson, *Outlines of the Literary History of Colonial Pennsylvania* (Lancaster, Pa., 1906), p. 55; Carl and Jessica Bridenbaugh, *Rebels and Gentlemen* (New York, 1942), pp. 27–28; and F. B. Tolles, *Penn. Mag. Hist. and Biog.*, LXXXI (1957), 137.

[38]*Caspipina's Letters* (Bath, 1777), II, 34, 35–36, quoted in Daniel J. Boorstin, *The Americans: The Colonial Experience* (New York, 1958), p. 316.

[39]Bridenbaugh, *Rebels and Gentlemen,* p. 116.

39

physics and Aristotelian logic...earned a loaf of bread,"[40] aptly characterized the prevailing climate of opinion. In short, here was an environment highly congenial to a pragmatist like young Benjamin, who having battled the New England saints and scholars shook the dust of Boston from his feet and journeyed southward with few regrets.

In the Philadelphia press, first as contributor to the *American Weekly Mercury*, then as editor of the *Pennsylvania Gazette* and *Poor Richard's Almanack*, Franklin once again identified himself with the leather-apron men. In Philadelphia the line was more sharply drawn than in Boston between the merchants and professional men, who never found Franklin quite socially acceptable, and the fraternity of artisans, laborers, and shopkeepers, the more ambitious of whom rose to swell the ranks of an emerging middle class. On one occasion, posing as "A Tradesman of Philadelphia," he defended the interests of these "middling People" against the "wealthy and powerful" Quakers, who dominated the Assembly, and an influential non-Quaker community of "Great and rich Men, Merchants and others."[41]

Andrew Bradford's *American Weekly Mercury* had been in existence a decade when Franklin and Joseph Breintnall, fellow members of the recently organized Junto, undertook the *Busy-Body* papers in 1729 as the first sustained literary venture in what was "primarily a news journal."[42] Franklin was incensed that his former em-

[40]Quoted in James Truslow Adams, *Provincial America, 1690–1763* (New York, 1927), p. 114.

[41]Labaree, III, 199–200. See also Smyth, VIII, 356.

[42]Anna J. DeArmond, *Andrew Bradford: Colonial Journalist* (Newark, Del., 1949), p. 45.

ployer Samuel Keimer should have started a newspaper, pretentiously entitled the *Universal Instructor in all Arts and Sciences: and Pennsylvania Gazette,* to forestall the publication of one that he intended to establish, and now sought with Breintnall to enliven the pages of the *Mercury* and make it a serious competitor to Keimer's paper.

In an advertisement of October 1, 1728, announcing the appearance shortly of the *Universal Instructor,* Keimer had remarked that "the late *Mercury* has been so wretchedly perform'd, that it has been not only a Reproach to the Province, but such a Scandal to the very Name of Printing, that it may, for its unparallel'd Blunders and Incorrectness, be truly stiled *Nonsense in Folio,* instead of a Serviceable News-Paper." He began at once to reprint Ephraim Chambers' *Cyclopaedia.* Having reached "ABO," he carried an article on abortion in the fifth number, whereupon Martha Careful threatened that if he published anything more of this kind, "my Sister Molly and my Self, with some others, are Resolved to run the Hazard of taking him by the Beard, at the next Place we meet him, and make an Example of him for his Immodesty"; Caelia Shortface added, "If thou proceed any further in that Scandalous manner, we intend very soon to have thy right Ear for it."[43] The following week, on February 4, 1729, the first number of the *Busy-Body* appeared.

The Busy-Body is a more nearly Addisonian character than Silence Dogood, especially Breintnall's Busy-Body, who censoriously declares:

A rash and precipitant Manner of Reasoning, with a Mixture of Satyr and Reflection, is now become fashionable;

[43]*American Weekly Mercury,* Jan. 28, 1729. This essay is reprinted in Labaree, I, 112–113, and there assigned to Franklin.

41

Humor and Cavil take Place of Argument, and a noisy
Buffoon is esteemed a Patron of his Country.... But a
truly honest Man, a Lover of his Country, would detest
such Practices, and employ his utmost Endeavours to effect
a Reconciliation.... Having no Regard to any separate
Views, his Behaviour would more resemble that of a Moder-
ator than a Partisan.[44]

While never so earthy and vernacular as Widow Dogood,
Franklin's Busy-Body is nonetheless dramatically conceived. I have continually observed, he declares, that
"what is every Body's Business is no Body's Business," and
I think fit therefore "to take *no Body's Business* wholly
into my own Hands; and, out of Zeal for the Publick
Good, design to erect my Self into a Kind of *Censor
Morum*." I am *"no Partyman, but a general Meddler";* I
have not shown "Partiality towards any Man, or Sett of
Men; but whatsoever I find nonsensically ridiculous, or
immorally dishonest, I have, and shall continue openly to
attack with the Freedom of an honest Man, and a Lover
of my Country."[45] Even before the Busy-Body had finished
presenting this account of himself Keimer launched an
attack:

That we have Party amongst us, is too obvious; and 'tis
difficult for a Man to be perfectly disengag'd. If he has no
sordid or tumultuous Views, Reason and good Judgement
will engage him on one Side; if *Passion* or *Prejudice* prevail,
these will compell him on the other; yet it is plain that a
Beauty and Merit attends the moderate and least violent.
The *Busy-Body* seems to be sensible of this, when he pretends
to be no Party-Man. But let him examine his own Heart,

[44]*American Weekly Mercury*, Mar. 13, 1729.
[45]Labaree, I, 115, 121, 135.

whether that be not inserted as an Attempt to screen himself from the Imputation of Malice or Prejudice.... It requires a great Genius and much good Nature, to manage with Decency and Humanity the Way of Writing which the *Busy-Body* would seem to imitate; feigned and imaginary Characters may excite Vertue and discourage Vice; but to figure out and apply them by gross Description, has the ill Effect which I take this Trouble to persuade the *Busy-Body* to avoid.[46]

Except for a paper on those who search fruitlessly for imaginary hidden treasure, Franklin's Busy-Body ranges over topics that lie safely within the conventional limits of the Augustan periodical essay: ridicule, virtue, evildoing, visitors who wear their welcome out. Only once, and then probably with Keimer in mind, does he come out of the neutral corner and indulge in personal abuse, inveighing: "O Cretico! Thou sowre Philosopher! Thou cunning States-man! Thou are crafty, but far from being Wise. When wilt thou be esteem'd, regarded and belov'd like Cato?" Whereupon Keimer retorted:

> What a confounded Noise and Racket,
> There is about your Weekly Pacquet?
> Some Parts good, and some Parts bad,
> Shew it has different Authors had.
> The author of the *Good*'s unknown,
> But all the *bad ones* are your own;
> And thus your own Stuff does infest,
> And basterdize all the rest.[47]

One feels that from the first Franklin's heart was not in this enterprise as it had so clearly been in the *Dogood*

[46]*Universal Instructor*, Feb. 25, 1729.
[47]*Ibid.*, Mar. 13, 1729.

43

papers; in any case, after the eighth paper he let Breintnall carry on the series alone, to a total of thirty-two. A fortnight after Franklin withdrew Keimer chortled, "The sudden Decease of the *Busy Body* has prov'd less shocking, because he was from his Birth a very weakly Child, and born with an incurable peccant Humour which continued to float over his whole Body, till at length it settled in one of his Legs with a Violent Tumour, upon which the most skilful Doctors advis'd him to an Amputation, but his Original Stock of Life being so very low and languid, 'tis said he expir'd under the Operation, and is to be interr'd this Evening in the most private Manner."[48]

Franklin's *Busy-Body* papers imitate the manner and matter of Addison more nearly than anything else he ever wrote. It was perhaps his awareness of this fact that led him to abandon his part in the undertaking as quickly as he did.

IV

The liveliness of the *Busy-Body* contributed to the failure of the *Universal Instructor,* just as Franklin had hoped. On October 2, 1729, he took over Keimer's newspaper, shortened the title to the *Pennsylvania Gazette,* and became an editor in his own right. Recalling how quickly the *Courant* had been drawn into factional disputes in Massachusetts and forced to take sides, the new editor judiciously applied "the principle of the open forum which English newspapers generally followed in the mid-eighteenth century."[49] "It is a Principle among Printers," he

[48]*Ibid.,* Apr. 10, 1729.
[49]Verner W. Crane, *Benjamin Franklin and a Rising People* (Boston, 1954), p. 25.

declared in 1740, "that when Truth has fair Play, it will always prevail over Falshood; therefore, though they have an undoubted Property in their own Press, yet they willingly allow, that any one is entitled to the Use of it, who thinks it necessary to offer his Sentiments on disputable Points to the Publick, and will be at the Expence of it."[50] At the same time he took care to exclude "all Libelling and Personal Abuse,"[51] convinced that "the Conductor of a News-paper," as he told Francis Hopkinson in 1782, "should, methinks, consider himself as in some degree the Guardian of his Country's Reputation, and refuse to insert such Writings as may hurt it. If People will print their Abuses of one another, let them do it in little Pamphlets, and distribute them where they think proper." The long and flourishing history of the *Gazette* testifies to the soundness of this editorial policy.

Having established such a policy, Franklin at once invited all those "who have long desired to see a good News-Paper in Pennsylvania" to "contribute towards the making This such."[52] The response to this invitation proving slight, he soon began to publish "little Pieces" of his own "which had been first compos'd for Reading in our Junto."[53] More important by far than the countless and frequently clever paragraphs he wrote for the *Gazette* between 1729 and 1748,[54] these essays cover the conventional range of subject matter, though with American colora-

[50]Labaree, II, 260.

[51]*Par. Text Ed.*, p. 244.

[52]Labaree, I, 158.

[53]*Par. Text Ed.*, p. 244.

[54]See Labaree, I, 164, and the sampling of *Gazette* extracts which follows in volumes I–III, printed at the end of each year.

tion: manners and morality,[55] philosophical reflection,[56] character,[57] humor,[58] and criticism.[59] In manner, too, they observe the conventions. Thus, adopting a technique developed long since by English journalists, he posed as "The Casuist," ready to answer queries he addressed to himself concerning cases of conscience. When asked, "Suppose *A* discovers that his Neighbour *B* has corrupted his Wife and injur'd his Bed: Now, if 'tis probable, that by *A*'s acquainting *B*'s Wife with it, and using proper Solicitations, he can prevail with her to consent, that her Husband be used in the same Manner, *is he justifiable in doing it?*," the Casuist replies: "The Philosopher said, with Regard to an Affront which he was urg'd to revenge, *If an Ass kicks me,*

[55]For example, "Reply to a Piece of Advice," *Pennsylvania Gazette*, Mar. 4, 1735; reprinted in Labaree, II, 21–26.

[56]"Self-Denial Not the Essence of Virtue," Feb. 18, 1735; reprinted in Labaree, II, 19–21.

[57]"Anthony Afterwit," July 10, 1732; "Celia Single," July 24, 1732; "Alice Addertongue," Sept. 12, 1732. Reprinted in Labaree, I, 237–248.

[58]"The Drinker's Dictionary," Jan. 13, 1737; reprinted in Labaree, II, 173–178. There is disagreement as to how original and "American" this dictionary is. On the one hand, Cedric Larson, *Am. Speech*, XII (1937), thinks "it quite possible that [Franklin] compiled the Dictionary himself" (p. 88); on the other, E. D. Seeber, *Am. Speech*, XV (1940), admitting that Franklin may have coined a few of the terms, warns, "In accepting Franklin's word that 'The Phrases in this Dictionary are not...borrow'd from Foreign Languages' we should not overlook England as a possible source for the majority of the *Dictionary*'s colloquialisms" (p. 104), and finds that of the 228 expressions only 90 are possible native American colloquialisms.

[59]"On Ill-Natur'd Speaking," July 12, 1733; "On Literary Style," Aug. 2, 1733; "On Amplification," June 17, 1736. Reprinted in Labaree, I, 327, 328–331; II, 146–149.

should I kick him again? So may the injur'd Man of Prudence and Virtue say, 'If a Fool has made himself wicked
and vicious, and has prevailed with an honest Woman to
become as bad as himself; should I also make my self
wicked and vicious, and corrupt another honest Woman,
that I may be even, or upon a Level, with him?'"[60] It is
an answer that discloses its author's own magnanimity,
being written with the same sort of mild irony that informs
The Way to Wealth. Franklin, whose first object in living
was to master the art of virtue, is here smiling at such
niggardly morality, though he speaks with seeming serious-
ness.

Although Franklin nowhere in the *Gazette* sustains a
persona through a series of essays as he had Silence Dogood
and the Busy-Body, in 1732 he did present three distinct
characters, each in the space of a single essay. Anthony
Afterwit, "an honest Tradesman, who never meant Harm
to any Body," indulges his wife's extravagances until
severely dunned. Then during her absence he makes some
alterations:

> I have turn'd away the Maid, Bag and Baggage (for what
> should we do with a Maid, who have (except my Boy) none
> but our selves). I have sold the fine Pacing Mare, and bought
> a good Milch Cow, with £3 of the Money. I have dispos'd
> of the Tea-Table, and put a Spinning Wheel in its Place,
> which methinks *looks very pretty:* Nine empty Canisters I
> have stuff'd with Flax; and with some of the Money of the
> Tea-Furniture, I have bought a Set of Knitting-Needles; for
> to tell you a Truth, which I would have go no farther, *I*

[60]*Pennsylvania Gazette*, June 26, July 3, 1732; reprinted in
Labaree, I, 234–235. For two other queries which the Casuist
answered, see Labaree, I, 163, 221–226.

begin to want Stockings. The stately Clock I have transform'd into an Hour-Glass, by which I gain'd a good round
Sum; and one of the Pieces of the old Looking-Glass, squar'd
and fram'd, supplies the Place of the Great One, which I
have convey'd into a Closet, where it may possibly remain
some Years.

If my wife "can conform to this new Scheme of Living,
we shall be the happiest Couple perhaps in the Province,
and, by the Blessing of God, may soon be in thriving
Circumstances." Two weeks later Celia Single complained
that Anthony's letter "has broken the Peace of several
Families, by causing Difference between Men and their
Wives." I was at Mrs. C – – ss's the other day when her
husband returned with some balls of thread. *"My Dear, says
he, I like mightily those Stockings which I yesterday saw
Neighbour Afterwit knitting for her Husband, of Thread
of her own Spinning."* A quarrel ensues, the upshot of
which is, as Celia learns from their maid, that "they dined
together pretty peaceably, (the Balls of Thread that had
caused the Difference, being thrown into the Kitchen Fire)
of which I was very glad to hear." Angered by the Gazetteer's severe reflections upon the idleness and extravagance
of women, Celia declares,

> I might mention Mr. Billiard, who spends more than he
> earns, at the Green Table; and would have been in Jail
> long since, were it not for his industrious Wife: Mr. Hussel-
> cap, who often all day long leaves his Business for the rattling
> of Half-pence in a certain Alley: Mr. Finikin, who has seven
> different Suits of fine Cloaths, and wears a Change every
> Day, while his Wife and Children sit at home half naked:
> Mr. Crownhim, who is always dreaming over the Chequer-
> board, and cares not how the World goes, so he gets the

48

Game: Mr. T'otherpot the Tavern-haunter; Mr. Bookish, the everlasting Reader; Mr. Tweedledum, Mr. Toot-a-toot, and several others, who are mighty diligent at any thing beside their Business.

Instead, I will merely advise you, Mr. Gazetteer, to entertain your readers in the future "with something else besides People's Reflections upon one another." These personae, one a bachelor recently married to an extravagant wife, the other a good-humored spinster irritated that her sex should be singled out for criticism, portray the world of the "middling People" in Pennsylvania vividly and with comic vigor.

In contrast, the portrait of Alice Addertongue verges on caricature. "I am a young Girl of about thirty-five," she informs the Gazetteer, "and live at present with my Mother."

I have no Care upon my Head of getting a Living, and therefore find it my Duty as well as Inclination, to exercise my Talent at CENSURE, for the Good of my Country folks. . . .

By Industry and Application, I have made my self the Center of all the *Scandal* in the Province, there is little stirring but I hear of it. . . . For besides the Stock of Defamation thus naturally flowing in upon me, I practice an Art by which I can pump Scandal out of People that are the least enclin'd that way. . . .

But alas, two great Evils have lately befaln me at the same time; an extream Cold that I can scarce speak, and a most terrible Toothach that I dare hardly open my Mouth: For some Days past I have receiv'd ten Stories for one I have paid; and I am not able to ballance my Accounts without your Assistance.

49

In a final comic twist the Gazetteer asks to be excused from printing the account she has sent him of *"4 Knavish Tricks, 2 crackt M – – – n – – ds, 5 Cu – – ld – ms, 3 drub'd Wives,* and *4 Henpeck'd Husbands," "such Things being in Reality* no News at all."* While Alice is a more conventional type than the homespun Anthony and Celia, a coarseness of expression as native to Franklin as his urbanity was acquired here serves to vitalize the character. All three personae point the way, even more clearly than Silence Dogood and the Busy-Body, to Richard and Bridget Saunders.

By 1735 Franklin had become so deeply engaged in civic projects and provincial business that he all but left off writing essays for the *Gazette;* in 1748 he turned the management of the newspaper and of his printing office over to his new partner, David Hall.[61] Toward the end of his life he would return to the tradition in which he had embarked on a literary career.[62] For the time being, the experience gained from venturing into this genre, first at Boston, then at Philadelphia, was valuable preparation for the aphoristic and polemical writing that lay ahead of him.

[61]See Labaree, III, 263–267.

[62]These late essays include: "On Sending Felons to America," Lib. Cong. MS, [1778?], printed in Smyth, IX, 628–630; "The Internal State of America," *Pennsylvania Gazette,* May 17, 1786, reprinted in *Wm. and Mary Quar.,* ser. 3, XV (1958), 223–227; "On the Abuse of the Press," Lib. Cong. MS, Mar. 30, 1788, printed in Smyth, IX, 639–642; and "A Letter concerning China," *The Repository* (London), II (May 1, 1788), 4–10, reprinted as "A Letter from China" in Smyth, IX, 200–208—the only example in Franklin's work of the foreign-visitor device.

III

The Almanac

ON December 28, 1732, the *Pennsylvania Gazette* announced as "JUST PUBLISHED, FOR 1733,"

> POOR RICHARD: An ALMANACK containing the Lunations, Eclipses, Planets Motions and Aspects, Weather, Sun and Moon's rising and setting, Highwater, &c. besides many pleasant and witty Verses, Jests and Sayings, Author's Motive of Writing, Prediction of the Death of his friend Mr. Titan Leeds, Moon no Cuckold, Batchelor's Folly, Parson's Wine and Baker's Pudding, Short Visits, Kings and Bears, New Fashions, Game for Kisses, Katherine's Love, Different Sentiments, Signs of a Tempest, Death a Fisherman, Conjugal Debate, Men and Melons, H. the Prodigal, Breakfast in Bed, Oyster Lawsuit, &c. by RICHARD SAUNDERS, Philomat.

Poor Richard's Almanack was by no means the first such production in Pennsylvania, where farmers, artisans, and shopkeepers demanded a literature of action. As early as 1686 Samuel Atkins had tried his hand at the form, and Daniel Leeds took his place the next year.[1] From the turn of the century the colony witnessed a steady flow of

[1] John Bach McMaster, *Benjamin Franklin as a Man of Letters* (Boston and New York, 1887), p. 99.

almanacs. When Franklin undertook his, no fewer than six others were being published at Philadelphia, several of them written and printed by men like Andrew Bradford, Samuel Keimer, and Thomas Godfrey whom he knew personally.

In his almanacs Franklin, the rising young editor, wrote with greater familiarity than he allowed himself in his more studied periodical essays; after all, as philomath he did not need to maintain the same dignity as in the *Gazette*. Considering *Poor Richard* "a proper Vehicle for conveying Instruction among the common People, who bought scarce any other Books," he "endeavour'd to make it both entertaining and useful."[2] He approached his task in seeming earnest, thereby escaping the prosaic dullness that characterized most colonial almanacs. In 1737 "Philomath," expressing what was certainly Franklin's attitude, specified "the Talents requisite in *an Almanack Writer*." Contending that *"Almanackorum scriptor nascitur non fit,"* he said that such a writer *"should be descended of a great Family, and bear a Coat of Arms";* that he should possess "a Sort of Gravity, which keeps a due medium between Dulness and Nonsense, and yet has a Mixture of both. . . . He shou'd write Sentences, and throw out Hints, that neither himself, nor any Body else can understand or know the meaning of"; and that he *"shou'd not be a finish'd Poet, but a Piece of one,* and qualify'd to write, what we vulgarly call Doggerel." "I could further prove to you, if I was to go about it," concluded Philomath, "That an *Almanack Writer* ought not only to be a Piece of a Wit, but a very Wag; and that he shou'd have the

[2]*Par. Text Ed.*, p. 242.

Art also to make People believe, that he is almost a Conjurer, &c."[3]

I

In the prefaces to *Poor Richard's Almanack* and occasionally in the verse Franklin created his most famous American personae, the homespun Richard Saunders and his clacking wife Bridget. "I might in this place attempt to gain thy Favour," Richard informs the reader in the first number,

> by declaring that I write Almanacks with no other View than that of the publick Good; but in this I should not be sincere; and Men are now a-days too wise to be deceiv'd by Pretences how specious soever. The plain Truth of the Matter is, I am excessive poor, and my Wife, good Woman, is, I tell her, excessive proud; she cannot bear, she says, to sit spinning in her Shift of Tow, while I do nothing but gaze at the Stars; and has threatned more than once to burn all my Books and Rattling-Traps (as she calls my Instruments) if I do not make some profitable Use of them for the good of my Family. The Printer has offer'd me some considerable share of the Profits, and I have thus begun to comply with my Dame's desire.[4]

His first almanac sells so well that at once he gains a measure of relief: "My Wife has been enabled to get a Pot of her own, and is no longer oblig'd to borrow one from a Neighbour; nor have we ever since been without something of our own to put in it. She has also got a pair of Shoes, two new Shifts, and a new warm Petticoat; and

[3]*Pennsylvania Gazette,* Oct. 20, 1737.

[4]Labaree, I, 311. Hereafter all quotations from *Poor Richard* will be identified by year and month in the body of the text.

53

for my part, I have bought a second-hand Coat, so good, that I am now not asham'd to go to Town or be seen there. These Things have render'd her Temper so much more pacifick than it us'd to be, that I may say, I have slept more, and more quietly within this last Year, than in the three foregoing Years put together" (1734). A prospering Richard assures his readers, "If the generous Purchaser of my Labours could see how often his *Fi'-pence* helps to light up the comfortable Fire, line the Pot, fill the Cup and make glad the Heart of a poor Man and an honest good old Woman, he would not think his Money ill laid out, tho' the Almanack of his Friend and Servant R. SAUNDERS were one half blank Paper" (1737). Lest they suppose him grown wealthy, though, he reminds them that the printer, though "I do not grudge it him," "runs away with the greatest Part of the Profit" (1739).

From the outset the *Almanack*'s purpose was wholly social. Like the Busy-Body, Richard professes and adheres to a neutrality in religion and politics. In 1746 he assures his public,

> Free from the bitter Rage of Party Zeal,
> All those we love who seek the publick Weal.

Indeed, other than his attacks on fellow philomaths like Titan Leeds and John Jerman, attacks for which Swift's Bickerstaff papers furnished a precedent, Franklin avoided polemics altogether, exhibiting instead that sweet reasonableness and moralistic bent so highly esteemed in the early eighteenth century.

As the Couranteers had entertained their readers with the age-old battle of the sexes, so now Franklin. To Richard's charge,

She that will eat her breakfast in her bed,
And spend the morn in dressing of her head,
And sit at dinner like a maiden bride,
And talk of nothing all day but of pride;
God in his mercy may do much to save her,
But what a case is he in that shall have her.

[Dec., 1733]

Bridget retorts,

He that for the sake of Drink neglects his Trade,
And spends each Night in Taverns till 'tis late,
And rises when the Sun is four hours high,
And ne'er regards his starving Family;
God in his Mercy may do much to save him,
But, woe to the poor Wife, whose Lot it is to have him.

[Dec., 1734]

The lines of battle thus early drawn, Bridget cries out against Richard's aspersions on her character: "What a peasecods! cannot I have a little Fault or two, but all the Country must see it in print! They have already been told, at one time that I am proud, another time that I am loud, and that I have got a new Petticoat, and abundance of such kind of stuff; and now, forsooth! all the World must know, that Poor Dick's Wife has lately taken a fancy to drink a little Tea now and then. A mighty matter, truly, to make a Song of! 'Tis true, I had a little Tea of a Present from the Printer last Year; and what, must a body throw it away?" (1738). When placed side by side with Mrs. Afterwit, Bridget seems the soul of modesty; in fact, her practicality, honesty, and industry call to mind rather the Widow Dogood. No matter, the battle raged on.

My sickly Spouse, with many a Sigh
Once told me,—Dicky I shall die:
I griev'd, but recollected strait,
'Twas bootless to contend with Fate:
So Resignation to Heav'n's Will
Prepared me for succeeding Ill;
'Twas well it did; for, on my Life,
'Twas Heav'n's Will to spare my Wife.
[Jan., 1740]

When he tells her that heaven will deny whatever she prays for, "Indeed! says Nell, 'tis what I'm pleas'd to hear; / For now I'll pray for your long life, my dear" (Sept., 1743). Finally, in what closes out this debate, there appeared an *"Epitaph on a Scolding Wife by her Husband,"* adapted from Dryden: "Here my poor Bridget's Corps doth lie, she is at rest,—and so am I" (Dec., 1744).

Although Richard Saunders has often been confused with his creator, the separate identity of the humble philomath grown affluent and his printer was clearly established from the opening number. So it is that Richard, in order to quash malicious rumors that there is no such man as he and that his productions are actually the work of the printer, publicly declares, *"That what I have written heretofore, and do now write, neither was nor is written by any other Man or Men, Person or Persons whatsoever"* (1736). So, too, that he holds the printer, not himself, accountable for most of the errata in one of the almanacs, remarking:

Printers indeed should be very careful how they omit a Figure or a Letter: For by such Means sometimes a terrible Alteration is made in the Sense. I have heard, that once, in a new Edition of the *Common Prayer,* the following Sentence, *We shall all be changed in a Moment, in the Twin-*

kling of an Eye; by the Omission of a single Letter, became, *We shall all be hanged in a Moment,* &c. to the no small Surprize of the first Congregation it was read to (1750).

This confusion between the author and his persona arises in part from the fact that after 1738 Richard the honest philomath tends to be obscured by the emergence of Richard the moralizing philosopher, a confusion later compounded by the avowedly didactic purpose of the often reprinted *Autobiography.* "Besides the usual Things expected in an Almanack," declares Richard in 1739, "I hope the profess'd Teachers of Mankind will excuse my scattering here and there some instructive Hints in Matters of Morality and Religion." From this time, but especially beginning in 1748, the year Franklin expanded his pamphlet from twenty-four pages to thirty-six, didactic and practical essays become more numerous and play a more prominent role in the *Almanack.*

Any final estimate of the character of Richard must take into account the 1758 Preface, known familiarly as *The Way to Wealth,* a work allied to popular tradesman books like Defoe's *Complete English Tradesman* and English conduct books like John Barnard's *Present for an Apprentice.* While Franklin's first object in living was to master the art of virtue and while he undoubtedly gave general assent to the wisdom of Poor Richard, here it is so narrowly concentrated and cast in so precise a narrative frame that Franklin probably did not mean the work to be taken altogether seriously.[5] But eighteenth-century

[5]Alfred Owen Aldridge, *Franklin and His French Contemporaries* (New York, 1957), p. 53, writes, "That Franklin himself did not take it seriously, the narrative elements with which he adorned it are ample proof."

France, identifying Franklin's attitude with Richard's, regarded it "as a work of sublime morality";[6] and since that time readers the world over have generally so interpreted it. Actually we see Richard, hearing himself quoted so liberally, enslaved by his own morality, a fact of which Franklin is clearly aware. Whereas the people at the auction, having approved the doctrine in Father Abraham's speech, "immediately practised the contrary, just as if it had been a common Sermon," Richard takes this prudential wisdom—and it is, of course, his own—so much to heart that he denies himself material for a new coat, even though the one he is wearing was secondhand when he bought it a quarter of a century before. And when he adds smugly, *"Reader,* if thou wilt do the same, thy Profit will be as great as mine," though we do not necessarily sympathize with the behavior of the others "at this Vendue of *Fineries* and *Knicknacks*," we smile at the foolish caution that prevents him from making a reasonable purchase. Franklin, who prized frugality as highly as any man, is here warning his public not to fall victim to a narrow and unimaginative exercise of it.[7]

At this point I should like to revise one judgment in John F. Ross's otherwise highly perceptive article on the character of Richard Saunders. Having distinguished carefully between the two Richards, Ross remarks:

[6]*Ibid.,* p. 59.
[7]Harold S. Larrabee, *Harper's Magazine,* CCXII (Jan., 1956), 66, says of Franklin, "His moral teaching—like that of John Dewey, now so much under attack—was a dynamic doctrine of 'open ends' rather than of fixed moral absolutes forcing all individuals into a single mold."

It is easy to see why Franklin let the original character go, and made no attempt to relate the maxims to the character of his star-gazer. He was interested in getting an almanac to press every fall, not in the depiction of character or the maintenance of literary consistency.... The early Richard was finally submerged by the famous farewell preface of 1758, wherein a shadowy Richard appears, only to introduce the speech of a wise old man, Father Abraham, who quotes maxim after maxim from the body of the almanacs.... That is, Franklin forced Richard to play a rôle.[8]

Granted that as Franklin built a comfortable living in the 1740's, he began to conceive of Richard as the complete American tradesman. Granted, too, that by the 1750's the *Almanack* was selling at the impressive rate of 10,000 copies a year.[9] I cannot accept the inference that he consciously forced Richard to play a role. It seems more probable that insofar as the conception of Richard underwent a change, it happened unconsciously. And if Franklin was not immediately concerned with maintaining literary consistency, how is it that the original Richard reappears in the 1750's—nowhere more memorably than in *The Way to Wealth,* where he is anything but "shadowy"? The enduring vitality of this, Franklin's most fully articulated persona, lies finally in the fact that over the space of twenty-five years the character of the indigent stargazer turned philomath is never totally submerged.

II

Balzac, in a statement that is true in spirit if not wholly in fact, once observed, "*Le canard est une trouvaille de*

[8]*PMLA,* LV (1940), 793–794.
[9]C. William Miller, *Stud. Bibliog.,* XIV (1961), 111.

*Franklin, qui a inventé le paratonnerre, le canard et la
république.*"[10] The earliest of Franklin's canards, recalling
Swift's hoax on John Partridge, was perpetrated at the
expense of a local rival, Titan Leeds. The equation:
Richard Saunders is to Titan Leeds as Isaac Bickerstaff is to
John Partridge: expresses the similarity in rhetorical
strategy, though in certain respects Richard resembles
Partridge more nearly than he does Bickerstaff. In the 1733
Preface Richard predicts the time of Titan's death to the
minute and, when Titan protests that he did not die at that
time, earnestly defends his prediction:

> Mr. Leeds was not only profoundly skilful in the useful
> Science he profess'd, but he was a Man of *exemplary So-
> briety,* a most *sincere Friend,* and an *exact Performer of his
> Word.* These valuable Qualifications, with many others so
> much endear'd him to me, that although it should be so,
> that, contrary to all Probability, contrary to my Prediction
> and his own, he might possibly be yet alive, yet my Loss of
> Honour as a Prognosticator, cannot afford me so much
> Mortification, as his Life, Health and Safety would give me
> Joy and Satisfaction (1734).

Titan's protests continuing, Richard retorts with pretended indignation:

> Having receiv'd much Abuse from Titan Leeds deceas'd,
> (Titan Leeds when living would not have us'd me so!) . . .
> I cannot help saying, that tho' I take it patiently, I take
> it very unkindly. And whatever he may pretend, 'tis un-
> doubtedly true that he is really defunct and dead. First be-
> cause the Stars are seldom disappointed. . . . Secondly, . . .
> for the Honour of Astrology, the Art professed both by him
> and his Father [Daniel] before him. Thirdly, . . . [because]

[10]*Illusions perdues* (Paris, 1879), II, 115.

his two last Almanacks...are not written with that *Life* his Performances use to be written with (1735).

In 1739, by Richard's account, the Bradfords, who continued to publish Titan's almanac, at last admit that he is dead. Whereupon Richard relates how, waking early one morning at his study table where he had fallen asleep, he discovered a letter from Titan confessing that he had indeed died at the time predicted, "with a Variation only of 5 min. 53 sec." Titan goes on to explain further:

Finding you asleep, I entred your left Nostril, ascended into your Brain, found out where the Ends of those Nerves were fastned that move your right Hand and Fingers, by the Help of which I am now writing unknown to you; but when you open your Eyes, you will see that the Hand written is mine, tho' wrote with yours (1740).

Here for the first time Franklin employs a rhetorical strategy that colored later writings like Polly Baker's Speech and the fictitious controversy involving English news writers. He initiates, carries forward, and closes out this hoax, not through malice, but for the pleasure to be gained from exploiting the comic implications of the fiction. Once Richard has predicted the time of Titan's death, pseudological proofs follow hard upon one another, the principal strategy being to seize upon the victim's every protest of innocence and turn it back upon him. Thus, in reply to Titan's declaration, "Saunders adds another GROSS FALSHOOD in his Almanack, viz. that by my own Calculation I shall *survive* until the 26th of the said Month October 1733, which is as *untrue* as the former," Richard asserts, "Now if it be, as Leeds says, *untrue* and a *gross Falshood* that he surviv'd till the 26th of October

61

1733, then it is certainly *true* that he died *before* that Time" (1735). The climactic letter in which Titan admits to having died at the time predicted, "with a Variation only of 5 min. 53 sec.," bears final witness to Franklin's high sense of invention. This Swiftian hoax is part of a continuing, good-humored attack on astrology in the pages of the *Almanack*. Not so incidentally, the sophistry Richard here displays lends subtlety to his character.

Franklin, who took himself less seriously than did his rival philomaths, has Richard declare:

> The noble Art [of astrology] is dwindled into Contempt; the Great neglect us, Empires make Leagues, and Parliaments Laws, without advising with us; and scarce any other Use is made of our learned Labours, than to find the best Time of cutting Corns, or gelding Pigs. This Mischief we owe in a great Measure to ourselves.... Urania has been betray'd by her own Sons; those whom she had favour'd with the greatest Skill in her divine Art, the most eminent Astronomers among the Moderns, the Newtons, Halleys, and Whistons, have wantonly contemn'd and abus'd her, contrary to the Light of their own Consciences (1751).

In the prefaces and essays such astrological lore as eclipses, weather predictions, and prophecies is constantly being held up to ridicule. Thus, Richard predicts two eclipses of the sun, "both, like Mrs. –––s's Modesty, and old Neighbour Scrape-all's Money, *Invisible*" (1734); and says of John Jerman's prediction, "He has done what in him lay (by sending them out to gaze at an invisible Eclipse on the first of April) to make *April Fools* of them all" (1744).

As for the weather, Richard asks that philomaths be allowed a few days' leeway, and, "if it does not come to pass accordingly, let the Fault be laid upon the Printer, who, 'tis very like, may have transpos'd or misplac'd it, perhaps for the Conveniency of putting in his Holidays" (1737). The year Bridget tampered with the almanac during her husband's absence she informs the reader, "Upon looking over the Months, I see he has put in abundance of foul Weather this Year; and therefore I have scatter'd here and there, where I could find room, some *fair, pleasant, sunshiny,* &c. for the Good-Women to dry their Clothes in" (1738). All in all, Richard is pleased to think that his weather predictions come to pass *"punctually* and *precisely* on the very Day, in some Place or other on this little *diminutive* Globe of ours" (1753).

Richard's "True PROGNOSTICATION, for 1739" is a skillful abstracting of the "Pantagruelian Prognostication" at the end of the Urquhart-Motteux translation of *Gargantua and Pantagruel,* with vernacular additions and substitutions made out of regard for an American audience. In a passage taken almost verbatim from Rabelais, Richard predicts: "During the first visible Eclipse Saturn is retrograde: For which Reason the Crabs will go sidelong, and the Rope-makers backward. The Belly will wag before, and the A——— shall sit down first." The passage continues: "Mercury will have his share in these Affairs, and so confound the Speech of People, that when a Pensilvanian would say PANTHER, he shall say PAINTER. When a New-Yorker thinks to say (THIS) he shall say (DISS) and the People in New-England and Cape-May will not be able to say (COW) for their lives, but will be forc'd to say (KEOW) by a certain involuntary Twist in the Root of their Tongues." To Rabelais' prediction, "This Year the Stone-blind shall see but very little; the Deaf shall hear but poorly; and the Dumb shan't speak very plain," Richard adds, "And it's much, if my Dame Bridget talks at all this Year." For Rabelais' "Salt-eel" he substitutes the more homely expression "Cowskin"; for "Apes, Monkeys, Baboons, and Dromedaries," the more familiar "Cats, Dogs and Horses"; for "your Hops of Picardy," the more nearly American "Orange Trees in Greenland"; and for "Wine" and "Herbs," the less exotic "Cyder" and "Turnips." In this burlesque Franklin exhibits skill in compressing and adapting a literary source to his own very different purpose.

III

In addition to prefaces and essays, colonial almanacs traditionally carried what Franklin advertised as "pleasant and witty Verses, Jests and Sayings," that is, proverbial matter and poetic borrowings. B. J. Whiting has defined the proverb as "an expression which, owing its birth to the people, testifies to its origin in form and phrase. It expresses what is apparently a fundamental truth...in homely language, often adorned, however, with alliteration and rhyme; it is usually true, but need not be."[11] Judging by Swift's *Complete Collection of Genteel and Ingenious Conversation,* two dialogues burlesquing proverbial expressions of the day, and by Lord Chesterfield's admonition that his son avoid "old sayings, and common proverbs; which are so many proofs of having kept bad and low company,"[12] it seems safe to accept Robert Newcomb's assertion that during the first part of the eighteenth century "the educated Englishman's attitude toward the

[11]*Harvard Studies and Notes in Philology,* XIV (1932), 302.

[12]July 25, 1741, *The Letters of Philip Dormer Stanhope. 4th Earl of Chesterfield,* ed. Bonamy Dobree (London, 1932), II, 461.

proverb was not very favorable."[13] As an artisan's son
Franklin had no such reservations, however; from the time
Silence Dogood announced that *"a Woman's Work is never
done,"* proverbial expression was an essential component of
his style.

Franklin filled the little spaces of his almanacs with what
Richard calls *"moral* Sentences, *prudent* Maxims, and *wise*
Sayings, many of them containing *much good Sense* in
very few Words, and therefore apt to leave *strong* and
lasting Impressions on the Memory of young Persons"
(1747). These proverbs were gleaned principally from
Thomas Fuller's *Gnomologia* (1732), *Introductio ad Pru-
dentiam* (1727), and *Introductio ad Sapientiam* (1731);
Lord Halifax's *Character of King Charles the Second: and
Political, Moral, Miscellaneous Thoughts and Reflections*
(1750); George Herbert's *Outlandish Proverbs* (1640);
James Howell's *Lexicon Tetraglotton* (1659); and Samuel
Richardson's *Collection of Moral and Instructive Senti-
ments* (1755).[14] Such sayings, especially those that appear
in the early numbers of the *Almanack,* usually reflect
Richard's interests.[15]

While most of Richard's comic sayings are given verbatim from the original source, on occasion Franklin, yield-

[13]Robert Howard Newcomb, "The Sources of Benjamin Franklin's
Sayings of Poor Richard" (unpublished dissertation, Univ. of Maryland, 1957), p. 46.

[14]Newcomb has uncovered most of the sources for the sayings in
Poor Richard. For his discussion of Franklin's borrowings from
Halifax, Montaigne, and Richardson, see *PMLA,* LXX (1955), 535–
539; *Mod. Lang. Notes,* LXXII (1957), 489–491; and *Jour. Eng. and
Germ. Phil.,* LVII (1958), 27–35.

[15]Newcomb, "Sources," p. 31.

ing to a coarseness that was native to him, modifies them
in the direction of the obscene or bawdy.

A good friend is my nearest relation. [Fuller, *Gn.*, No. 151]
Relation without friendship, friendship without power,
power without will, will without effect, effect without
profit, and profit without vertue, are not worth a farto.
[*Poor Richard's Almanack*, Apr., 1733]

A Fort which begins to parley is half gotten. [Howell, *It.
Prov.*, p. 12]
The Woman who hearkens, and the town which treats, the
one will yield, the other will do. [Howell, *Fr. Prov.*, p. 5]
Neither a Fortress nor a Maidenhead will hold out long
after they begin to parly. [*PRA*, May, 1734]

The pun, a recognizable feature in the proverb, is so
habitual to Franklin that he will introduce one where
none is present in the original.

The good wife is made by the man. [Howell, *Sp. Prov.*, p. 14]
Good wives and good plantations are made by good husbands. [*PRA*, Aug., 1736]

The comic element present in such sayings further vivifies
Franklin's most vital comic creation and goes far toward
counteracting the stereotype of Richard the prudential
moralist that persisted throughout the "inner-directed"
nineteenth century and still lingers today.

As a proverb stylist who often recast what he borrowed,
Franklin was guided by such neoclassic ideals as perspicuity, elegance, and cadence. In accommodating foreign
sayings to an American audience, he habitually familiarizes
and simplifies the diction.

Nor wife, nor wine, nor horse ought to be praised. [Howell,
It. Prov., p. 12]

66

Never praise your Cyder, Horse, or Bedfellow. [*PRA*, Mar., 1736]

A yeoman upon his legs is higher than a prince upon his knees. [Fuller, *Gn.*, No. 488]

A Plowman on his Legs is higher than a Gentleman on his Knees. [*PRA*, May, 1746]

Go neither to the Physician upon every distemper, nor to the Lawyer upon every brabble, nor to the pot upon every thirst. [Howell, *Sp. Prov.*, p. 7]

Don't go to the doctor with every distemper, nor to the lawyer with every quarrel, nor to the pot for every thirst. [*PRA*, Nov., 1737]

He tightens the syntax of many sayings and expresses the meaning in a narrower compass, sometimes employing alliteration or rhyme.

That cheese is wholesomest which comes from a Miser. [Howell, *Sp. Prov.*, p. 23]

The misers cheese is wholesomest. [*PRA*, Feb., 1737]

As soon as men have understanding enough to find a fault, they have enough to see the danger of mending it. [Halifax, *Misc.*, p. 244]

Men take more pains to mask than mend. [*PRA*, Apr., 1757]

A ship under sail, a man in complete armor, a woman with a great belly are three of the handsomest sights. [Howell, *Eng. Prov.*, p. 2]

A Ship under sail and a big-bellied Woman,
Are the handsomest two things that can be seen common.
[*PRA*, June, 1735]

But since Franklin does not believe in economy for its own sake, he may see fit to expand the original saying. Such expansion is usually the result of supplying the saying with an introduction (often a personification), clarifying its sense by extending it, or appending a moral close.

He is a greater Liar than an epitaph. [Howell, *It. Prov.*, p. 2]

Here comes Glib-tongue: who can out-flatter a Dedication; and lie, like ten Epitaphs. [*PRA*, Dec., 1742]

Happy those who are convinced so as to be of the general opinions. [Halifax, *Polit.*, p. 227]

Singularity in the right, hath ruined many: Happy those who are Convinced of the general Opinion. [*PRA*, Oct., 1757]

A quiet Conscience sleeps in Thunder. [Fuller, *Gn.*, No. 375]
A quiet Conscience sleeps in Thunder,
But Rest and Guilt live far asunder. [*PRA*, July, 1747]

When all sins grow old covetousness grows young. [Herbert, No. 18]

When other Sins grow old by Time,
Then Avarice is in its prime,
Yet feed the Poor at Christmas time. [*PRA*, Dec., 1757]

To secure precision he modifies sayings in the direction of concreteness.

The tongue talks at the head's cost. [Herbert, p. 308]

The Tongue offends, and the Ears get the Cuffing. [*PRA*, Nov., 1757]

Slander would not stick, if it had not always something to lay hold of. [Halifax, *Misc.*, p. 255]

Act uprightly, and despise Calumny; Dirt may stick to a Mud Wall, but not to polish'd Marble. [*PRA*, Sept., 1757]

Revisions like these all make for greater perspicuity.

Such ornament as Richard's sayings possess is consistent with the responsible use of rhetoric enjoined by the Port-Royalists and Locke. Franklin at times introduces a metaphor into an original saying, at others amplifies or gives greater precision and consistency to one already present.

> Nothing can be humbler than Ambition, when it is so disposed. [Halifax, *Moral*, p. 232]
>
>> Nothing humbler than *Ambition*, when it is about to climb. [*PRA*, Nov., 1753]
>
> Who riseth late, trots all day, because he is behind hand with business. [Howell, *Sp. Prov.*, p. 27]
>
>> He that riseth late, must trot all day, and shall scarce overtake his business at night. [*PRA*, Aug., 1742]
>
> That which is given shines, that which is eaten stinks. [Howell, *Fr. Prov.*, p. 8]
>
>> What's given shines,
>> What's receiv'd is rusty. [*PRA*, July, 1735]

Sometimes he supplies an example to point up and color a saying.

> Necessity has no law. [Howell, *Eng. Prov.*, p. 9]
>
>> *Necessity* has no Law; I know some Attorneys of the name. [*PRA*, Oct., 1734]

However elegantly Franklin dresses up Richard's sayings, he carefully avoids making a show of rhetoric.

Cadence, which John Hughes defined as "a Disposing of the Words in such Order, and with such Variation of Periods, as may strike the Ear with a sort of musical Delight," is markedly present in the sayings Franklin recasts. Frequently he strives for a more balanced expression, or one that is less mechanically balanced.

It is better to have an egg today than an hen tomorrow. [Howell, *It. Prov.*, p. 1]

An Egg today is better than a Hen to-morrow. [*PRA*, Sept., 1734]

Thou shouldst grace thy House; not thy House thee. [Fuller, *Prud.*, No. 1796]

Grace then thy House, and let not that grace thee. [*PRA*, Apr., 1739]

A Man had as good go to Bed to a Razor, as to be intimate with a foolish friend. [Halifax, *Moral*, p. 235]

To be intimate with a foolish Friend, is like going to bed to a Razor. [*PRA*, Sept., 1754]

When one Knave betrayeth another, the one is not to be blamed, nor the other to be pitied. [Halifax, *Moral*, p. 237]

When Knaves betray each other, one can scarce be blamed, or the other pitied. [*PRA*, Feb., 1758]

To strengthen the rhythm of the sentence he often employs alliteration.

A Melon and a woman are hard to be known. [Howell, *Sp. Prov.*, p. 4]

Men and Melons are hard to know. [*PRA*, Sept., 1733]

Men should do with their hopes as they do with tame fowl, cut their wings that they may not fly over the wall. [Halifax, *Moral*, p. 237]

Cut the Wings of your Hens and Hopes, lest they lead you a weary Dance after them. [*PRA*, Feb., 1754]

Having early achieved a flexible command of the English sentence, Franklin knows how to refine the syntax of his source and make it more euphonious.

Who goes far to marry, either goes to deceive, or to be deceived. [Howell, *Sp. Prov.*, p. 13]

He that goes far to marry, will either deceive or be deceived. [*PRA*, Mar., 1735]

Do not Do it if thou wilt not have it known. [Howell, *It. Prov.*, p. 6]

Do not do that which you would not have known. [*PRA*, Feb., 1736]

Resolving to serve well, and at the same time to please, is generally resolving to do what is not to be done. [Halifax, *Polit.*, p. 215]

To serve the Publick faithfully, and at the same time please it entirely, is impracticable. [*PRA*, Oct., 1758]

The skill with which Franklin shaped his proverbial borrowings suggests that by the time he launched the *Almanack*, in his twenty-seventh year, he was on his way to becoming one of the great makers of the English sentence. Whereas proverbs merely serve to fill up the spaces in the almanacs, in his letters public and private and in the *Autobiography* they form an integral part of the work. Franklin's proverbial manner of expression was undoubtedly one reason the genteel critic Joseph Dennie charged him with being "the founder of that Grubstreet sect, who have professedly attempted to degrade literature to the level of vulgar capacities, and debase the polished and current language of books, by the vile alloy of provincial idioms, and colloquial barbarism, the shame of grammar, and akin to any language, rather than English."[16] As a Boston critic had deplored the plain prose of the *Dogood* papers, so Dennie's social bias ruled out proverbial expres-

[16]*The Port Folio* (Philadelphia), I (Feb. 14, 1801), 54.

sion. How infinitely poorer and less idiosyncratic Franklin's style would be without it!

"The Verses on the Heads of the Months...not many of them are of my own Making," confesses Richard. "If thou hast any Judgment in Poetry, thou wilt easily discern the Workman from the Bungler. I know as well as thee, that I am no *Poet born;* and it is a Trade I never learnt, nor indeed could learn.... Why then should I give my Readers *bad Lines* of my own, when *good Ones* of other People's are so plenty?" (1747). More numerous and frequently of greater length than poems of his own composition are those Franklin borrowed from seventeenth- and eighteenth-century English sources, notably Dryden, Pope, Swift, Gay's *Fables,* Young's *Love of Fame,* Savage's *Public Spirit,* and two miscellanies, Sir John Mennes and James Smith's *Wits Recreation* (1640) and the anonymous *Collection of Epigrams* (1735–1737).[17] In fact, over a twenty-five-year period (1733–1758) most of the genres popular in the early eighteenth century—epigrams, topographical poems, georgics, satires, odes, fables, epistles—appeared in the pages of *Poor Richard's Almanack.*[18]

Generally speaking, Franklin made few changes in his poetic borrowings; thus Savage's *Public Spirit,* cut and revised, runs at the heads of the months in 1752. Consider, though, the case of an *Almanack* poem for January 1734:

[17]See W. P. Mustard, *Nation,* LXXXII (Mar. 22, Apr. 5, 1906), 239, 279; Newcomb, "Sources," chapter five. Newcomb, *Phil. Quar.,* XL (1961), 270–280, has demonstrated what omissions, additions, and revisions Franklin made in the process of adapting English epigrams from *Wits Recreations* and *A Collection of Epigrams* to suit the mood and format of the *Almanack.*

[18]Newcomb, "Sources," p. 167.

From a cross Neighbour, and a sullen Wife,
A pointless Needle, and a broken Knife;
From Suretyship, and from an empty Purse,
A Smoaky Chimney and a jolting Horse;
From a dull Razor, and an aking Head,
From a bad Conscience and a buggy Bed;
A Blow upon the Elbow and the Knee,
From each of these, *Good L--d deliver me.*

These lines are abstracted from the first third of "A
Letany," in the "Fancies and Fantasticks" section of *Wits
Recreation:*

From a proud Woodcock, and a peevish wife,
A pointlesse Needle, and a broken Knife,
From lying in a Ladies lap,
Like a great fool that longs for pap,
   And from the fruit of the three corner'd tree,
   Vertue and goodnesse still deliver me.

From a conspiracy of wicked knaves,
A knot of villains, and a crew of slaves,
From laying plots for to abuse a friend,
From working humours to a wicked end,
   And from the wood where Wolves and Foxes be,
   Vertue and goodnesse still deliver me.

From rusty Bacon, and ill roasted Eeles,
And from a madding wit that runs on wheels,
A vap'ring humour, and a beetle head,
A smoky chimney, and a lowsie bed,
   A blow upon the elbow and the knee,
   From each of these, goodnesse deliver me.

From setting vertue at too low a price,
From losing too much coyn at Cards and Dice.
From surety-ship, and from an empty purse,

73

Or any thing that may be termed worse;
    From all such ill, wherein no good can be,
    Vertue and goodnesse still deliver me.[19]

This poem, addressed to a seventeenth-century English audience, ranges widely and bawdily through the manifold layers of London life. Franklin, writing for less sophisticated American readers, retains only those portions of it that do not conflict with his purpose; lines 2–3, the first half of line 4, line 7, and most of line 8 in his poem are taken over verbatim from his source. Because his eye is fixed on the emerging characters of Richard and Bridget Saunders, he sees fit to eliminate the whole of the second stanza and the bawdy reference in lines 3–5 of his source and invents such details as "cross Neighbour," "jolting Horse," and "dull Razor" in order to strengthen the domestic atmosphere. The same consideration governs his substitutions: "buggy" is a more homely, alliterative description of a bed than "lowsie." In drawing upon "A Letany" (many details of which were alien to the American scene) to create a far shorter poem that would appeal to his immediate public, Franklin shows himself in this instance to be a workman, not a bungler.

In 1792, the year Robert Bailey Thomas launched the now famous *Farmer's Almanac,* Reverend William Smith praised *Poor Richard's Almanack* as "the Farmers' Philosopher, the Rural Sage, the Yeomens' and Peasants' Oracle."[20] Among the countless almanacs that flourished in colonial times Franklin's stands in the first rank, both for

[19]*Facetiae. Musarum Deliciae: or, The Muses Recreation...* (London, 1817), II, 436.

[20]*Eulogium on Benjamin Franklin...*(Philadelphia, 1792), p. 20, quoted in C. E. Jorgenson, *New Eng. Quar.,* VIII (1935), 556.

the matter that Smith admired and for its manner of expression. No other American philomath created and developed within his pages such original types as Richard and Bridget Saunders; in subtlety no other equaled Franklin's hoax on Titan Leeds. Although Moses Coit Tyler has called Nathaniel Ames's *Astronomical Diary and Almanack* (1726–1764) "in most respects better than Franklin's,"[21] the best that can be said for it is that it had a much larger subscription.[22] Certainly Ames's sayings fall short of Franklin's in respect to perspicuity, elegance, and cadence. What finally assured the general excellence and favorable reception of *Poor Richard* is the fact that here, as on so many later occasions, Franklin seems to be relaxing after the day's labor and enjoying himself.

[21]*History of American Literature*, II, 122.

[22]According to Samuel Briggs, Ames's *Almanack* had an annual circulation of 60,000 copies in the period 1726–1764 (*Essays, Humor, and Poems of Nathaniel Ames,* p. 20n).

IV

The Letter to the Press

THE letter to the press or editorial, like the periodical essay, is less personal in tone than the familiar essay and more dramatic in form. In the journalistic practice of the eighteenth century it enjoyed prestige as a literary form. Internationally famous were the antiministerial letters of "Junius," first printed in the London *Public Advertiser* (1769–1771). During the second half of his life Franklin addressed 149 letters to the American, English, and French press. All but six of these were written in the years 1758–1775, during most of which time he was colonial agent in London. They let us glimpse the man in a more relaxed posture than his official duties allowed him to assume, and reveal him as a political moderate who, in language more homespun than legalistic, put the welfare of America ahead of that of England whenever the interests of the two clashed.

Close friend of William Strahan, who became King's Printer in 1770, and of the editor Henry S. Woodfall, who connived in several of his journalistic tricks, Franklin the colonial agent was well circumstanced to operate—unofficially, to be sure—as press agent also. And well qualified, too. He described himself, and it was no overstatement, as "one who had lived long in America, knew the people and their affairs extremely well—and was equally well acquainted with the temper and practices of government officers."[1] Ministerial writers he characterized as "your coffee-house talkers...mere rhetoricians, tongue-pads and scribes...ever bawling for war on the most trifling occasions, and...the most blood-thirsty of mankind."[2] One of them, probably John Mein, called him in turn "this living emblem of Iniquity in Grey Hairs."[3] When this war of words waxed hottest in the press, Franklin took his own advice most to heart: "Passion, Invective & Abuse, serve no Cause. They show that a Man is angry; but not always that he has reason to be angry."[4] And indeed his own sweet reasonableness never deserted him.

In his progress from provincial to intercolonial to imperial statesman—witness the expanding argument in *Plain Truth* (1747), the Albany *Plan of Union* (1754), and the letters to Governor Shirley (1754)—Franklin ever showed himself to be a federalist.[5] By 1757, the year he embarked on the first of two diplomatic missions to England, he had come to that view of empire he would hold until disabused by Wedderburn's "invective ribaldry" against him at the Cockpit in January 1774. The American colonies he envisioned as member states in a British com-

[1]*Benjamin Franklin's Letters to the Press, 1758–1775,* ed. Verner W. Crane (Chapel Hill, 1950), p. 81. Hereafter referred to as Crane.

[2]Crane, p. 83.

[3]*Ibid.,* p. 248.

[4]*Ibid.,* p. 119.

[5]See especially Labaree, III, 195; V, 415, 449–450.

monwealth of nations, autonomous except for the allegiance they owed the Crown. Although such a view conflicted with the theory of mercantilism, once again being revived by the Grenville, Townshend, and North Ministries after several decades of "salutary neglect," he held to it firmly throughout the years of his agency. "The British empire," he asserted in 1770, "is not a single state; it comprehends many; and, though the Parliament of Great Britain has arrogated to itself the power of taxing the colonies, it has no more right to do so, than it has to tax Hanover. We have the same King, but not the same legislatures."[6] Pointedly he asked: "Are they [meaning Ireland and America] not Parts of the same Whole, Members of the same Body? Why would you swell the Hand at the Expence of the Limbs, and give your Empire Rickets?"[7] Whatever his immediate objective, whether seeking advantageous peace terms in the Seven Years' War, working for the repeal of the Stamp Act and Townshend Revenue Act, or trying to prevent the passage of the Coercive Acts, this dominion view of empire underlay the particular argument.

At this period in his life constitutionalists within the Anglo-American community replaced the Boston divines and Harvard scholars of a former time as his natural enemies. In essential agreement with the Port-Royalists that logic is "the Art of directing reason aright, in obtaining the knowledge of things," Franklin did not argue from legal precedent but appealed to that reason he thought fixed and universal in human nature. He was of a mind

[6]Smyth, V, 280.

[7]"Plainman" (Benjamin Franklin): fragment "Courage, Britains!," Amer. Philos. Soc. MS, [1765–1775], B F85 v. 78.

with his Scottish friend Lord Kames that "rude ages exhibit the triumph of authority over reason.... In later times, happily, reason hath obtained the ascendant: men now assert their native privilege of thinking for themselves; and disdain to be ranked in any sect, whatever be the science."[8] So it was that, when confronted with America's claims to legislative autonomy, he readily admitted, "I am not Lawyer enough to decide this question."[9] One such lawyer was John Dickinson, with whom he had tangled in the bitterly contested Pennsylvania campaign of 1764. In the *Letters from a Farmer in Pennsylvania* (1767–1768) Dickinson applied Pitt's distinction between internal and external taxation in an effort to prove the unconstitutionality of the Townshend Revenue Act. Whereupon Franklin, grown impatient with such nice distinctions in the interval since his examination before Commons in February 1766, wrote his son William: "The more I have thought and read on the subject, the more I find myself confirmed in opinion, that no middle doctrine can be well maintained, I mean not clearly with intelligible arguments. Something might be made of either of the extremes; that Parliament has a power to make *all laws* for us, or that it has a power to make *no laws* for us; and I think the arguments for the latter more numerous and weighty, than those for the former."[10] In contrast with the "Colonist's Advocate" letters, Franklin's most ambitious and sustained effort in this genre, the *Farmer's Letters* are weighted with legal proofs and possess little rhetorical

[8]*Elements of Criticism* (8th ed.; London, 1805), I, 10.
[9]Crane, p. 136.
[10]Smyth, V, 115.

color. The one man argues his case empirically, the other from constitutional, charter, and natural rights.

From at least as early as 1722, the year the *Courant* office advertised *Cato's Letters* as for sale, young Benjamin had been aware of the letter to the press as a distinct genre. Silence Dogood, abandoning for a space her nonpartisan tone, quoted from them in the course of her attacks on censorship of the press and religious hypocrisy. Although Franklin kept the *Pennsylvania Gazette* an open forum throughout the years he was editor and carefully avoided letting the *Almanack* give offense to church and state, he spoke out politically in such pamphlets as *Plain Truth,* wherein he brings his argument for the defense of Pennsylvania to a close with these impassioned words:

> *May the* GOD *of* WISDOM, STRENGTH *and* POWER, *the Lord of the Armies of Israel, inspire us with Prudence in this Time of* DANGER; *take away from us all the Seeds of Contention and Division, and unite the Hearts and Counsels of all of us, of whatever* SECT *or* NATION, *in one Bond of Peace, Brotherly Love, and generous Publick Spirit; May he give us Strength and Resolution to amend our Lives, and remove from among us every Thing that is displeasing to him; afford us his most gracious Protection, confound the Designs of our Enemies, and give* PEACE *in all our Borders, is the sincere Prayer of*

> A TRADESMAN of Philadelphia.

From 1755 onward he labored and spoke out so emphatically and persuasively against proprietary government that twice the Pennsylvania Assembly sent him to England, first to petition that the proprietary estates be taxed, then to secure a royal charter. What is here important, Franklin's journalistic forays on behalf of the antiproprietary party made him master of the patterns, figures, and tropes essential to a polemical style by the time he went to work as press agent in London.

I

Franklin's thoughts on empire yeasting over and the traditional molds that would have contained them in an earlier age now standing in need of modification, he made the letter to the press into a more flexible vehicle for argument serious and satirical than did his English contemporary, "Junius." When not drafted as conventional letters to the editor, they are conceived as anecdote, annotations, a list of queries, or cast in a more belletristic form like colloquy, fable, parody, or fictitious controversy.

Anecdote, long a favorite device of his, is the controlling pattern in three letters.[11] In the second of these, the talk in Parliament of requiring the Americans to make payment for the stamps they should have used while the Stamp Act was in force reminds Franklin of

> the Frenchman that used to accost English and other Strangers on the Pont-Neuf, with many Compliments, and a red hot Iron in his Hand; *Pray Monsieur Anglois,* says he, *Do me the Favour to let me have the Honour of thrusting this hot Iron into your Backside?* Zoons, what does the fellow mean! Begone with your Iron or I'll break your Head! *Nay Monsieur,* replies he, *if you do not chuse it, I do not insist upon it. But at least, you will in Justice have the Goodness to pay me something for the heating of my Iron.*

[11]*Ibid.,* IV, 397–398; V, 14–15; Crane, Document No. 117. See my *Political Satire in the American Revolution, 1763–1783* (Ithaca, 1960), wherein several of Franklin's letters to the press are discussed in greater detail than in the present chapter.

Occasionally, as he had in *Dogood* 13, Franklin ends on an anecdote. He concludes a protest against the partial repeal of the Townshend Revenue Act then being contemplated thus:

A collector on the King's highway, who had rifled the passengers in a stage coach, desirous to shew his great civility, returned to one a family seal, to another a dear friend's mourning ring, which encouraged a third to ask a watch that had been his grandmother's? 'Zounds, says he, have you no conscience? presently you will all expect your money again! a pack of unreasonable dogs and b — — s; I have a great mind to blow your brains out.'[12]

It is not surprising, in view of Franklin's early acquaintance with *Pilgrim's Progress* and Xenophon's *Memorabilia,* that three of his letters to the press take the form of colloquy.[13] In the second of these, an Englishman, a Scotchman, and an American are heard discoursing on the subject of slavery. When it is charged that America is heavily populated with Negroes, indentured servants, and convicts, the American reminds the Englishman who it was that forced them upon the Americans in the first place. Then, seizing the offensive, he points to the colliers and other poor laborers in Britain and to the impressment of sailors and soldiers as forms of slavery more terrible than any that exist in America.

Parody, that species of high burlesque which "adopts the manner of a specific work,"[14] is a satiric pattern Franklin employed early and late. Six of his letters to the press are

[12]Crane, p. 200.

[13]Labaree, VI, 296–306; Crane, Doc. No. 91; Smyth, VII, 82–86 (misdated 1777).

[14]David Worcester, *The Art of Satire* (Cambridge, Mass., 1940), p. 48.

parodies,[15] the most famous of these being "An Edict by the King of Prussia." Written with such an air of authenticity that only his closest associates smoked it, the "Edict" is in actuality an ironic expression of colonial grievances against mercantilism dating back, some of them, to the previous century. If history chanced to play into his hands, it was not chance that enabled Franklin to meet the occasion with the wholly appropriate jargon of state diplomacy —a language at once precise, involuted, unembellished, euphemistic.[16]

Fictitious controversy is in large part a sophistication of the planted letter, a convention he had employed previously in the *Dogood, Busy-Body,* and *Casuist* papers. In the first of two pairs of letters cast in this form,[17] Franklin, tempted to the hoax by late rumors in the English press concerning the Duke of York's travels, concocted further hints as to his peregrinations, hoping they might prove "instructive to the News-writers," and planted them in Woodfall's *Public Advertiser* on May 15, 1765, over the signature of "The Spectator." The following week, now writing as "A Traveller," he complained that the hints given out by "an ingenious Correspondent that calls himself *the* SPECTATOR" might do great injury to the public "as well as to those good People," the news writers: After all, the Traveller observes, by "the *We hears* they give us of this and t'other intended Voyage, or Tour of this and t'other great Personage, . . . we are supplied with abundant Fund of Dis-

[15]Crane, Doc. Nos. 8, 116, 135; Smyth, VII, 27–29; VIII, 437–447; X, 87–91.

[16]George Simson, *Am. Lit.,* XXXII (1960), 152–157, locates the legal sources of the "Edict."

[17]Crane, Doc. Nos. 16–17, 63–64.

course." I can assure you "on the Faith of a Traveller" that some of "the Articles of News, that seem improbable, . . .are serious Truths." "It is objected by superficial Readers" that "the establishing Manufactures in the Colonies to the Prejudice of those of this Kingdom" is "not only improbable but impossible."

The very Tails of the American Sheep are so laden with Wool, that each has a Car or Waggon on four little Wheels to support and keep it from trailing on the Ground. Would they caulk their Ships? would they fill their Beds? would they even litter their Horses with Wool, if it was not both plenty and cheap? . . . All this is as certainly true as the Account, said to be from Quebec, in the Papers of last Week, that the Inhabitants of Canada are making Preparations for a Cod and Whale Fishery this Summer in the Upper Lakes. Ignorant People may object that the Upper Lakes are fresh, and that Cod and Whale are Salt-water Fish: But let them know, Sir, that Cod, like other Fish, when attacked by their Enemies, fly into any Water where they think they can be safest; that Whales, when they have a Mind to eat Cod, pursue them wherever they fly; and that the grand Leap of the Whale in that Chace up the Fall of Niagara is esteemed by all who have seen it, as one of the finest Spectacles in Nature!

The Traveller concludes:

Thus much I thought it necessary to say, in favour of an honest Set of Writers, whose comfortable Living depends on collecting and supplying the Printers with News, at the small Price of Six-pence an Article; and who always show their Regard to Truth, by contradicting such as are wrong in a subsequent Article—for another Six-pence, to the great Satisfaction and Improvement of us Coffee-house Students in History and Politics, and the infinite Advantage of all future Livies, Rapins, Robertsons, Humes, Smollets, and Macaulays, who may be sincerely inclin'd to furnish the World with that *rara Avis,* a true History.

What begins as a spoof on rumormongers in the press evolves into a skillfully disguised defense of America's right to domestic manufacturing. There is further irony in the fact that two months before Franklin invented this controversy the Stamp Act, which acted as a spur to such manufacture, had been made law.

II

In contrast to the essentially lighthearted, social tone of his periodical essays and almanac writings, Franklin approached his duties as press agent in dead earnest. In the half century separating the *Dogood* papers from the letters to the press, his manner took on a deeper and more elusive coloring. Not that he ever abandoned completely the urbanity early acquired from the example of Addison, in underlying rhetorical organization these later writings resemble more nearly the manner of Defoe and Swift. What he said of two well-known letters to the English press, the "Edict" and "Rules by Which a Great Empire May be Reduced to a Small One," holds equally for all his letters, serious as well as satirical:

Such papers may seem to have a tendency to increase our divisions; but I intend a contrary effect, and hope by comprising in little room, and setting in a strong light the grievances of the colonies, more attention will be paid to them by our administration, and that when their unreasonableness is generally seen, some of them will be removed to the restoration of harmony between us.[18]

[18]Smyth, VI, 153.

Striving always for neoclassical restraint, Franklin limits himself to those rhetorical figures and tropes that can be most fully controlled. Occasionally he employs figures in an effort to achieve unity within the letter; more often, though, they are merely intended to impart color. Analogy, when chosen to ensure unity, several times takes the form of an historical equation. In the "Edict," for example, he constructs the equation: England is to Prussia as America is to England: according to which Frederick the Great can make the same imperial demands of England that England had for years been making of her American colonies.[19] He was not always so successful. Although he personally preferred the "Rules," the analogy he introduces at the outset proves a less efficient vehicle than the *reductio ad absurdum* which informs the "Edict," and soon he is forced to abandon it. "In the first place," the letter begins, "you are to consider, that a great empire, like a great cake, is most easily diminished at the edges. Turn your attention, therefore, first to your *remotest* provinces; that, as you get rid of them, the next may follow in order." Such a beginning promises well. "By carefully making and preserving such distinctions, you will (to keep to my simile of the cake) act like a wise gingerbread-baker, who, to facilitate a division, cuts his dough half through in those places where, when baked, he would have it *broken to pieces*." Still excellent. But then, apparently at a loss how to develop it farther, he drops the figure altogether.[20]

[19]In two other letters he constructs the following equations: Athenian orators are to Sicily as English coffeehouse orators are to America (Crane, Doc. No. 42); France is to Corsica as England is to America (Crane, Doc. No. 77).

[20]Smyth, VI, 127–128. Antonio Pace, *Benjamin Franklin and Italy*

The instances in which analogy effectively imparts rhetorical color range widely through physical and human nature. In 1760, urging the British nation to debate the advantages and disadvantages of making an early peace and not act hastily, Franklin advises, "Light often arises from a collision of opinions, as fire from flint and steel; and if we can obtain the benefit of the *light,* without danger from the *heat* sometimes produc'd by controversy, why should we discourage it?"[21] As an advocate of total, not partial, repeal of the Townshend Revenue Act, he asks the North Ministry, "How do we shew ourselves wiser than the Savages of Louisiana, who, to come at the Fruit, cut down the Tree?"[22] To point up the hardships which smuggling works on those who pay the lawful duty, he puts the following question: "What should we think of a Companion, who, having sup'd with his Friends at a Tavern, and partaken equally of the Joys of the Evening with the rest of us, would nevertheless contrive by some Artifice to shift his share of the reckoning upon others, in order to go off scot free?"[23] At a time when Parliament, angered by the demonstrations in America "about a paltry three-pence Duty on Tea," was voting coercive measures against Massachusetts, Franklin, here signing himself "A Londoner," warns, "But we are disgusted with their free gifts; we want to have something that is obtain'd by force, like a mad Landlord who should refuse the willing payment of his full Rents, and chuse to take less by way of Robbery."[24]

Repetition, another conventional rhetorical figure, may

(Philadelphia, 1958), p. 5, suggests that the "Rules" is a parody of Machiavelli's *The Prince.*

[21]Smyth, IV, 35.　　　　　　　　[22]Crane, p. 179.
[23]Smyth, V, 62.　　　　　　　　[24]*Ibid.,* VI, 217.

take the form of a refrain with variations.[25] Or, repetition and alliteration may reinforce one another to produce strongly accented expression, as in the sentence, "The People, who think themselves injured in Point of Property, are discontented with the Government, and grow turbulent; and the Proprietaries using their Powers of Government to procure for themselves what they think Justice in their Points of Property, renders those Powers odious."[26] Sometimes Franklin exploits another's use of repetition; in his *Preface to the Speech of Joseph Galloway*, for example, he makes the words *"fundamentally wrong and unjust,"* which John Penn had used in all six articles of his gubernatorial message of May 17, 1764, an ironic motif.[27] Sometimes he seizes on another's phrase and turns it against him; a ministerial writer during the Stamp Act controversy having described the New Englanders as "descended from the Stiff-Rumps in Oliver's Time," Franklin works the expressions, "those very Oliverian Stiff-Rumps," "as stiff-rump'd as the others," and "'tis not unlikely they may set their Rumps more stiffly against this Method of Government," into the first two paragraphs of his annotated reply.[28] All in all, he employs repetition sparingly but with considerable imaginative skill.

Exclamation, too, he uses to good advantage. Waxing sarcastic in 1751 over the practice of exporting English convicts to the Southern colonies, he exclaims: "Our *Mother* knows what is best for us. What is a little *House-breaking, Shoplifting,* or *Highway Robbing;* what is a *Son*

---

[25]For example: "If it be a good principle...stick to that principle, and go thorough-stitch with it" (Smyth, V, 536–537); "Otherwise you will grow able to pay your debts" (Crane, pp. 97–99).

[26]Smyth, IV, 229.   [27]*Ibid.,* IV, 324–332.   [28]*Ibid.,* IV, 393–394.

now and then *corrupted* and *hang'd,* a Daughter *debauch'd* and *pox'd,* a Wife *stabb'd,* a Husband's *Throat cut,* or a Child's *Brains beat out* with an Axe, compar'd with this 'IMPROVEMENT and WELL PEOPLING of the Colonies!'"[29] Franklin does not apostrophize. And he seldom indulges in invective, although on one occasion he describes the armed Indians on the Susquehanna and the Ohio as "Rum-debauched, Trader-corrupted Vagabonds and Thieves."[30]

As for tropes, Franklin, in keeping with Lamy's insistence on clarity and proportion, uses only simile and metaphor with any frequency. In one letter he declares that the only remedy for the constant struggle in Pennsylvania between the proprietors, the Assembly, and the people is "an immediate *Royal Government,* without the Intervention of Proprietary Powers, which, like unnecessary Springs and Movements in a Machine, are so apt to produce Disorder."[31] In another he reflects bitterly that the Lords present during Wedderburn's abusive attack on him in 1774 were "purposely invited as to a Bull-baiting."[32] At a time when partial repeal of the Townshend Revenue Act threatened to cause the collapse of the colonial boycott, Franklin expostulates with *"those* ENGLISHMEN *who virulently write and talk against his* COUNTRYMEN." "If the American Trade is of so little Consequence to this Nation...that your Merchants and Manufacturers do not miss it,...cannot you leave [the Americans] (like froward Children that quarrel with their Bread and Butter) to punish themselves by going without it?"[33]

Arguing the advantages of royal government over pro-

[29]Labaree, IV, 133.
[31]*Ibid.,* IV, 231.
[33]*Ibid.,* pp. 214–215.

[30]Smyth, IV, 307.
[32]Crane, p. 245.

prietary, Franklin asks Pennsylvanians, "When the direct and immediate Rays of Majesty benignly and mildly shine on all around us, but are transmitted and thrown upon us thro' the Burning-Glass of Proprietary Government, can your Sensibilities feel no Difference?"[34] Over the English signature "N. N." *(non nominatus)* he gives "a full and particular account of the rise and present state of our misunderstanding with the Colonies" and closes on a forceful medical metaphor:

> What remedy, if any, the wisdom of Parliament shall think fit to apply to these disorders, a little time will shew. Mean while, I cannot but think that those writers, who busily employ their talents in endeavouring to exasperate this nation against the Colonies, are doing it a very ill office: For their virulent writings being dispersed among the inhabitants of the Plantations...do in some degree irritate the Colonists against a country which treats them, as they imagine, so injuriously.... For harsh treatment may increase the inflammation, make the cure less practicable, and in time bring on the necessity of an amputation; death indeed to the severed limb, weakness and lameness to the mutilated body.[35]

Elsewhere he elaborates on the parental metaphor so frequently employed in this time of colonial struggle: "We call Britain the mother country; but what good mother would introduce thieves and criminals into the company of her children to corrupt and disgrace them?"[36] In the spring of 1774, when ministerial writers talked "of nothing but Troops and Fleets, and Force, of blocking up Ports, destroying Fisheries, abolishing Charters, &c. &c.,"

[34]Smyth, IV, 349.   [35]Crane, p. 220.
[36]Smyth. V, 216.

Franklin asks pointedly: "Did ever any Tradesman succeed, who attempted to drub Customers into his Shop? And will honest JOHN BULL, the Farmer, be long sattisfied with Servants, that before his Face attempt to kill his *Plow Horses?*"[37] Sometimes his metaphors are more homely still, as when, accepting the Stamp Act as a *fait accompli,* he writes Charles Thomson: "We might as well have hindered the sun's setting. But since it is down, my Friend, and it may be long ere it rises again, let us make as good a night of it as we can. We may still light candles."[38]

Franklin, as we have seen in the last chapter, deserves to stand among the great makers of the English sentence. Nowhere does he exhibit greater skill in the management of parallel and balanced construction than in his letters to the press. In the course of a letter defending the performance of the Americans in the Seven Years' War against the aspersions of a ministerial writer, he answers the charge that the New Englanders behaved rashly before Louisbourg in 1745 in the following manner:

Is there [no merit] in the indefatigable labour the troops went through during the siege, performing the duty both of men and horses; the hardship they patiently suffered for want of tents and other necessaries; the readiness with which they learned to move, direct, and manage cannon, raise batteries, and form approaches; the bravery with which they sustained sallies; and finally, in their consenting to stay and garrison the place after it was taken, absent from their business and families, till troops could be brought from England for that purpose, though they undertook the service on a promise of being discharged as soon as it was over, were unprovided for so long an absence, and actually

[37]*Ibid.,* VI, 218.   [38]Crane, p. 36.

suffered ten times more loss by mortal sickness through want of necessaries, than they suffered from the arms of the enemy?[39]

In carrying the parallelism of this rhetorical question, itself the last in a series of six, down to the second degree of subordination, he is careful to avoid monotony; the gerund "consenting" which introduces the final substantive construction imparts variety, as does the structural shift from the substantives in the first part of the sentence to the compound predicate within the concessive clause in the second part. In other letters he achieves parallelism by repeating a short clause[40] or, as in this gerund construction, a substantive:

> It is *right*, O ye Americans! for us to charge you with *dreaming* that you have it in your power to make us a bankrupt nation; by engaging us in new wars; with *dreaming* that you may thereby encrease your own strength and prosperity; with *dreaming* that the seat of government will then be transported to America, and Britain dwindle to one of its provinces.[41]

Within the clause itself he employs word-coupling, sometimes strengthening it with alliteration; thus, "Cowardice and cruelty are indeed almost inseparable companions."[42]

Through balanced construction Franklin often avoided a mechanical ordering of the parts, as in the sentence, "Hence the instances of transported thieves advancing their fortunes in the colonies are extremely rare; if there really is a single instance of it, which I very much doubt; but

[39]Smyth, V, 213–214.
[40]See Smyth, IV, 309–310; V, 210–211; Crane, p. 208.
[41]Crane, p. 96.
[42]*Ibid.*, p. 44.

93

of their being advanced there to the gallows the instances are plenty."[43] If "instances" be made the *a* term, "advancing" and "advanced" the *b*, and "rare" and "plenty" the *c*, it can be seen that he has achieved variety within balance: abc/bac; moreover, the parenthetical insertion of the conditional clause, by tending to obscure the balance itself, intensifies the subtle rhythm of the sentence. Balance may be achieved by skillful repetition, as here of the word "most": "Unwise men are often most obstinate when they are most in the wrong";[44] or by alliteration: "The Victorious of this year may be the vanquish'd of the next."[45] Infrequently Franklin employed antithesis; in a letter designed to discourage an intended act for preventing emigration to America, he introduces it at the end of the following sentence:

> Our estates, far from diminishing in value through a want of tenants, have been in that period [the last 150 years] more than doubled; the lands in general are better cultivated; their increased produce finds a ready sale at an advanced price, and the complaint has for some time been, not that we want mouths to consume our meat, but that we want meat for our number of mouths.[46]

Proverbial expressions, traditionally characterized by parallelism and balance, are frequently incorporated into the prose pattern of the letters to the press. Richard Saunders' saying of 1757, "Act uprightly, and despise Calumny; Dirt may stick to a Mud Wall, but not to polish'd Marble," reappears at the outset of Franklin's defense against Wedderburn's harangue of 1774: "Splashes of Dirt thrown upon my Character, I suffered while fresh to remain: I

[43]Smyth, V, 215.   [44]Crane, p. 142.
[45]Smyth, IV, 34.   [46]*Ibid.*, VI, 292.

did not chuse to spread by endeavouring to remove them, but rely'd on the vulgar Adage *that they would all rub off when they were dry.*"[47] Less imaginatively, proverbs are sometimes simply set down intact within the sentence. In answer to a Grenvillite writer who doubted whether the Americans could keep a resolution to drink no more English tea, Franklin replies, "I question whether the army proposed to be sent among them, would oblige them to swallow a drop more of tea than they chuse to swallow; for, as the proverb says, though one man may *lead* a horse to water, ten *can't make him drink.*"[48] Sometimes they occur as separate sentences within the paragraph. Deploring the fact that the Pennsylvania Assembly of 1764, deliberating whether or not to petition for a royal charter, did not at any time consult their constituents, Franklin observes, "Wisdom in the Mind is not, like Money in the Purse, diminish'd by Communication to others."[49] Occasionally a paragraph is brought to a close with a proverbial expression. Among the arguments advanced in *The Interest of Great Britain Considered* that Canada rather than Guadeloupe be claimed at the end of the Seven Years' War, he assures his English audience that the present loyalty of the Americans makes them useful allies; the paragraph continues, "While the government is mild and just, while important civil and religious rights are secure, such subjects will be dutiful and obedient," and concludes with this warning: "The waves do not rise but when the winds blow."[50] Realizing the value of cli-

[47]*Ibid.,* VI, 258.

[48]Smyth, IV, 396. See also Smyth, V, 161, and Crane, p. 235, wherein the proverb supplies the key thought of the letter.

[49]Smyth, IV, 339.   [50]*Ibid.,* IV, 72.

max, Franklin ends one letter with a proverb; finding the English, "who either directly or indirectly have been concern'd in making the very Laws they break," more blameworthy than American smugglers against whom they exclaim, he concludes, "The old saying is true now as ever it was, *One man may better steal a horse, than another look over the hedge.*"[51]

With the passage of time Franklin's diction tended to become purer. The underlying purpose of his letters to the press required that he write more formally than he had in his newspaper essays and in the *Almanack;* even so, the language here is not altogether devoid of the idiomatic and colloquial vigor that characterizes those earlier writings. Some words carry metaphorical overtones, like "halloo'd" in the following question: "Will [the colonies] have reason to consider themselves any longer as subjects and children, when they find their cruel enemies halloo'd upon them by the country from whence they sprung, the government that owes them protection as it requires their obedience?"[52] In answer to the Grenvillite writer who charged that the Americans did not find Indian corn "an agreeable, or easy digestible breakfast," Franklin replies that it "is one of the most agreeable and wholesome grains in the world," and sets down several localisms: "Pray let me, an American, inform the gentleman...that samp, hominy, succatash, and nokehock, made of it, are so many pleasing varieties; and that johny or hoecake, hot from the

[51]*Ibid.,* V, 65.

[52]*Ibid.,* IV, 76. Other metaphorical expressions are *"Punto"* (Smyth, IV, 304), "thorough-stitch" (Smyth, V, 536), "heart-burning" (Smyth, V, 79), "Steel-proof" (Crane, p. 184).

fire, is better than a Yorkshire muffin."[53] He employs a colloquialism in denouncing John Mein's assertions of parliamentary sovereignty: "He thrusts us into the throne cheek-by-jole with Majesty."[54] A final example of the range of vigorous diction that colors these letters is the following humorous expression, one that reflects his continuing concern for the virtues of industry, frugality, and sobriety. To those sentimentalists who defend the English poor against the rich, Franklin replies that "the condition of the poor here [in England] is, by far, the best in Europe," and concludes:

> SIX *days shalt thou labour*. This is as positive a part of the commandment, as that which says, *The* SEVENTH *day thou shalt rest*. But we remember well to observe the indulgent part, and never think of the other. *Saint Monday* is generally as duly kept by our working people as *Sunday;* the only difference is, that, instead of employing their time cheaply at church, they are wasting it expensively at the alehouse.[55]

III

The most important of the rhetorical devices that color the letters to the press and help unify certain of them is the pseudonym. This device not only effectively concealed from the official class what Franklin's left hand was doing but sometimes renders the satire, when his intention is satiric, ironical. Moreover, such pseudonymity enabled him

[53]Smyth, IV, 395.

[54]*Ibid.*, VI, 217. Other colloquialisms are "Snips" [for tailors] (Smyth, IV, 398); *"stick in my stomach"* [said of Indian corn] (Crane, p. 52); "But the deuce a bit" (Smyth, V, 536); "in a Nut-Shell" (Crane, p. 197).

[55]Smyth, V. 127. See Smyth, V, 538; *Par. Text Ed.*, p. 118, for other uses of this expression.

97

to mediate between extremes of political opinion and at the same time assess the differences more objectively; for, as he had observed years before, "When the Writer conceals himself, he has the Advantage of hearing the Censure both of Friends and Enemies, express'd with more Impartiality."[56]

Some of the letters are written in an assumed English, a few in an American character. Over the signature "New-England," his most fully developed American character, Franklin introduces himself to the printer as "a native of *Boston*, in *New-England*," and continues:

> I do not concern myself in your *London* election; nor do I believe that any of my countrymen think it of importance to them, whether you choose Alderman *T* [Barlow Trecothick], your representative, or reject him. And yet I hear great clamour, as if his nomination were to promote a *Boston* interest. He may be, for aught I know, a man of abilities, and a friend of ours: But, should he get into P—t, what is one man among five or six hundred? A drop in the bucket. . . .
>
> I sit down, Sir, after much patience, merely to take some notice of the invective and abuse, that have, on this occasion, been so liberally bestowed on my country, by your writers who sign themselves *Old England, a Londoner, a Liveryman of London,* &c. &c. [By the way, Mr. Printer, should I have said liberally or illiberally? Not being now it seems allowed to be an *Englishman,* I ought modestly to doubt my *English,* and submit it as I do to your correction.]

Though he may recriminate a little against "the productions of a few unknown angry writers, heated by an election contest, who rave against *America,* because a candi-

LETTER TO THE PRESS

date they would decry once lived there," New-England
assures the printer: "*Boston man* as I am, Sir, and inimical,
as my country is represented to be, I hate neither *England*
or *Englishmen,* driven (though my ancestors were) by
mistaken oppression of former times, out of this happy
country, to suffer all the hardships of an *American* wilderness. I retain no resentment on that account."[57] Such
American characters as this, though not aptronymous, are
a faint echo of the personae Franklin had created in his
newspaper essays and almanac writings.

Over one of his favorite English signatures, "N. N.,"
Franklin writes, "Surely, if we are so much [the Americans'] superiors, we should shew the superiority of our
breeding by our better manners! Our slaves they may be
thought: But every master of slaves ought to know, that
though all the slave possesses is the property of the master,
his *good-will* is his own."[58] But it was as "The Colonist's
Advocate," the only instance in which he carried a pseudonym through a series of letters, that he developed an English character most fully, though even here the character
remains shadowy. Keenly aware that within the English
official class there was widespread ignorance of the American colonies and indifference to colonial interests, he
sought, as an advocate for total repeal of the Townshend
Revenue Act, to win the confidence of his English readers
at once by assuring them, "The impartial Publick will
judge, from my Manner of treating the Subject, in the
following Numbers,...what Opportunities I have had,
during some Years Service in America, of knowing the
Inclinations, Affections, and Concerns of the Inhabitants

[57]Crane, pp. 113, 116, 115.
[58]*Ibid.,* p. 42.

99

in the Provinces of that extensive Continent."[59] Trusting that the British nation will hear him out, the Advocate frankly pleads the cause of America in his fourth letter:

> To assume the Title of the *Colonist's Advocate,* is to undertake the Defence of Three Millions of the most valuable Subjects of the British Empire, against Tyranny and Oppression, brought upon them by a wrong-headed Ministry. It is to call the Attention of Government to the Injuries of the brave and free Emigrants from these Realms, who first, without the least Charge to us, obtained, and have, for many Years, at the Expence of their Sweat and their Blood, secured for themselves, and the Mother Country, an unmeasurable Territory, from whence Riches, Power, and Honour have, for many Centuries, been flowing in upon us; and (had not the evil Genius of England whispered in the Ear of a certain Gentleman [Grenville], "George! be a Financier") would, for Ages to come, have continued to flow in the same happy Channel. I beg Justice for those brave People, who, in Confidence of our Protection, left their native Country, pierced into Woods, where no humanized Foot had, from the Creation, trod; who rouzed the deadly Serpent in his Hole, the Savage Beast in his Den, and the brutal Indian in his Thicket, and who have made us the Envy and the Terror of Europe. The Colonists have made our Merchants Princes, while themselves are, for the most Part, Farmers and Planters. They have employed our Hands, increased our People, consumed our Manufactures, improved our Navy, maintained our Poor, and doubled, or trebled our Riches.[60]

After the eleventh letter the Advocate broke off his suit, for at this juncture Lord North's motion in Commons to

[59]*Ibid.,* p. 168.
[60]*Ibid.,* p. 177.

retain the three-pence tax on tea convinced Franklin that total repeal would be defeated. As indeed it was.

As journalists from the turn of the century had so conclusively shown, the persona or mask, as distinct from the pose, can be made to serve the cause of satire well. Among Augustan writers none excelled Swift in the use of this device.[61] Without arguing for direct influence, it can be demonstrated that Franklin's ironic masks, like those of Swift, are of two major kinds: that of the spectator or detached observer; and the situational, in which the satirist relinquishes the role of observer and the "self-developing irony of the situation" speaks for itself directly to the reader.[62] When he adopts the role of spectator Franklin appears as either the impartial historian[63] or the modest proposer.[64] On September 5, 1773, a well-meaning correspondent writes from Danzig, "We have long wondered here at the supineness of the English nation, under the Prussian impositions upon its trade entering our port," and encloses Frederick's edict "Given at Potsdam, this twenty-fifth day of the month of August, one thousand seven hundred and seventy-three, and in the thirty-third year of our reign." What renders this hoax more plausible is the impression the correspondent manages to convey in a post-

[61]In addition to Swift, Roger L'Estrange, John Tutchin, G. P. Marana, Ned Ward, Addison, Steele, and Defoe made extensive use of the persona. See William Bragg Ewald, *The Masks of Jonathan Swift* (Oxford, 1954), pp. 4–7.

[62]John M. Bullitt, *Jonathan Swift and the Anatomy of Satire* (Cambridge, Mass., 1953), pp. 57, 60–61; Ricardo Quintana, *Univ. Tor. Quar.*, XVII (1948), 135.

[63]Crane, Doc. Nos. 52, 60; Smyth, VI, 118–124.

[64]Labaree, IV, 130–133; Crane, Doc. No. 30; Smyth, VI, 127–137; Crane, Doc. Nos. 131, 132.

script of being simply an impartial witness to the matter at hand:

> Some take this Edict to be merely one of the King's *Jeux d'Esprit:* others suppose it serious, and that he means a quarrel with England; but all here think the assertion it concludes with, "that these regulations are copied from acts of the English parliament respecting their colonies," a very injurious one; it being impossible to believe, that a people distinguished for their love of liberty, a nation so wise, so liberal in its sentiments, so just and equitable towards its neighbours, should, from mean and injudicious views of petty immediate profit, treat its own children in a manner so arbitrary and tyrannical![65]

Like Defoe's *Shortest Way with the Dissenters,* the "Edict" deceived Englishmen when it first appeared.[66]

Franklin felt still more at home in the Swiftian guise of modest proposer. At the time Parliament was debating whether to repeal the Stamp Act, he declares, here signing himself "Pacificus," "I shall think myself happy if I can furnish any Hints that may be of public Utility," and proceeds, with apparent good humor and impartiality, to propose a plan for conquering America frighteningly like that in which Burgoyne and Howe were to have cooperated a decade later.[67] And when in 1774 a British officer named Clarke was so rash as to boast that "with a Thousand British grenadiers, he would undertake to go from one end of America to the other, and geld all the Males, partly by

[65]Smyth, VI, 124.

[66]See Franklin's letter of Oct. 6, 1773, to his son William, Smyth, VI, 146.

[67]Crane, Doc. No. 30.

force and partly by a little Coaxing,"[68] Franklin, writing over the signature "A Freeholder of Old Sarum," points out the advantages that would arise from the execution of this scheme, taking care at every ironic turn to stay within the realm of the possible.[69]

In the case of the situational mask personae are created "who embody and illustrate the ironic contradictions between what *seems* to them and what, as the reader knows, actually *is*."[70] In "The Sale of the Hessians" (1777) the irony present in the many euphemisms, the epigram "Glory is true wealth," and the mock-heroic allusion to Thermopylae spring from the situation itself; after all, Schaumbergh's reason for commending Hohendorf on so careful a reckoning of the Hessians killed at Trenton is purely mercenary.[71] In the first part of the "Supplement to the *Boston Independent Chronicle*" (1782) Captain Gerrish, horror-struck by the packages of American scalps he has intercepted but anxious to do his duty, is the innocent, well-meaning vehicle for Franklin's attack on "the English barbarities in America, particularly those committed by the savages at their instigation";[72] in the second part an unnamed correspondent is made the vehicle, in

[68]Franklin to Strahan, Aug. 19, 1784, Smyth, IX, 261.

[69]Crane, Doc. No. 132.

[70]Bullitt, *Swift,* p. 61.

[71]Smyth, VII, 27–29. Written in French and first published (in all probability) on March 10, 1777, "The Sale of the Hessians" was first ascribed to Franklin by John Bigelow in 1874. See Durand Echeverria, *Proc. APS,* XCVII (1954), 427–431, for the early publication history of this letter, and my *Political Satire in the American Revolution,* pp. 192–194, for an analysis of it.

[72]Franklin to Dumas, May 3, 1782, Smyth, VIII, 448.

order to expose the piratical war England was waging against America.[73] But because (to paraphrase Swift) the pathetic part threatens to swallow up the rational,[74] the situational mask does not succeed so well here as in the "Sale."

In answer to James Jackson's speech in the House of Representatives, opposing the memorial of the Pennsylvania Society for Promoting the Abolition of Slavery that Congress do all that lies in its power to abolish the institution of slavery in America, Franklin on March 23, 1790, having less than a month to live, addressed his final letter to the press, "On the Slave Trade," to Andrew Brown, editor of the Philadelphia *Federal Gazette*. Congressman Jackson's speech puts "Historicus" (Franklin's signature) in mind of "a similar One made about 100 Years since by Sidi Mehemet Ibrahim, a member of the Divan of Algiers,...against granting the Petition of the Sect called *Erika,* or Purists, who pray'd for the Abolition of Piracy and Slavery as being unjust." Thinking it may be instructive, Historicus offers a translation of Ibrahim's speech:

> If we forbear to make Slaves of [Christians], who in this hot Climate are to cultivate our Lands? Who are to perform the common Labours of our City, and in our Families? ... We have now above 50,000 Slaves in and near Algiers. This Number, if not kept up by fresh Supplies, will soon diminish, and be gradually annihilated. If we then cease taking and plundering the Infidel Ships, and making Slaves of the Seamen and Passengers, our Lands will become of no Value for want of Cultivation; the Rents of Houses in the City will sink one half; and the Revenues of Government arising from its Share of Prizes be totally destroy'd!

[73]Smyth, VIII, 437–447.   [74]*Works of Swift,* VIII, 206.

And for what? To gratify the whims of a whimsical Sect, who would have us, not only forbear making more Slaves, but even to manumit those we have.

Who, asks Ibrahim, "is to indemnify their Masters for the Loss?" Certainly the Erika can't. "And if we set our Slaves free, what is to be done with them? Few of them will return to their Countries; they know too well the greater Hardships they must there be subject to. . . . Is their Condition then made worse by their falling into our Hands? No; they have only exchanged one Slavery for another, and I may say a better; for here they are brought into a Land where the Sun of Islamism gives forth its Light, and shines in full Splendor, and they have an Opportunity of making themselves acquainted with the true Doctrine, and thereby saving their immortal Souls."

I repeat the Question, What is to be done with them? I have heard it suggested, that they may be planted in the Wilderness, where there is plenty of Land for them to subsist on, and where they may flourish as a free State; but they are, I doubt, too little dispos'd to labour without Compulsion, as well as too ignorant to establish a good government, and the wild Arabs would soon molest and destroy or again enslave them. . . . If some of the religious mad Bigots, who now teaze us with their silly Petitions, have in a Fit of blind Zeal freed their Slaves, it was not Generosity, it was not Humanity, that mov'd them to the Action; it was from the conscious Burthen of a Load of Sins, and Hope, from the supposed Merits of so good a Work, to be excus'd Damnation.

"Let us then hear no more of this detestable Proposition, the Manumission of Christian Slaves," he concludes, "the Adoption of which would, by depreciating our Lands and

Houses, and thereby depriving so many good Citizens of
their Properties, create universal Discontent, and provoke
Insurrections, to the endangering of Government and producing general Confusion." Historicus in closing puts a
question to the editor: "And since like Motives are apt
to produce in the Minds of Men like Opinions and Resolutions, may we not, Mr. Brown, venture to predict, from this
Account, that the Petitions to the Parliament of England
for abolishing the Slave-Trade, to say nothing of other
Legislatures, and the Debates upon them will have a
similar Conclusion?"

Here again, and for the same reason as in the "Sale"
and "Supplement," Franklin adopts a situational mask.
In order to conceal the anger he experienced at Jackson's
speech, he constructs an historical equation: Christians are
to Algerine pirates as Negro slaves are to American and
European slavers: which not only unifies the letter but
allows him to explore an ironical situation with the aim of
exposing Christian slavers as worse even than the Algerine
pirates then preying on American and European shipping
in Mediterranean waters.[75] Here, too, Franklin's manner
resembles that of Swift in "letting the same words express
incompatible values," in presenting simultaneously "the
'official version' and the 'real meaning' in the same term."[76]
On close examination Ibrahim's apparent show of humanity proves to be a cover for his conviction that the
practice of a brutal and absolute tyranny over fellow

[75]The analogy between Christians and Algerine pirates may have
been suggested by Benjamin Lay's *All Slave-Keepers...Apostates,*
a book Franklin had published in 1737. See A. S. Pitt, *Bul. Friends'
Hist. Assn.,* XXXII (1943), 29–30.

[76]Price, *Swift's Rhetorical Art,* pp. 24–25.

human beings should be continued; what is worse, when Ibrahim has finished speaking, the Divan passes the following resolution: "The Doctrine, that Plundering and Enslaving the Christians is unjust, is at best *problematical;* but that it is the Interest of this State to continue the Practice, is clear; therefore let the Petition be rejected." In Franklin's heart of hearts, of course, the doctrine of the Erika was no more problematical than the one recently advanced by the Pennsylvania Quakers, with whom he was of one mind.

In the letters to the press, the most rhetorical of his public writings, Franklin reached beyond the leather-apron class at Boston and Philadelphia, for whom his essays and almanacs had first of all been intended, to a far larger, transatlantic audience.[77] In order to sway this Anglo-American public, first to the view that the American colonies should be given dominion status within the British Empire, then that they should be granted independence, he favored polemic statement to urbane, arguing his case seriously or satirically as the occasion seemed to demand. The fact that his efforts as press agent at London ended in failure in no sense diminishes the literary merit of these editorials. For clarity, vigor, and humor of expression they represent a high order of journalism. What is finally important, his instinct for selecting the appropriate pattern and for controlling it by such devices as the ironic mask makes it clear that in time of revolution Franklin the polemicist came of age.

[77]Many of Franklin's letters to the English press were reprinted in America. See John J. Zimmerman, *Penn. Mag. Hist. and Biog.,* LXXXI (1957), 351–364, for a discussion of the letters relative to the Stamp Act which William Goddard reprinted in the *Pennsylvania Chronicle* in 1767.

V

The Personal Letter

WE turn now from Franklin's public writings to those of a more private nature: letters, bagatelles, autobiography. Studying the correspondence of mid-century English writers like Cowper, Gray, and Walpole, one is inclined to agree with Chauncey Tinker that the letter "was the chosen medium of the age, as the periodic essay was of the earlier period and as the drama was of the Elizabethan age."[1] Within this genre a distinction must be drawn between the genuinely personal letter, addressed to a single individual with no thought to publication, and—what is the subject of the next chapter—the familiar letter, wherein the writer poses, self-consciously revealing a side of himself, and in effect reaches beyond his audience of one to a larger public. In what is more accurately a description of the personal letter than of the familiar, Hannah More declares:

> What I want in a letter is a picture of my friend's mind, and the common sense of his life. I want to know what he is saying and doing: I want him to turn out the inside of his heart to me, without disguise, without appearing better

[1]*The Salon and English Letters* (New York, 1915), p. 252.

than he is, without writing for a character. I have the same feeling in writing to him. My letter is therefore worth nothing to an indifferent person, but it is of value to my friend who cares for me.[2]

Among the genres in which the eighteenth century wrote none is more closely allied to conversation than the letter. As John Dennis observes in his Preface to *Letters upon Several Occasions* (1696), "the Style of a Letter [is] neither to come quite up to that of Conversation, nor yet to keep at too great a distance from it."[3] The "honest plainness of Speech" Franklin admired in his Nantucket relatives[4] and the "seeming diffidence" he always recommended in conversation mark his own epistolary style. Inclined by nature to prefer "the language of Artizans, Countrymen, and Merchants, before that, of Wits, or Scholars," he is more pronouncedly colloquial in the personal letter than in either the essay or the letter to the press. He is more spontaneous, too; he wished mightily that "all correspondence was on the foot of writing and answering when one can, or when one is disposed to it, without the compulsions of ceremony."[5] In both respects he lies closer to the tradition of Cicero and Quintilian than to that of Seneca. Even though the *Institutio Oratoria* focuses on oratory rather than on letter writing, in Book VIII Quintilian sets

[2]William Roberts, *Memoirs of the Life and Correspondence of Mrs. Hannah More* (London, 1834), I, 51, quoted in Tinker, *Salon*, p. 247.

[3]Quoted in William Henry Irving, *The Providence of Wit in the English Letter Writers* (Durham, 1955), p. 120.

[4]*The Letters of Benjamin Franklin and Jane Mecom*, ed. Carl Van Doren (Princeton, 1950), p. 327.

[5]Smyth, V, 24.

forth a theory of style held by many eighteenth-century letter writers, Franklin among them:

> Those words which are obviously the result of careful search and even seem to parade their self-conscious art, fail to attain the grace at which they aim and lose all appearance of sincerity because they darken the sense and choke the good seed by their own luxuriant overgrowth.... Cicero long since [in *De Oratore*, I. iii, 12] laid down this rule in the clearest of language, that the worst fault in speaking is to adopt a style inconsistent with the idiom of ordinary speech and contrary to the common feeling of mankind.[6]

Franklin in turn, in recommending that fourth-class boys at the English School in Philadelphia "should be put on Writing Letters to each other on any common Occurrences, and on various Subjects, imaginary Business, &c.," insists that they "be taught to express themselves clearly, concisely, and naturally, without affected Words, or high-flown Phrases." Here were stylistic ideals he practiced all his life.

I

Franklin's personal correspondence with men of three centuries and two continents extends over a period of sixty-five years, from the letter in 1725 offering Sir Hans Sloane some American curiosities for the Royal Society to the one he sent Thomas Jefferson nine days before his death on the vexing question of western boundaries. It is with the letters that are predominantly social rather than with those that are official or scientific that this chapter and the next have directly to do. But first a word about these other two.

[6]*The Institutio Oratoria of Quintilian,* trans. H. E. Butler (London and New York, 1921), III, 189, 191.

From the time he set up as printer at Philadelphia through a quarter century of diplomatic negotiations in London and Paris to the presidency of the Pennsylvania Council at the end of his life, Franklin corresponded steadily and increasingly with the officialdom of two continents—with long-time American friends like Joseph Galloway, Charles Thomson, and George Washington, Massachusetts politicians, Congressmen engaged in foreign affairs, fellow commissioners abroad, foreign diplomats, military personalities like John Paul Jones and the Marquis de Lafayette. The most recent gathering of such letters is of those he exchanged with the English lawyer Richard Jackson, who was appointed agent for Pennsylvania in 1763, "to solicit and transact the Affairs thereof at the Court of *Great-Britain* for the ensuing year." In one of the few unofficial moments in this correspondence Franklin describes life at Fort Pitt: "The People have Balls for Dancing, and Assemblies for Religious Worship, but as they cannot yet afford to maintain both a Clergyman and a Dancing-master, the Dancingmaster reads Prayers and one of Tristram Shandy's Sermons every Sunday."[7]

His scientific letters reflect the contemporary interest in such areas of investigation as light, heat, electricity, geology, astronomy, and mathematics.[8] He numbered among his far-flung correspondents James Bowdoin of Boston, Cadwallader Colden of New York, John Lining of Charleston, Peter Collinson of London, Lord Kames of Edin-

[7]*Letters and Papers of Benjamin Franklin and Richard Jackson, 1753–1785,* ed. Carl Van Doren (Philadelphia, 1947), p. 94.

[8]A convenient and judicious selection of the scientific letters is to be found in *The Ingenious Dr. Franklin,* ed. Nathan G. Goodman (Philadelphia, 1931).

burgh, Barbeu Dubourg of Paris, Jan Ingenhousz of Vienna, and Giovanni Battista Beccaria of Turin. The scientific correspondence, like the official, is not in the main belletristic, though for vigor, clarity, and humor of expression few eighteenth-century writers on science were Franklin's equal. Occasionally he gives such letters a social turn; for example, having praised D'Alibard's electrical experiment, he graciously adds, "The Time I spent in Paris, and in the improving Conversation and agreable Society of so many learned and ingenious Men, seems now to me like a pleasing Dream, from which I was sorry to be awaked by finding myself again at London."[9]

The social letters are variously addressed to members of his family, Deborah, William, Sarah and Richard Bache, his sister Jane Mecom; personal friends in Britain like David Hartley, David Hume, Lord Kames, Richard Price, Jonathan Shipley, William Strahan, and Benjamin Vaughan; and younger women, notably Catharine (Ray) Greene, Georgiana and Catherine Shipley, and Mary (Stevenson) Hewson.[10] It was a happy marriage, this between Deborah Read making the daily round as mother, housewife, keeper of accounts, and the man of an ever-widening world, in whose parlor merchants, politicians,

[9] Smyth, V, 95.

[10] Since the appearance of the Smyth edition many other of Franklin's social letters have been printed. The most important of these appear in *Benjamin Franklin's Autobiographical Writings*, ed. Carl Van Doren (New York, 1945); *Benjamin Franklin and Catharine Ray Greene: Their Correspondence, 1755–1790*, ed. William G. Roelker (Philadelphia, 1949); *The Letters of Benjamin Franklin and Jane Mecom;* and Whitfield J. Bell, Jr., "'All Clear Sunshine': New Letters of Franklin and Mary Stevenson Hewson," *Proc. APS*, C (1956), 521–536.

and scientists often congregated. About the time their daughter Sarah was born Franklin sang:

> In Peace and good Order, my Household she keeps
>> Right Careful to save what I gain
> Yet chearfully spends, and smiles on the Friends
>> I've the Pleasures to entertain.
>
> . . . . .
>
> Am I Laden with Care, she takes off a large Share,
>> That the Burthen ne'er makes [me] to reel,
> Does good Fortune arrive, the Joy of my Wife,
>> Quite doubles the Pleasures I feel.
>
> . . . . .
>
> Were the fairest young Princess, with Million in Purse
>> To be had in Exchange for my Joan,
> She could not be a better Wife, mought be a Worse,
>> So I'd stick to my Joggy alone
>>> My dear Friends
> I'd cling to my lovely ould Joan.[11]

There is little reason to doubt that he was thinking of Deborah when he composed this song.

Franklin's strong sense of family prompted him to correspond with his "dear Debby" during the years he was colonial agent in England, as though unconsciously making amends for the neglect he had shown her on the occasion of his first stay there before their marriage. No sooner had he taken up his London residence in 1757 than he confesses to her, "At this time of life, domestic comforts afford

[11]"Song," Amer. Philos. Soc. MS, [c. 1742], printed in Labaree, II, 353–354. In addition to the evidence herein cited to establish Franklin's authorship, Dr. Cabanis identified this poem as *"une chanson sur l'anniversaire de son union avec madame Franklin,"* *Oeuvres posthumes de Cabanis* (Paris, 1825), V, 265n.

the most solid satisfaction, and my uneasiness at being absent from my family, and longing desire to be with them, make me often sigh in the midst of cheerful company."[12] He hastened to send her English china, linens and yard goods, and household appliances; the china jug "I fell in Love with...at first Sight; for I thought it look'd like a fat jolly Dame, clean and tidy, with a neat blue and white Calico Gown on, good natur'd and lovely, and put me in mind of—Somebody."[13] In 1766 he declares that had the Stamp Act not been repealed and had "the Trade between the two Countries totally ceas'd, it was a Comfort to me to recollect, that I had once been cloth'd from Head to Foot in Woollen and Linnen of my Wife's Manufacture, that I never was prouder of any Dress in my Life, and that she and her Daughter might do it again if it was necessary."[14] Though he need never have doubted the good sense of the wife who practiced the frugality he preached, shortly before Sarah's marriage to Richard Bache he cautions her:

> I would only advise that you do not make an expensive feasting Wedding, but conduct every thing with Frugality and Oeconomy, which our Circumstances really now require to be observed in all our Expences.... If we were young enough to begin Business again, it might be another Matter;—but I doubt we are past it; and Business not well managed ruins one faster than no Business.[15]

When the Baches's first child was born, he praised the grandmother for not interfering with the mother's discipline, and adds this anecdote:

[12]Labaree, VII, 364–365. [13]Ibid., VII, 383.
[14]Smyth, IV, 449. [15]Ibid., V, 31–32.

There is a story of two little Boys in the Street; one was crying bitterly; the other came to him to ask what was the Matter? I have been, says he, "for a pennyworth of Vinegar, and I have broke the Glass, and spilt the Vinegar, and my Mother will whip me." No, she won't whip you, says the other. Indeed, she will, says he. *What,* says the other, *have you then got ne'er a Grandmother?*[16]

Kept apart from her for all but two of the last seventeen years of their marriage by the continuing demands of his agency, Franklin tenderly recalls their many years as man and wife: "It seems but t'other Day since you and I were rank'd among the Boys & Girls, so swiftly does Time fly! We have however great Reason to be thankful that so much of our Lives has pass'd so happily; and that so great a Share of Health and Strength remains, as to render Life yet comfortable."[17] That was in 1773. On December 19, 1774, three months before he was at liberty to come home, Debby died. How poignant his final letter to her sounds! especially when we realize that she may not have lived to read it:

It is now nine long Months since I received a Line from my dear Debby. I have supposed it owing to your continual Expectation of my Return; I have feared that some Indisposition has rendered you unable to write.... This will serve to acquaint you that I continue well, Thanks to God.—It would be a great pleasure to me to hear that you are so.[18]

He searched long and often without success for ways to fill the void her death left in his life. When in Philadelphia, he visited regularly at the home of his daughter,

[16]*Ibid.,* V, 282–283.   [17]*Ibid.,* VI, 4.
[18]*Autobiographical Writings,* p. 340.

"to whose filial Care of me and Attention to me I owe much of my present Happiness";[19] when abroad, he felt "the Want of that tender Care of me, which might be expected from a Daughter, and would give the World for one."[20] Official duties required that he spend more than half of his remaining years in France. The better to establish a home at Passy, he took two of his grandsons with him. It was in part the desire to create a real home away from home that led him to negotiate matches for them, intending Temple for Mme Brillon's Cunegonde and Benny for Mary Hewson's Eliza, but each time the plans fell through. In 1786 he at last had the pleasure of seeing Mary, long a widow, cross the Atlantic with her three children and settle near him in Philadelphia. All of this is a sharp reminder that this man of world renown longed always for the hearthside.

Three children were born to Franklin, a natural son William (*c.* 1731–1813) and, by Deborah, Francis Folger (1732–1736) and Sarah (1743–1808). "The Doctor by his Wife Deborah had no children," noted Ezra Stiles in his diary; "but by his first Concubine he had that are still living a Son the Governor & a Daughter married to Mr. Bache."[21] It is through precisely such misrepresentations as this that the image of Franklin the philanderer gained headway even in his lifetime. While ever a conscientious parent, the time came when the affection he continued to show his daughter was withheld from his son, and largely for reasons political. Later he would recall the proverb,

[19]Smyth, IX, 504.

[20]*Ibid.,* VIII, 455.

[21]May 6, 1777, *The Literary Diary of Ezra Stiles,* ed. F. B. Dexter (New York, 1901), II, 159.

> My Son is my Son till he take him a Wife;
> But my Daughter's my Daughter all Days of her Life.[22]

William Franklin was appointed royal governor of New Jersey in 1762; by the eve of the Revolution his father felt compelled to tell him, "You, who are a thorough Courtier, see every thing with Government Eyes."[23] In June 1776, by the father's account, William's "People took him Prisoner, and sent him under a Guard into Connecticut";[24] two years later he made his way to England, where he lived out his life in exile. Theirs was an estrangement re-enacted many times in this period. When William sought to be reconciled after the war, the father wrote, "It will be very agreable to me; indeed nothing has ever hurt me so much and affected me with such keen Sensations, as to find myself deserted in my old Age by my only Son; and not only deserted, but to find him taking up Arms against me, in a Cause, wherein my good Fame, Fortune and Life were all at Stake."[25] But the breach proved permanent. In bequeathing the bulk of his large estate to other members of his family and a pittance to his son, Franklin explained, "The part he acted against me in the late war, which is of public notoriety, will account for my leaving him no more of an estate he endeavoured to deprive me of."[26]

Of all Franklin's personal correspondences none lasted longer or gives a greater sense of continuity to his life than that he carried on with his youngest sister, the beloved Jane. On January 6, 1727, when she was fifteen, he writes her for the first time:

[22]Smyth, IX, 656. [23]*Ibid.*, VI, 241.
[24]*Ibid.*, VII, 51. [25]*Ibid.*, IX, 252.
[26]*Ibid.*, X, 494.

I have been thinking what would be a suitable present for me to make, and for you to receive, as I hear you are grown a celebrated beauty. I had almost determined on a tea table, but when I considered that the character of a good housewife was far preferable to that of being only a pretty gentlewoman, I concluded to send you a *spinning wheel,* which I hope you will accept as a small token of my sincere love and affection.[27]

Six months later she became the bride of Edward Mecom, a Boston saddler. From the outset death laid its hand on the marriage; of twelve children born to them only one survived her, and she spent the last third of her life a widow. She bore these losses with a fortitude that commanded the admiration of her brother and all who knew her. In turn, her pride in the man who would one day stand before kings was boundless. When their brother Peter Franklin died in 1766, she reminds him: "You & I only are now left. my Affection for you has all ways been so grate I see no Room for Increec, & you have manifested yrs to mee in such Large measure that I have no Reason to suspect Itts strength."[28] When in far-off Passy he expressed the hope that they might spend their last days together, she replies, "If this could be Accomplished it would give me more joy than any thing on this side Heaven could posally do."[29] As it turned out, she ended her days in her native Boston and he his in Philadelphia.

Wherever public duty required him to serve, in Pennsylvania, England, or France, Franklin struck up literary acquaintances with women younger than himself and thus lived out his life in one unchanging springtime. In 1755,

[27]Labaree, I, 100.   [28]*Franklin-Mecom Letters,* p. 93.
[29]*Ibid.,* p. 194.

BENJAMIN FRANKLIN

for example, he began to correspond with Caty Ray, a
Rhode Island girl of wit. Early in their friendship, and
before her marriage to William Greene, he grows bold:
"You must practise *Addition* to your Husband's Estate, by
Industry and Frugality; *Subtraction* of all unnecessary Expences; *Multiplication* (I would gladly have taught you
that myself, but you thought it was time enough, and
wou'dn't learn) he will soon make you a Mistress of it. As
to *Division,* I say with Brother Paul, *Let there be no Divisions among ye.*"[30] Several years later, at a time when she
was safely married, he returned to this conceit, only now
there is a variation: "[Mrs. Franklin] bids me say, she
supposes you proceeded regularly in your Arithmetick and
that, before you got into *Multiplication,* you learnt *Addition,* in which you must often have had Occasion to say,
One that I CARRY, *and two, makes Three.*—And now I
have writ this, she bids me scratch it out again. I am loth
to deface my Letter, so e'en let it [stand]."[31]

One of the few Anglican clergymen in England who
sympathized with the American struggle for independence,
and Franklin's friend partly for this reason, was Jonathan
Shipley, Bishop of St. Asaph's. It was at Chilbolton, the
Shipley home, that Franklin drafted the first part of the
Autobiography during a visit in the summer of 1771. On
August 13 of that year, he escorted eleven-year-old Kitty,
the youngest of the Bishop's five daughters, back to school
in London. That night, in a letter he thought "too trifling"
for her to show the Bishop, he gave Mrs. Shipley a charm-

[30]Labaree, VI, 225.

[31]*Franklin-Greene Correspondence,* p. 33. There is no record of a
child being born to Caty at this time.

ing account of the carriage journey, in the course of which he and Kitty chose a suitable husband for each of the Shipley girls: for Georgiana, "a country gentleman that loved travelling and would take her with him"; for Betsy, "a good, honest, sensible city merchant who will love her dearly and is very rich"; for Emily, a Duke; for Anna Maria, an Earl; and for Kitty (who never married), "an old General that has done fighting," for then, as Kitty explained, "you know I may be a rich young widow."[32] The following year Franklin lamented "the unfortunate end of poor MUNGO," Georgiana's squirrel, and sent her an epitaph "in the monumental style and measure."[33] And after the war he composed one of his more serious bagatelles, "The Art of Procuring Pleasant Dreams," for Kitty.

II

Whether at Boston, Philadelphia, London, or Paris, Franklin knew how to adjust to the intellectual climate in which he found himself. One does not have to look far, therefore, to find support for Gerald Stourzh's assertion that culturally and intellectually Benjamin Franklin was an Englishman at heart.[34] In 1763 he declared:

> Of all the enviable Things England has, I envy it most its People. Why should that petty Island, which compar'd to America, is but like a stepping-Stone in a Brook, scarce enough of it above Water to keep one's Shoes dry; why,

[32]*Autobiographical Writings,* pp. 268–270. Although the letter is dated August 12, 1771, Van Doren reasons convincingly that it must have been written Tuesday night, August 13.

[33]Smyth, V, 438.

[34]*Benjamin Franklin and American Foreign Policy* (Chicago, 1954), p. 96.

I say, should that little Island enjoy in almost every Neighbourhood, more sensible, virtuous, and elegant Minds, than we can collect in ranging 100 Leagues of our vast Forests?[35]

Small wonder, then, that he should remember his tour of Scotland in 1759, in the course of which he rubbed against such stimulating minds as Hume, Kames, and Robertson, as "six weeks of the *densest* happiness I have met with in any part of my life."[36] Whenever he contemplated settling permanently in England, though, he was constrained by his "Affection to Pensilvania, and long established Friendships and other connections there" and by Debby's "invincible Aversion to crossing the Seas."[37] To the end of his life he often thought with great pleasure, as he told an English friend in 1787, "on the happy Days I pass'd in England with my and your learned and ingenious Friends, who have left us to join the Majority in the World of Spirits."[38]

Mary Stevenson—or Polly, as Franklin preferred to address her—stands in the first rank of these English friends.[39] She was eighteen at the time he took lodgings at her mother's London home in Craven Street in the summer of 1757. It was yet another case, a notable one to be sure, of his being attracted to a younger woman and she

[35]Smyth, IV, 194.

[36]*Ibid.*, IV, 6. See J. Bennett Nolan, *Benjamin Franklin in Scotland and Ireland, 1759 and 1771* (Philadelphia, 1938), chapters 4–6.

[37]Smyth, IV, 10.   [38]*Ibid.*, IX, 556.

[39]About 170 letters and other manuscripts, the bulk of them now in the possession of the American Philosophical Society, passed between the Franklin and Stevenson-Hewson families. For some of the biographical details in the account that follows I am indebted to Whitfield Bell's article, cited above.

to him. Though from the first his heart proved large enough to hold Polly's affection for him and return it in abundance, like other women of his close acquaintance she had to learn that she must share it with others. When she protests that he also loves her friend, Dorothea Blount, he pays her a teasing compliment: "I cannot conceive that any Inconvenience can arise from my loving young Ladies and their believing that I love them. Therefore you may assure your Friend Dolly that she judges right.—I love all good Girls because they are good, and her for one Reason more, because you love her."[40]

The duties of his agency kept Franklin in London most of the year, whereas Polly lived with her wealthy Aunt Tickell in Wanstead and Kensington, visiting Craven Street infrequently. Soon they were corresponding regularly. As essays and almanac writings had often afforded him a diversion from the more serious business of making his mark in the provincial world of Philadelphia, so now (and later in France) he sought to relax from ceaseless diplomatic negotiations by writing social letters. He is at once delighted by "the Ease, the Smoothness, the Purity of Diction, and Delicacy of Sentiment" that always appear in Polly's letters.[41] "You can scarce conceive the Pleasure your Letters give me," he writes her during the interval he was back in Philadelphia. "Blessings on his Soul, that first invented Writing, without which, I should, at this Distance, be as effectually cut off from my Friends in England, as the Dead are from the Living."[42]

[40]Franklin to Polly, Jan. 9, 1765, Franklin Papers, Amer. Philos. Soc., B F85.7, 9.

[41]Franklin to Polly, June 10, 1763, Smyth, IV, 201.

[42]Franklin to Polly, Mar. 14, 1764, Smyth, IV, 217.

Soon after they met he agreed to instruct her in natural science: "Our easiest Method of Proceeding I think will be, for you to read some Books that I may recommend to you; and, in the Course of your Reading, whatever occurs, that you do not thoroughly apprehend, or that you clearly conceive and find Pleasure in, may occasion either some Questions for further Information, or some Observations that show how far you are satisfy'd and pleas'd with your Author. These will furnish Matter for your Letters to me, and, in consequence of mine also to you."[43] You should, moreover, "enter in a little Book short Hints of what you find that is curious, or that may be useful; for this will be the best Method of imprinting such Particulars in your Memory, where they will be ready, either for Practice on some future Occasion, if they are Matters of Utility, or at least to adorn and improve your Conversation, if they are rather Points of Curiosity."[44] Within three weeks she has a question: "You obligingly condescended to satisfy my Curiosity about the Barometer, and by your explanation I clearly conceived the cause of the rise and fall of the Mercury; but, upon looking at it after you were gone, I was puzzled to find out how the Air has access to the end of the Tube, which you told me was left open to receive its pressure, it being cover'd with Wood."[45] He is quick to reply: "'Tis a very sensible Question you ask, how the Air can affect the Barometer, when its Opening appears covered with Wood? If indeed it was so closely covered as to admit of no Communication of the outward

[43]Franklin to Polly, May 1, 1760, Smyth, IV, 11.

[44]Franklin to Polly, May 17, 1760, Smyth, IV, 19.

[45]Polly to Franklin, June 6, 1760, Bradford Collection, Amer. Philos. Soc., B F84.bra, 11.

Air to the Surface of the Mercury, the Change of Weight in the Air could not possibly affect it. But the least Crevice is sufficient for the Purpose; a Pinhole will do the Business. And if you could look behind the Frame to which your Barometer is fixed, you would certainly find some small Opening."[46] She looks and finds the opening. "You can't imagine how important I felt to find you thought me worthy so much of your time and attention. I thank you, my dear Preceptor, for your Indulgence in satisfying my Curiosity, and for the pleasing Instruction you give, which I will endeavour shall not be lost."[47]

During the next two years their correspondence ranged widely, touching on such diverse subjects as two ways of contracting a chimney, barometric pressure, the warm spring water at Bristol, air and evaporation, water spouts, insects, the behavior of electric fluid on a Leyden jar, river tides, salt water made fresh by distillation, the absorption of heat, and the action of fire. In these letters, as elsewhere in his scientific writings, the explanations are vigorously clear and often humorous. "You assert your Opinion with so much Modesty," she assures him, "and maintain your Argument with such Clearness, that every sensible Heart must be charm'd, and every unprejudic'd Mind convinc'd."[48] When the pupil asks why the water at Bristol becomes warm by pumping though it is not so at the spring, the instructor cautions her not to make hypotheses until she is sure of the facts; he relates an anecdote to underscore the point:

[46]Franklin to Polly, June 11, 1760, Smyth, IV, 20.

[47]Polly to Franklin, June 23, 1760, Bradford Collection, B F85.bra, 12.

[48]Polly to Franklin, Apr. 27, 1761, Bradford Collection, B F85.bra, 16.

This Prudence of not attempting to give Reasons before one is sure of Facts, I learned from one of your Sex, who, as Selden tells us, being in company with some Gentlemen that were viewing and considering something which they call'd a Chinese Shoe, and disputing earnestly about the manner of wearing it, and how it could possibly be put on; put in her Word, and said modestly, *Gentlemen, are you sure it is a Shoe? Should not that be settled first?*[49]

The social obligations Polly felt compelled to discharge, living as she did with her aunt, infringed on the time she might otherwise have devoted to these scientific studies. "The continual Engagements I am in," she complains, "prevent my [spend]ing as much time as I should chuse in the pursuit of Knowledge. I would not be thought to speak from an Affectation of Wisdom, or a Discontent at my Situation; but I cannot help wishing I might employ some of that time in reading, which is devoted to the Card Table."[50] Even though she insists that "attending to you is my Darling Amusement,"[51] her interest in science began to flag. "Have you finish'd your Course of Philosophy?" he chides. "No more Doubts to be resolv'd? No more Questions to ask? If so, you may now be at full Leisure to improve yourself in Cards."[52] "I confess you have just Reason to complain of me," she admits, "and my Indolence merits your severe Rebuke. Your Letter fill'd me with Confusion, and I assure you it will be a Spur to my Indus-

[49]Franklin to Polly, Sept. 13, 1760, Smyth, IV, 26.

[50]Polly to Franklin, Jan. 13, 1761, Bradford Collection, B F85.bra, 15.

[51]Polly to Franklin, May 19, 1761, Bradford Collection, B F85.bra, 17.

[52]Franklin to Polly, Mar. 8, 1762, Smyth, IV, 148.

try."[53] But the social demands of her life and her own temperament got the better of this early enthusiasm. By the time Franklin was ready to return to America in 1762, he found that his role as her scientific tutor was all but played out.

Not so his role as moral tutor. Early in their acquaintance he cautions her:

> The Knowledge of Nature may be ornamental, and it may be useful; but if, to attain an Eminence in that, we neglect the Knowledge and Practice of essential Duties, we deserve Reprehension. For there is no Rank in Natural Knowledge of equal Dignity and Importance with that of being a good Parent, a good Child, a good Husband or Wife, a good Neighbour or Friend, a good Subject or Citizen, that is, in short, a good Christian. Nicholas Gimcrack, therefore, who neglected the Care of his Family, to pursue Butterflies, was a just Object of Ridicule, and we must give him up as fair Game to the satyrist.[54]

Deeply impressed by his piety, Polly soon resolved to pattern her character upon his. Though far more of a formalist than he, she agreed that Christianity requires no more than "the strict discharge of moral obligation."[55] Whenever she wearied of her aunt's company, he reminds her that "nothing can contribute to true Happiness, that is inconsistent with Duty; nor can a course of Action, conformable to it, be finally without an ample Reward."[56]

[53]Polly to Franklin, Mar. 10, 1762, Bradford Collection, B F85.bra, 49.

[54]Franklin to Polly, June 11, 1760, Smyth, IV, 22.

[55]Polly to Franklin, [Summer 1761?], Bradford Collection, B F85.bra, 49.

[56]Franklin to Polly, Oct. 28, 1768, Smyth, V, 181.

BENJAMIN FRANKLIN

It was advice that Polly did not forget when she became a mother and a widow. Less by precept than by the example of his life he continued to be her moral guide until death claimed him.

So great was her affection for him that during his absence on the continent in 1761 she declares, "I don't know whether to say I fear or I hope this won't reach you before you leave Holland, for I don't care how soon we have you on our Island again, and I wish you had no Attachments ever to draw you from it again, that is I wish your Attachments were all here."[57] He on his side dreamed of a match between her and his son. In the summer of 1762, as he made ready to sail for America, there was an exchange of letters, the more affectionate since so far as either of them then knew they would not see each other again. "It will be yet 5 or 6 Weeks before we embark, and leave the old World for the New," he writes. "I fancy I feel a little like dying Saints, who, in parting with those they love in this World, are only comforted with the Hope of more perfect Happiness in the next."[58] "May you my dear Saint enjoy all the Felicity you Promise yourself in the New World!" she replies, pursuing the conceit, "and May it be long ere you are remov'd to that other World where only your Votary can hope to meet you!"[59] News of his son William's engagement to Elizabeth Downes reaching him at Portsmouth where he had gone to embark, he sat down and wrote one of the tenderest letters he ever penned:

[57]Polly to Franklin, Sept. 10, 1761, Bradford Collection, B F85.bra, 20.

[58]Franklin to Polly, June 7, 1762, Smyth, IV, 158.

[59]Polly to Franklin, June 11, 1762, Bradford Collection, B F85.bra, 23.

This is the best Paper I can get at this wretched Inn, but it will convey what is intrusted to it as faithfully as the finest. It will tell my Polly how much her Friend is afflicted, that he must, perhaps, never again, see one for whom he has so sincere an Affection, join'd to so perfect an Esteem; who he once flatter'd himself might become his own, in the tender Relation of a Child, but can now entertain such pleasing Hopes no more. Will it tell *how much* he is afflicted? No, it cannot.[60]

Before he knew he would be commissioned to England a second time he wrote longingly from Philadelphia: "Business, publick and private, devours all my Time. I must return to England for Repose. With such Thoughts I flatter myself, and need some kind Friend to put me often in mind, that *old Trees cannot safely be transplanted*."[61] "Don't let them tell you 'old trees cannot safely be transplanted,'" comes her comforting answer. "I have lately seen some fine tall firs remov'd from Kensington to the Queen's Palace without injury, and Why should not the valuable North American plants flourish here?"[62] Franklin was back at his Craven Street lodgings in December 1764, and they resumed their epistolary friendship, only now the talk was chiefly social. In the fall of 1767 he sent her a vivid account of his trip to France with Sir John Pringle—the chaise ride to Dover; the Channel crossing, during which "the Sea laid Claim" to many a hearty breakfast; poor peasants laboring on the roads and fair women at the capital ("As to Rouge, they don't pretend to

[60]Franklin to Polly, Aug. 11, 1762, Smyth, IV, 173–174.

[61]Franklin to Polly, Mar. 14, 1764, Smyth, IV, 217.

[62]Polly to Franklin, May 24, 1764, Bradford Collection, B F85.bra, 28.

imitate Nature in laying it on"); attending a *Grand Couvert* at Versailles; French politeness—and concludes playfully, "This Letter shall cost you a Shilling, and you may consider it cheap, when you reflect that it has cost me at least 50 Guineas to get into the Situation, that enables me to write it."[63]

The same year he composed birthday verses for her, prefacing them with an explanation and apology calculated to amuse a young woman of wit such as she.

A Muse, you must know, visited me this Morning!... This Muse appear'd to be no Housewife. I suppose few of them are. She was *drest* (if the Expression is allowable) in an *Undress,* a kind of slatternly *Negligée,* neither neat nor clean, nor well made; and she has given the same sort of Dress to my Piece. On reviewing it, I would have reform'd the Lines, and made them all of a Length, as I am told Lines ought to be; but I find I can't lengthen the short ones without stretching them on the Rack, and I think it would be equally cruel to cut off any Part of the long ones. Besides the Superfluity of *these* makes up for the Deficiency of *those;* and so, from a Principle of Justice, I leave them at full Length, that I may give you, at least in one Sense of the Word, *good Measure.*[64]

One stanza, the second of three, will suffice to give the flavor of this birthday greeting:

> God, who values only Souls,
> Has given yours that outward Case,
> In which (as Time his Season rolls)
> It may, while here below, improve,
> Till, fit for Heav'n above,

[63]Franklin to Polly, Sept. 14, 1767, Smyth, V, 48–54.
[64]Franklin to Polly, June 17, 1767, Smyth, V, 30, 31.

> It shall be brought there, to increase
> The Happiness of the Place,
> Where all is Joy and all is Love.[65]

Two years later Polly made him a pair of ruffles for Christmas and accompanied the gift with a poem that reads in part,

> For you my fancy and my skill I tried—
> For you my needle with delight I plied—
> Proud ev'n to add a trifling grace to you,
> From whom philosophy and virtue too
> I've gain'd: if either can be counted mine,
> In you they with the clearest lustre shine.[66]

In 1767, by Franklin's account in a letter to his wife, Polly's match with "a mean-spirited mercenary Fellow... not worthy so valuable a Girl as she is in every Respect, Person, Fortune, Temper and excellent Understanding" was broken off. "The Difference was about Money-Matters."[67] In August 1769, during a stay at Margate with her aunt, Polly met William Hewson. "A very sensible physician," she assures Franklin, who had just returned from the Continent. "I would not have you or my mother surprised, if I should run off with this young man.... He engaged me so deeply in conversation, and I was so much pleased with him, that I thought it necessary to give you warning, though I assure you he has made no *proposal*. How I rattle! This flight must be owing to this new

[65]June 15, 1767, Polly's copy of "You'd have the Custom broke, you say," Bradford Collection, B F85.bra, 2.

[66]"Verses, by a lady. Addressed to dr. Franklin, with a pair of worked ruffles, Dec. 1769," *American Museum* (Philadelphia), VII (June, 1790), Appendix, 43–44.

[67]Franklin to Deborah, June 22, 1767, Smyth, V, 33.

acquaintance, or to the joy of hearing my old one is returned to this country."[68] "Possibly, if the Truth were known," he replies, "I have Reason to be jealous of this same insinuating, handsome young Physician; but, as it flatters more my Vanity, and therefore gives me more Pleasure, to suppose you were in Spirits on acc^t of my safe Return, I shall turn a deaf Ear to Reason in this Case, as I have done with Success in twenty others."[69] Soon Dr. Hewson did propose, and when Polly, whose heart had already spoken, courteously consulted Franklin his answer was equally generous:

> His Person you see; his Temper and his Understanding you can judge of; his Character, for any thing I have ever heard, is unblemished; his Profession, with the Skill in it he is suppos'd to have, will be sufficient to support a Family; and, therefore, considering the Fortune you have in your Hands (tho' any future Expectation from your Aunt should be disappointed), I do not see but that the Agreement may be a rational one on both sides.... I am sure that were I in his situation in every respect, knowing you so well as I do, and esteeming you so highly, I should think you a Fortune sufficient for me without a Shilling.... I shall be confident, whether you accept or refuse, that you do right. I only wish you may do what will most contribute to your Happiness, and of course to mine.[70]

On July 10, 1770, Franklin was present to give the bride away. "Your Mother desires me to express abundance of Affection for you, and to Mr. Hewson," he informs her a fortnight later; "and to say all the proper Things for her, with respect to the rest of your Friends there. But you

[68]Polly to Franklin, Sept. 1, 1769, Smyth, V, 224.
[69]Franklin to Polly, Sept. 2, 1769, Smyth, V, 225.
[70]Franklin to Polly, May 31, 1770, Smyth, V, 256.

can imagine better than I can write. Sally [Sally Franklin, an English cousin] and little Temple join in best Wishes of Prosperity to you both. Make my sincere Respects acceptable to Mr. Hewson, whom, exclusive of his other Merits, I shall always esteem in proportion to the Regard he manifests for you." Then, foreseeing the changes that this marriage will bring in their friendship, he gently adds: "We like your Assurances of continued Friendship, un-impair'd by your Change of Condition, and we believe you think as you write; but we fancy we know better than you. You know I once knew your Heart better than you did yourself. As a Proof that I am right, take notice,— that *you now think this the silliest Letter I ever wrote to you, and that Mr. Hewson confirms you in that Opinion.*"[71] In spite of the loneliness he now experienced, Franklin did not (though he may have been tempted) pose as the jealous father who has just lost an only daughter. Instead, he entertained her with "The Cravenstreet Gazette," wherein he pictures himself only as "the *great* Person (so called from his enormous Size) of a certain Family in a certain Street."

In 1771 Franklin stood as godfather for William, the first of three children born to the Hewsons. "He resembles you in many particulars," the mother tells him. "He is generally serious, no great Talker, but sometimes laughs very hearty; he is very fond of being in his *Birth day Suit,* & has not the least apprehension of *catching cold* in it; he is never troubled with the Airophobia, but always seems delighted with fresh Air."[72] "His being like me in so

[71]Franklin to Polly, July 24, 1770, Smyth, V, 269, 270.

[72]Polly to Franklin, Nov. 2, 1771, Bradford Collection, B F85.bra, 36. Franklin had described "the *tonic* or bracing method" of cold-air bathing in a letter of July 28, 1768, to Dubourg (Smyth, V, 152–153).

many Particulars pleases me prodigiously," replies the god-father; "and I am persuaded there is another, which you have omitted, tho' it must have occurr'd to you while you were putting them down. Pray let him have every thing he likes; I think it of great Consequence while the Features of the Countenance are forming; it gives them a pleasant Air, and, that being once become natural and fix'd by Habit, the Face is ever after the handsomer for it, and on that much of a Person's good Fortune and Success in Life may depend."[73] In the summer of 1772 the Hewsons moved into the Craven Street house, and Mrs. Stevenson and her American boarder to another on the same street. For the time that they were close neighbors there was little need to correspond. The Hewsons' second child, Thomas, was born in 1773. The following year was a time of loss and gain for Polly, as Franklin explains in a letter to his sister Jane:

> Mrs Stevenson presents her Respects to you. Her Daughter Mrs Hewson, who lost her Husband in May, has lately got a third Child, a Girl [Elizabeth], born 5 Months after its Father's Death: A melancholy Circumstance!—But her Aunt, a Sister of Mrs Stevenson, dying lately, and leaving her Fortune to Mrs Hewson, which was considerable, puts her into easy Circumstances, and will enable her to bring up her Children decently.[74]

Now that a new generation was coming along Franklin again dreamed of marriage, this time between Polly's daughter Elizabeth and his grandson Benjamin Bache (b.

[73]Franklin to Polly, Nov. 25, 1771, Smyth, V, 346.

[74]Franklin to Jane, Sept. 26, 1774, *Franklin-Mecom Letters*, p. 148. Dr. Hewson had died on May 1 of an infection contracted while dissecting.

1769). From Philadelphia he writes her in 1775, half in jest, half in earnest, "Ben, when I delivered him your Blessing, inquired the Age of Elizabeth, and thought her yet too young for him; but, as he made no other Objection, and that will lessen every day, I have only to wish being alive to dance with your Mother at the Wedding."[75] And from Passy two years later: "I have with me here my young Grandson, Benja. Franklin Bache, a special good Boy. I give him a little French Language and Address, and then send him over to pay his Respects to Miss Hewson."[76] Though Polly spoke of Benny as "my future son-in-law"[77] and though Franklin entrusted him to her care for a time in 1784, nothing came of this dream either.

In March 1775, his second mission as colonial agent now at an end, Franklin departed for America. In a letter of 1779 to Mrs. Stevenson, who had looked after his needs for so many years, he recalls Craven Street with affection:

It is always with great Pleasure, when I think of our long continu'd Friendship, which had not the least Interruption in the Course of Twenty Years (some of the happiest of my Life), that I spent under your Roof and in your Company. ...Be assured, my dear Friend,...that, if Circumstances would permit, nothing would afford me so much Satisfaction, as to be with you in the same House, and to experience again your faithful, tender Care, and Attention to my Interests, Health, and Comfortable Living, which so long and steadily attach'd me to you, and which I shall ever remember with Gratitude.[78]

[75]Franklin to Polly, July 8, 1775, Smyth, VI, 410–411.

[76]Franklin to Polly, Jan. 12, 1777, Smyth, VII, 10.

[77]Polly to Franklin, Apr. 8, 1781, Bache Collection, Amer. Philos. Soc., B F85.BA.

[78]Franklin to Mrs. Stevenson, Jan. 25, 1779, Smyth, VII, 220–221.

Polly, of course, had formed a large part of his happiness there. Now war would keep them apart for a decade, during most of which time the letters that passed between them were constantly liable to seizure. She cannot think why their letters should be stopped, since she has no political intelligence to impart and no purpose would be served by his sending her any.[79] What she does retail is domestic news. "We drank your health today; the person who first proposed the toast was my Son William, who took up his glass of wine & water (for he is still very sober) & said 'my Doctor papa's health.'"[80] "My letters," she explains, "are a kind of private newspaper, I give the articles just as they happen to occur without regard to order or connection. I fancy this kind will be most pleasing to you, as it will not require an answer, & will make you feel somewhat like having your English friends about you."[81] The war itself distressed them both. "I who have no political animosity," she writes, "cannot rejoice at the success of either nation, but feel for all the evil that the war produces."[82] He for his part, even as peace was approaching, waxes bitter: "All Wars are Follies, very expensive, and very mischievous ones. When will Mankind be convinced of this, and agree to settle their Differences by Arbitration? Were they to do it, even by the Cast of a Dye, it would be better than by Fighting and destroying each other."[83]

After her husband's death in 1774 Polly had the full

[79]Polly to Franklin, Apr. 27, 1778, Bache Collection, B F85.BA.
[80]Polly to Franklin, Sept. 5, 1776, Bache Collection, B F85.BA.
[81]Polly to Franklin, Sept. 8, 1776, Bache Collection, B F85.BA.
[82]Polly to Franklin, Jan. 11, 1779, Bradford Collection, B F85.bra, 39.
[83]Franklin to Polly, Jan. 27, 1783, Smyth, IX, 12.

responsibility of rearing the children. Within six years she was able to inform Franklin:

> You know that my affairs are settled in a manner that affords me a competent income.... The retirement of our situation [at Cheam] gives me time to do many things for my children, which in the bustle of the world I could not do.... I am thankful for the great blessing of three children with sound constitutions, perfect forms, good understandings, and amiable dispositions.[84]

Her domestic management meets with his unqualified approval:

> You cannot be more pleas'd in talking about your Children, your Methods of Instructing them, and the Progress they make, than I am in hearing it, and in finding, that, instead of following the idle Amusements, which both your Fortune and the Custom of the Age might have led you into, your Delight and your Duty go together, by employing your Time in the Education of your Offspring. This is following Nature and Reason, instead of Fashion; than which nothing is more becoming the Character of a Woman of Sense and Virtue.[85]

On January 1, 1783, Polly's mother died. "The Departure of my dearest Friend," he tells her, "greatly affects me.... The last Year carried off my Friends Dr. Pringle, and Dr. Fothergill, Lord Kaims, and Lord le Despencer. This has begun to take away the rest, and strikes the hardest. Thus the Ties I had to that Country, and indeed to the World in general, are loosened one by one, and I shall soon have no Attachment left to make me unwilling to follow."[86] Three years earlier he had urged Polly to

[84]Polly to Franklin, Apr. 2, 1780, Bache Collection, B F85.BA.
[85]Franklin to Polly, June 13, 1782, Smyth, VIII, 455–456.
[86]Franklin to Polly, Jan. 27, 1783, Smyth, IX, 11.

join him at Passy, "in which Village you might find Lodging or a small House, sufficient to accommodate your self, good Mother & Children. There are in the Village a Number of Boarding Schools, in which the young ones might soon learn the Language, and a Number of good Families that form a most amiable Society."[87] Now, feeling "the Infirmities of Age come on so fast, and the Building to need so many Repairs, that in a little time the Owner will find it cheaper to pull it down and build a new one," he renewed his proposal.[88]

In the fall of 1784 he went so far as to dispatch Temple, the natural son of his natural son William and now his heir, to fetch her over to France. Unable to go at that time, Polly sent the grandfather a complimentary if candid letter concerning his emissary.

> We are all pleased with our old Friend Temple changed into young Franklin. We see a strong resemblance of you, and indeed saw it when we did not think ourselves at liberty to say we did, as we pretended to be as ignorant as you supposed we were, or chose we should be. I believe you may have been handsomer than your Grandson is, but then you never were so genteel; and if he has a little less philosophy he has more polish. To have such a young man to run off with one, and yet to stay behind, argues great virtue or great stupidity. *Les Belles Françoises* will be at no loss which to term it; my country women will not marvel so much, as at forty-five we are expected to be prudent.[89]

At the end of the year she did go and wintered happily at Passy. Afterwards they both recalled the visit with

[87]Franklin to Polly, Jan. 10, 1780, Franklin Papers, B F85.7, 16.
[88]Franklin to Polly, Mar. 19, 1784, Smyth. IX, 181.
[89]Polly to Franklin, Oct. 25, 1784, Bache Collection, B F85.BA.

pleasure. "I cannot say even if I had time all that I feel for your kindness," she writes him from Dover, "but my thoughts have incessantly turned to Passy as I have proceeded from it."[90] "I pass'd a long Winter, in a manner that made it appear the shortest of any I ever past," he assures her. "Such is the Effect of pleasing Society, with Friends one loves.... M. le Veillard, in particular, has told me at different times, what indeed I knew long since, *C'est une bien digne Femme, cette Madame Hewson, une très aimable Femme.*" In a postscript he adds: "My love to William, and Thomas, and Eliza, and tell them I miss their chearful Prattle. Temple being sick, and Benjamin at Paris, I have found it very *triste* breakfasting alone, and sitting alone, and without any Tea in the Evening."[91]

Released from his diplomatic mission to France at last, Franklin sailed for home in July 1785. Back at Philadelphia, he was (as he tells Polly) "plung'd again into public Business, as deep as ever."[92] He assures her, though, that he still finds time to enjoy life:

> I have public business enough to preserve me from *ennui,* and private amusement besides in conversation, books, my garden, and *cribbage*. Considering our well-furnished, plentiful market as the best of gardens, I am turning mine, in the midst of which my house stands, into grass plots and gravel walks, with trees and flowering shrubs. Cards we sometimes play here, in long winter evenings; but it is as they play at chess, not for money, but for honour, or the pleasure of beating one another.... As to public amusements...we

[90]Polly to Franklin, Apr. 26, 1785, Bradford Collection, B F85.bra, 44.

[91]Franklin to Polly, May 5, 1785, Smyth, IX, 323.

[92]Franklin to Polly, Oct. 30, 1785, Smyth, IX, 474.

jog on in life as pleasantly as you do in England; anywhere but in London, for there you have plays performed by good actors. That, however, is, I think, the only advantage London has over Philadelphia.[93]

He had long hoped she would bring her family to America. "Give me leave to flatter myself," he once hinted, "that my being made happier in my last Years by your Neighbourhood and Society may be some Inducement to you."[94] Finally, from the Capes of Delaware on October 17, 1786, Polly announced her arrival, asking him to procure suitable lodgings: "Three beds for ourselves and one for my maid, that & one room to eat in is all we care for."[95]

In letters after this time to English friends and relatives Polly gives intimate glimpses of her long-time American friend, now past fourscore, in whose company she spent her days so agreeably. "Dr. Franklin is now quite well," she informs her sister-in-law in 1788. "In a very short time he will lay down his office of President of Council & Govr. of the State, having served three years, and the Constitution does not admit of any one continuing longer in office, otherwise I have no doubt but he would be chosen again."[96] Shortly after his death she describes the fortitude he exhibited in the face of unceasing pain:

> No repining, no peevish expression, ever escaped him, during a confinement of two years, in which, I believe, if every moment of ease could be added together the sum

[93]Franklin to Polly, May 6, 1786, Smyth, IX, 511–512.

[94]Franklin to Polly, Sept. 7, 1783, Smyth, IX, 90.

[95]Polly to Franklin, Oct. 17, 1786, Bradford Collection, B F85.bra, 46.

[96]Polly to Barbara Hewson, Oct. 21, 1788, Hewson film, Amer. Philos. Soc.

would not amount to two whole months. When the pain was not too violent to be amused, he employed himself with his books, his pen, or in conversation with his friends; and upon every occasion displayed the clearness of his intellect and the cheerfulness of his temper. Even when the intervals from pain were so short, that his words were frequently interrupted, I have known him to hold a discourse in a sublime strain of piety.[97]

Franklin bequeathed to her "one of my silver tankards marked for her use during her life, and after her decease I give to her daughter *Eliza*. I give to her son, *William Hewson,* who is my godson, my new quarto Bible, Oxford edition, to be for his family Bible, and also the botanic description of the plants in the Emperor's garden at Vienna, in folio, with coloured cuts. And to her son, *Thomas Hewson,* I give a set of *Spectators, Tatlers,* and *Guardians* handsomely bound."[98] Five years later, on October 14, 1795, Polly herself died, having spent her final years at Bellemead, Temple's home near Bristol, Pennsylvania.

In 1782 Franklin had reminded Polly, "It is now a Quarter of a Century since our Friendship commenc'd; and, tho' we lived much of the time together, it has never been interrupted by the smallest Misunderstanding or Coolness."[99] "Our Friendship," he added a few months later, "has been all clear Sunshine, without the least Cloud in its Hemisphere."[100] The letters, which are the true index of their abiding affection for each other, had made it so.

[97]Polly to Thomas Viny, May 5, 1790, quoted in *The Works of Benjamin Franklin,* ed. Jared Sparks (Boston, 1836–1840), I, 531.
[98]Smyth, X, 508.
[99]*Ibid.,* VIII, 585.
[100]*Ibid.,* IX, 12.

III

Whereas the tone of Franklin's letters to the press shades off into irony, in the personal letters his instinct is toward the comic. Having told Dubourg how as a boy he was drawn across a pond by means of a kite, he concludes: "I have never since that time practised this singular mode of swimming, though I think it not impossible to cross in this manner from Dover to Calais. The packet-boat, however, is still preferable."[101] Sometimes the comic effect depends upon obscene and bawdy reference, more frequently present in this and other types of private writing than in his public. He explains his objection to a line in an acrostic on Jane Franklin's name ("Kindness of heart by words express") thus:

'Tis pity that good works, among some sorts of people, are so little valued, and good words admired in their stead: I mean seemingly pious discourses, instead of humane benevolent actions. Those they almost put out of countenance, by calling morality *rotten morality*—righteousness *ragged righteousness*, and even filthy rags—and when you mention virtue, pucker up their noses as if they smelt a stink; at the same time that they eagerly snuff up an empty canting harangue, as if it was a posey of the choicest flowers: so they have inverted the good old verse, and say now

A man of deeds and not of words
Is like a garden full of

I have forgot the rhyme, but remember 'tis something the very reverse of perfume.[102]

Elsewhere he informs James Read:

Your copy of Kempis, must be a corrupt one, if it has that

[101]*Ibid.*, V, 545.　　　　　[102]*Franklin-Mecom Letters*, pp. 67–68.

passage as you quote it, *in omnibus requiem quaesivi, sed non inveni, nisi in angulo cum libello.* The good father understood pleasure (requiem) better, and wrote, *in angulo cum puella.* Correct it thus, without hesitation. I know there is another reading, *in angulo puellae;* but this reject, tho' more *to the point,* as an expression too indelicate.[103]

In view of the colloquial and spontaneous nature of personal correspondence, it is not surprising that such rhetorical figures as analogy, repetition, proverb, and pun should abound in Franklin's personal letters, official and scientific as well as social. Two analogies that refer, appropriately enough, to the field of ceramics serve to underscore his thoughts on empire. "We are in your Hands as Clay in the Hands of the Potter," he warns Collinson, shortly after tax-minded George Grenville became first minister; "and so in one more Particular than is generally consider'd: for as the Potter cannot waste or spoil his Clay without injuring himself, so I think there is scarce anything you can do that may be hurtful to us, but what will be as much or more so to you."[104] Contemplating the rift in the Anglo-American community after a year of war, he reminds William Howe, then poised off Sandy Hook, bearing an olive branch in one hand and a sword in the other, "Long did I endeavour, with unfeigned and unwearied Zeal, to preserve from breaking that fine and noble China Vase, the British Empire; for I knew, that, being once broken, the separate Parts could not retain even their Shares of the Strength and Value that existed in the Whole, and that a perfect Reunion of those Parts could scarce ever be hoped for."[105] Repetition he uses to give this

[103]Labaree, III, 39–40. [104]Smyth, IV, 243.
[105]*Ibid.*, VI, 460–461.

account of a proposed "Party of Pleasure on the Banks of SchuylKill" in 1749 a comic turn: "A Turky is to be killed for our Dinners by the Electrical Shock; and roasted by the electrical Jack, before a Fire kindled by the Electrified Bottle; when the Healths of all the famous Electricians in England, France and Germany, are to be drank in Electrified Bumpers, under the Discharge of Guns from the Electrical Battery."[106] In the course of a letter to Collinson on the Sugar Act of 1764 he introduces a proverb and proceeds to amplify it: "Therefore what you get from us in Taxes you must lose in Trade. The Cat can yield but her skin. And as you must have the whole Hide, if you first cut Thongs out of it, 'tis at your own Expence."[107] Another proverb effectively points up why he addressed the "Rules" and "Edict" to the British nation in 1773: "A little Sturdiness when Superiors are much in the Wrong, sometimes occasions Consideration. And there is truth in the Old Saying, That *if you make yourself a Sheep, the Wolves will eat you.*"[108] An alchemical pun is gracefully imbedded in his letter of 1754 to the Royal Society acknowledging receipt of the Copley gold medal: "I know not whether any of your learned Body have attain'd the ancient boasted Art of *multiplying* Gold; but you have certainly found the Art of making it infinitely *more valuable.*"[109] Observing that clay medallion likenesses of him have become fashionable in France, he playfully tells his daughter Sarah: "It is said by learned etymologists, that the name *doll,* for the images children play with, is de-

[106]Labaree, III, 364–365.
[107]Smyth, IV, 243.
[108]*Franklin-Mecom Letters*, p. 143.
[109]Labaree, V, 334.

rived from the word IDOL. From the number of *dolls* now made of [your father's face], he may be truly said, *in that sense,* to be *i-doll-ized* in this country."[110]

In his personal correspondence Franklin relies heavily on simile and metaphor to ensure clarity and impart color, frequently recruiting such tropes from the New Science of the seventeenth and eighteenth centuries. "Now waves once raised, whether by the wind or any other power," he writes, describing the effects of oil poured on water, "have the same mechanical operation, by which they continue to rise and fall, as a *pendulum* will continue to swing a long time after the force ceases to act by which the motion was first produced; that motion will, however, cease in time; but time is necessary."[111] Learning that his oldest sister would not budge from the house in Unity Street, Boston, where she had lived for years, Franklin tells Jane: "As *having their own Way,* is one of the greatest Comforts of Life, to old People, I think their Friends should endeavour to accommodate them in that, as well as in any thing else.— When they have long liv'd in a House, it becomes natural to them, they are almost as closely connected with it as the Tortoise with his Shell, they die if you tear them out of it."[112] He sometimes extends the simile over a long reach, as here in a letter to Caty Ray written in the period of his electrical experiments:

I left New England slowly, and with great Reluctance: Short Days Journeys, and loitering Visits on the Road, for three or four Weeks, manifested my Unwillingness to quit a Country in which I drew my first Breath, spent my earliest

[110]Smyth, VII, 347.
[111]*Ibid.*, VI, 164.
[112]*Franklin-Mecom Letters*, p. 57.

and most pleasant Days, and had now received so many fresh
Marks of the People's Goodness and Benevolence, in the
kind and affectionate Treatment I had every where met
with. I almost forgot I had a Home; till I was more than
half-way towards it; till I had, one by one, parted with all
my New England Friends, and was got into the western
Borders of Connecticut, among meer Strangers: then, like
an old Man, who, having buried all he lov'd in this World,
begins to think of Heaven, I begun to think of and wish
for Home; and as I drew nearer, I found the Attraction
stronger and stronger.[113]

In keeping with the colloquial tone that informs the
personal letter, Franklin's metaphors are usually homely.
"I have continu'd to work till late in the Day," he writes
his sister Jane in 1785; "tis time I should go home, and
go to Bed."[114] And on the occasion of his election to the
presidency of the Pennsylvania Council he tells his old
friends, the Bards: "But I had not firmness enough to
resist the unanimous desire of my country folks; and I
find myself harnessed again in their service for another
year. They engrossed the prime of my life. They have
eaten my flesh, and seem resolved now to pick my bones."[115]
But because metaphor is a more studied ornament than
simile, Franklin's are sometimes contrived. In answer to
Strahan, who described England's political disorders in
1784, he draws one out from what had long been their
common profession:

Here are near two Months that your Government has been
employed in *getting its form to press;* which is not yet fit to

[113]Labaree, V, 503.
[114]*Franklin-Mecom Letters*, p. 236.
[115]Smyth, IX, 476.

work on, every Page of it being *squabbled,* and the whole ready to fall into *pye.* The Founts too must be very scanty, or strangely *out of sorts,* since your *Compositors* cannot find either *upper* or *lower case Letters* sufficient to set the word ADMINISTRATION, but are forc'd to be continually *turning for them.*[116]

Occasionally he refines a metaphor in such a way that it becomes in effect a conceit. Writing from Philadelphia, he gives one of Caty Ray's domestic remarks this metaphysical turn:

You have spun a long Thread, 5022 Yards! It will reach almost from Block Island hither. I wish I had hold of one End of it, to pull you to me: But you would break it rather than come. The Cords of Love and Friendship are longer and stronger, and in Times past have drawn me farther; even back from England to Philadelphia. I guess that some of the same kind will one day draw you out of that Island.[117]

As letter writer Franklin was most active during the second half of his life, as though he knew instinctively that he must master the writer's craft at all points before giving himself wholeheartedly to this delightful but infinitely demanding pursuit. The special charm and intimacy that characterize the successful letter, personal or familiar, require not only a dynamic and adaptable personality but grace, clarity, and vigor of expression, qualities that are come by only through long years of practice. Thus, in his public utterances as essayist, philomath, and polemicist Franklin may be described as serving an apprenticeship against the time when he felt equal to the demands of this more intimate form of communication. The range

[116]*Ibid.,* IX, 172.
[117]Labaree, VI, 183–184.

and flexibility of his epistolary style will only become fully apparent when the publication of *The Papers of Benjamin Franklin*, which will include all the important letters he sent and received and all third-party letters, is completed some years hence. Only then, as I have tried to show in a limited way by reconstructing his epistolary friendship with Polly, will we be in a position to study and come to know fully Franklin the letter writer.

VI

The Familiar Letter

THE familiar letter is even more closely allied to conversation than the personal. Georgiana Shipley was reminded by certain bagatelles Franklin sent her of "those happy hours we once passed in your society when we were never amused without learning some usefull Truth & when I first acquired a taste *pour la conversation badinante et réfléchie*."[1] The adjectives *"badinante"* and *"réfléchie"* characterize Franklin's familiar letters as well as the excellent talk which was the inspiration for them. The great exemplar of the familiar letter in eighteenth-century England was Horace Walpole. William Hazlitt had him immediately in mind when he wrote:

> Letters are certainly the honestest records of great minds, that we can become acquainted with; and we like them the more, for letting us into the follies and treacheries of high life, the secrets of the gay and the learned world, and the mysteries of authorship. We are ushered, as it were, behind

[1] Smyth, VIII, 162n.

the scenes of life; and see gay ladies and learned men, the wise, the witty, and the ambitious, in all the nakedness, or undress at least, of their spirits.[2]

Admittedly the distinction between the personal and the familiar letter is highly subjective, since the success of both sub-genres depends finally on the degree of intimacy they achieve, on the writer's knowledge of his correspondent and his ability to tune in at the right wave length. The special quality of salon talk imparted to the familiar letter a self-consciousness that is its distinguishing feature. Rousseau has characterized such talk as flowing easily and naturally,

> neither dull nor frivolous, full of knowledge without being pedantic, gay but not noisy, polished without affectation, gallant and not merely insipid, playful but not ambiguous. Everything is discussed in order that every one may be able to say something, but no subject is plumbed to its depth for fear of becoming tedious. It is brought up quite by the way and rapidly disposed of, but precision gives an elegance to conversation in that every one gives his opinion in as few words as possible. No one attacks another's point of view with warmth, and the latter does not defend it with any obstinacy. People indulge in discussion in order to enlighten themselves, but stop before it can degenerate into a dispute.[3]

If one allow for the more clearly self-conscious posturing in the salon, this characterization goes far toward defining the special charm of the familiar letters that passed between Franklin and certain French ladies of his close acquaint-

[2]*The Complete Works of William Hazlitt* (London, 1930–1934), XVI, 141, quoted in Watson, *Magazine Serials,* p. 70.

[3]Quoted in Louis Ducros, *French Society in the Eighteenth Century* (New York and London, 1927), pp. 338–339.

ance.[4] It is no accident that the bulk of his familiar letters were written during and after his nine-year sojourn in France, where the salon attained its highest refinement and where the writer has traditionally been held in high esteem.]

An excellent example, and a letter whose particular wit it is hard to imagine Franklin conceiving before this time, is the well-known one addressed to Sarah Bache in 1784. Prompted by news of the formation of the Society of the Cincinnati, the father, echoing a sentiment he had expressed long ago in a *Courant* essay on titles of honor, writes his daughter: "Honour, worthily obtain'd (as for Example that of our Officers), is in its Nature a *personal* Thing, and incommunicable to any but those who had some Share in obtaining it. Thus among the Chinese, the most ancient, and from long Experience the wisest of Nations, honour does not *descend,* but *ascends.*" "This *ascending* Honour is therefore useful to the State, as it encourages Parents to give their Children a good and virtuous Education. But the *descending Honour,* to Posterity who could have no Share in obtaining it, is not only groundless and absurd, but often hurtful to that Posterity." Let me prove my case by mathematical demonstration:

In nine Generations, which will not require more than 300 years (no very great Antiquity for a Family), our present

[4]The most significant of these correspondents were Mmes Brillon, De Forbach, D'Houdetot, Helvétius, La Freté, and Le Roy, and Mlle Le Veillard. In addition to the familiar letters printed in Smyth and in other editions already noted, see *Les amitiés américaines de Madame D'Houdetot,* ed. Gilbert Chinard (Paris, 1924) and *Benjamin Franklin's Letters to Madame Helvétius and Madame La Freté,* comp. Luther S. Livingston (Cambridge, Mass., 1924).

Chevalier of the Order of Cincinnatus's Share in the then existing Knight, will be but a 512th part. . . .

Let us go back with our Calculation from this young Noble, the 512th part of the present Knight, thro' his nine Generations, till we return to the year of the Institution. . . . One Thousand and Twenty-two Men and Women [are] contributors to the formation of one Knight. And, if we are to have a Thousand of these future knights, there must be now and hereafter existing One million and Twenty-two Thousand Fathers and Mothers, who are to contribute to their Production, unless a Part of the Number are employ'd in making more Knights than One. Let us strike off then the 22,000, on the Supposition of this double Employ, and then consider whether, after a reasonable Estimation of the Number of Rogues, and Fools, and Royalists and Scoundrels and Prostitutes, that are mix'd with, and help to make up necessarily their Million of Predecessors, Posterity will have much reason to boast of the noble Blood of the then existing set of Chevaliers de Cincinnatus.

While obviously Franklin hoped by such political arithmetic to fix in Sally's mind the true meaning of honor, it seems clear that in this instance he is reaching beyond her to instruct aristocratic-minded Americans and even Europeans in the post-Revolutionary period.[5]

[5]Smyth, IX, 161–168. The letter was published in London that same year under circumstances recounted in Durand Echeverria, *Mirage in the West* (Princeton, 1957), pp. 56–57. Sainte-Beuve, not comprehending Franklin's strategy, said of it, "He brings everything down to arithmetic and strict reality, assigning no part to human imagination." *Portraits of the Eighteenth Century, Historic and Literary,* trans. K. P. Wormeley (New York and London, 1905), I, 324.

I

Whereas Gerald Stourzh finds Franklin culturally and intellectually an Englishman, Morris Bishop calls France "his spiritual home. [There] he found intellectual companionship and social satisfactions more appropriate and welcome to his character than anything he had known in America."[6] In contrast to Doctor Johnson, who obstinately wore the same brown clothes, black stockings, and plain shirt in Paris he was accustomed to wearing in London, the American Doctor had not been in the French capital a week in 1767 before—he is writing to Polly Stevenson— "my Taylor and Perruquier had transform'd me into a Frenchman. Only think what a Figure I make in a little Bag-Wig and naked Ears!"[7] Granting that Franklin always adjusted to the cultural climate in which he found himself, it is probably fair to say that at no other time in his life was this climate so precisely defined for him or more bracing than in 1776–1785, the years he lived near Paris.

Initially he shared the eighteenth-century Anglo-American fear of France. As late as August 1767, when he was on the point of traveling there with Sir John Pringle, he still thought of her as "that intriguing nation [who] would like very well to...blow up the coals between Britain and her colonies."[8] Once on French soil, though, his attitude quickly softened. "It seems to be a Point settled here universally," he observes, "that Strangers are to be treated with Respect; and one has just the same Deference shewn one here by being a Stranger, as in England by being a Lady."[9] The friendships he formed at this time—and they

[6]*Daedalus,* LXXXVI (1957), 226.
[7]Smyth, V, 54.   [8]*Ibid.,* V, 47.   [9]*Ibid.,* V, 53.

continued his principal ones there for some years to come—were with "learned and ingenious Men,"[10] men like Condorcet, whom he described "as a great Mathematician" and, after reading his *Éloge de Michel de l'Hôpital,* "as one of the first among the Politicians of Europe";[11] D'Alibard, French translator of his *Experiments and Observations on Electricity* (1752), whom he praised as "the first of Mankind, that had the Courage to attempt drawing Lightning from the Clouds to be subjected to your Experiments";[12] the physicist Le Roy, whose wife, when Franklin commended her for the courage she had shown in going up in a balloon, replied, "If that conveyance could have transported me toward you, I would have been in seventh heaven";[13] and Dr. Dubourg, whose two-volume *Oeuvres de M. Franklin* (1773) marked the first important French edition of his writings. "Would to God," Franklin exclaimed to Du Pont de Nemours in 1770, "I could take with me [to America] Messrs. du Pont, du Bourg, and some other French Friends with their good Ladies! I might then, by mixing them with my Friends in Philadelphia, form a little happy Society that would prevent my ever wishing again to visit Europe."

At the end of 1776 Franklin sailed from Philadelphia, commissioned by the Congress to help negotiate a treaty of alliance with France; successful in this, he continued at Paris, serving as minister plenipotentiary even beyond the war's end. So relentless were the demands of his post and so uncertain was the state of his health that not once in the nine years he was there did he leave the capital and its

[10]*Ibid.,* V, 95. [11]*Ibid.,* VII, 68. [12]*Ibid.,* V, 94.

[13]*Ibid.,* X, 455. In this and later quotations the translations from the French are my own unless indicated otherwise.

suburbs; as a consequence, he probably "saw little of France except the best of her—her most enlightened men, her most pleasing women, her most pleasant places."[14] As late as 1788, with revolution in the air, he could still express the hope, "When this fermentation is over and the troubling parts subsided, the wine will be fine and good, and cheer the hearts of those who drink it."[15]

"Figure me in your mind as jolly as formerly," he wrote Emma Thompson shortly after his arrival, "and as strong and hearty, only a few years older; very plainly dress'd, wearing my thin gray strait hair, that peeps out under my only *Coiffure,* a fine Fur Cap, which comes down my Forehead almost to my Spectacles. Think how this must appear among the Powder'd Heads of Paris!"[16] He set up his residence in Passy at the Hôtel Valentinois, whose owner, Donatien Le Ray de Chaumont, showed him every courtesy. "I live in a fine airy House upon a Hill, which has a large Garden with fine Walks in it, about $\frac{1}{2}$ an hours Drive from the City of Paris," he informs his sister Jane. "I have got into a good Neighborhood, of very agreable People who appear very fond of me; at least they are pleasingly civil: so that upon the whole I live as comfortably as a Man can well do so far from his Home & his

[14]Parton, *Franklin,* II, 412. See also the later judgments of E. E. Hale and E. E. Hale, Jr., *Franklin in France* (Boston, 1888), II, 390–391, and of Smyth, X, 361. Occasionally Franklin mentions how the masses in Europe lived; for example, in "The Internal State of America" he speaks of "the few rich and haughty Landlords, the multitude of poor, abject, and rack'd Tenants, and the half-paid and half-starv'd ragged Labourers" (Smyth, X, 120).

[15]Smyth, IX, 673.

[16]*Ibid.,* VII, 26.

Family."[17] Settling down in the midst of an ever-widening circle of friends, he soon felt rejuvenated; so much so that in 1780 he told his old friend Thomas Bond, "Being arrived at seventy [his age when he came to France], and considering that by travelling further in the same road I should probably be led to the grave, I stopped short, turned about, and walked back again; which having done these four years, you may now call me sixty-six."[18]

His social life centered at three points. There was the Hôtel itself, where he always dined on Sundays, "with such Americans as pass this Way; and I then have my Grandson Ben, with some other American Children from his school."[19] There was also the Masonic lodge of the Nine Sisters, whose membership ranged widely as had that of the Junto and where he counted among his friends and correspondents the moralist La Rochefoucauld, who would eulogize him in 1790, and Le Veillard, mayor of Passy, a neighbor whose judgment he valued so highly that he sent him a fair copy of the *Autobiography* in 1789. Most important of all were the great homes in the neighborhood, especially those kept by Mme Brillon at Passy, Mme Helvétius at Auteuil, and the Comtesse d'Houdetot at Sannois, where "this man's Performance, and the marriage of the Duke de Richelieu, fill up much more of our present Conversation, than any thing that relates to the War."[20] Such stimulating diversions soon prompted him to take pen in hand.

For more than half a century Franklin had been cor-

[17]*Franklin-Mecom Letters,* pp. 171, 172.

[18]Smyth, VIII, 37.

[19]*Ibid.,* VII, 223.

[20]*Ibid.,* VIII, 31.

responding extensively with family, friends, and the official-dom of two continents; now, when he was writing in a foreign tongue, he suddenly felt unsure of his grammar and idiom. While he might say to Le Roy, "If it is more easy for you to write in French, do not give yourself the trouble of writing in English, as I understand your French per-fectly well,"[21] he apologized for his own letters. "I have just been writing a French Letter to Mademoiselle Chau-mont," he informs her father; "but it costs me too much time to write in that Language, and after all 'tis very bad French, and I therefore write to you in English, which I think you will as easily understand; if not, ma chère amie Sophie, can interpret it for you."[22] In the present century Franklin's written French has been not inaccurately de-scribed as "semi-wild" and even *"fantaisiste."*[23] Even so, such letters were a principal source of relaxation during these busy years and the friendships strengthened through them so precious to him that he continued to correspond after returning to America.

II

"I have abundance of Acquaintance," Franklin told Mrs. Stevenson in 1779, "dine abroad Six Days in seven." He was counting in this busy social schedule the many times he dined with Mme Helvétius at Auteuil, less than a league from Passy. Paying her what was high tribute indeed, Abbé Morellet, who with Abbé de la Roche and Dr.

[21]*Ibid.,* V, 194.
[22]*Ibid.,* IX, 542.
[23]J. J. Jusserand, "Franklin in France," in *Essays Offered to Her-bert Putnam,* ed. W. W. Bishop and A. Keogh (New Haven, 1929), p. 231; *Les amitiés américaines de Madame D'Houdetot,* pp. 32–33.

Cabanis dwelt under her roof for more than fifteen years in Platonic intimacy, recalled, "We lived very peaceably with the same friend, who did not exhibit for any one of the three, a preference which would have displeased the other two."[24] Over the years there gathered at her home, in addition to these three and Franklin, Chamfort, Condorcet, D'Alembert, Roucher, and Turgot.[25] The salon over which *"Notre Dame d'Auteuil,"* as her friends called her, presided may well have been as stimulating as the more famous ones Mmes du Deffand and Necker kept in nearby Paris. Trying to account for the power by which Mme Helvétius attracted so brilliant an array, Franklin once told her:

> I see that statesmen, philosophers, historians, poets, and men of learning of all sorts are drawn around you, and seem as willing to attach themselves to you as straws about a fine piece of amber. It is not that you make pretentions to any of their sciences; and if you did, similarity of studies does not always make people love one another. It is not that you take pains to engage them; artless simplicity is a striking part of your character.... We find in your sweet society that charming benevolence, that amiable attention to oblige, that disposition to please and be pleased, which we do not always find in the society of one another. It springs from you; it has its influence on us all, and in your company we are not only pleased with you, but better pleased with one another and with ourselves.[26]

[24]*Mémoires inédits de l'abbé Morellet* (Paris, 1822), I, 380, quoted in Aldridge, *Franklin and His French Contemporaries,* p. 162.

[25]Antoine Guillois, *Le salon de Madame Helvétius* (Paris, 1894), p. 34.

[26]Smyth, X, 442.

Like Morellet's it was a high compliment, one she had earned full right to.

For Franklin alone she broke a habit she had followed since the death of her famous husband and once a week accompanied Cabanis or one of the abbés to his home.[27] "When she honours you with a visit, it is on foot," chides the Gout in the famous Dialogue. "She walks all hours of the day, and leaves indolence, and its concomitant maladies, to be endured by her horses. In this, see at once the preservative of her health and personal charms. But when you go to Auteuil, you must have your carriage, though it is no farther from Passy to Auteuil than from Auteuil to Passy."[28] The conviviality Franklin discovered at her salon, so different from the domestic comforts he enjoyed by Mrs. Stevenson's sober hearth, called to mind a time forty years before, when he had regaled himself with members of the Junto in tavern and parlor; whereupon he sent La Roche a drinking song ("Fair Venus calls") written at that earlier time, explaining, "'Tis a singer, my dear Abbé, who exhorts his companions to seek *happiness* in *love,* in *riches,* and in *power.* They reply, singing together, that happiness is not to be found in any of these things; that it is only to be found in *friends* and *wine.* To this proposition the singer at last assents."[29] And to Morellet he sent proofs, scriptural and otherwise, in support of the saying, *"In vino veritas."*[30] The pleasant memory of "the

[27]Guillois, *Le salon de Madame Helvétius,* pp. 42–43.

[28]*Autobiographical Writings,* p. 486.

[29]*Ibid.,* pp. 477–478.

[30]Smyth, VII, 436–438. The French text of this letter is printed in Morellet's *Mémoires,* I, 303–306, with the five drawings (based on the original designs) explained in the postscript; Morellet says that Temple Franklin prepared them.

Auteuil *Academy of Belles Lettres*"[31] lingered after he
returned to Philadelphia. He writes Mme Helvétius:

At ten o'clock this morning, I thought of you, of your home,
your board, your friends, etc. At this hour, said I, they are all
dining, M. le Roy, M. Hennin, Abbés de la Roche and
Morellet, M. Cabanis, perhaps a few of the little stars [her
daughters]. Madame waits upon the whole company with
as much ease as delight. But, alas, I was not there to take
part in the pleasing conversation full of common sense, wit,
and friendship with which her meals are always seasoned.[32]

Their constant attendance upon each other encouraged
Mme Helvétius and Franklin to undertake a familiar
correspondence. Soon they had entered into verbal love-
making very like that practiced in the salon. His chance
remark in a letter of September 12, 1779, to Cabanis,
written in the third person, may indeed have had its basis
in fact; in any case, from it sprang one of the most popular
anecdotes told about Franklin in France. He confides:

If that lady is fond of spending her days with him he would
like just as much to spend his nights with her; and as he has
already given her a great many days, though he had so few
left to give, she would seem ungrateful to have never given
him a single one of her nights, which continually flow by as
pure loss, without making anyone happy except Poupou
[her lap dog].[33]

She had lost her husband in 1771 and he his wife three

31Smyth, IX, 577.
32*Ibid.*, IX, 470.
33*Ibid.*, VII, 375. The *American Museum*, X (Oct., 1791), 176,
published an early version of this story, wherein the fashionable lady
remains anonymous. Faÿ, *Franklin, Apostle,* p. 468, conjectures that
the lady in question may have been either Mme Helvétius or Mme
Brillon; the former seems to me the more likely candidate.

years later. This fact alone makes his proposal of marriage, whether advanced in earnest or in play, appear anything but indecorous. She refused him, just as she had earlier refused Turgot, and by that act called forth one of his most skillfully contrived letters: "Distressed by your barbarous resolution pronounced so positively last night, to remain single the rest of your life in honor of your dear husband," the letter begins, "I withdrew to my quarters, fell upon my bed, and, thinking I was dead, found myself in the Elysian Fields." There I discovered M. Helvétius, who "asked me a thousand things about the war and about the present state of religion, liberty, and government in France," but not once about his wife. When I asked him why not, he explained that he had "taken another wife, the most like her that I could find; she is not, it is true, altogether so beautiful, but she has as much good sense, a little more wit, and she loves me infinitely. Her continual study is to please me." "'I perceive,' said I, 'that your former wife is more faithful than you are; for several good offers of marriage have been made her, but she has refused them all.'" The new Mme Helvétius coming toward us, "I recognized her instantly as Mrs. Franklin, my former American wife. I claimed her, but she told me coldly: 'I was your good wife forty-nine years and four months, nearly half a century; be content with that. Here I have formed a new connection, which will last to eternity.'" "Displeased with this refusal of my Eurydice," Franklin concludes, "I immediately resolved to leave those ungrateful shades and return to this good world, to behold the sun and you again. Here I am! Let us avenge ourselves."[34]

[34]Gilbert Chinard, *Proc. APS*, CIII (1959), 727–734, transcribes the recently discovered manuscript copy of this letter annotated by

Seeking to overcome Mme Helvétius' resolve to live in single estate, Franklin confronts her in this letter with the knowledge that her husband and his wife have entered into a heavenly union and asks her, in effect, whether this fact is not sufficient provocation for their entering into one of their own on earth. Locating the action in the Elysian Fields rather than in a Christian heaven is highly appropriate; not only is the choice of a classical setting well suited to eighteenth-century French taste, it also establishes a worldly atmosphere wholly in keeping with Franklin's purpose. Here, as so often in other familiar letters and in the bagatelles, he tempers wit with tact to produce a pleasing blend.

Franklin did not at once abandon the courtship. He asks Mme Helvétius to heed the flies in his room who present her their respects: "There only remains one thing for us to wish in order to assure the permanence of our good fortune; permit us to say it

Bizz izzzz *ouizz a ouizzzz izzzzzzz*, etc.

Henceforth it is your responsibility to see that [yours and his] be made into a single household."[35] When they parted in 1785, he declared, "It seems to me things are badly arranged in this world below when I see that human

---

Franklin; I have based my translation on this copy. The letter was printed in April 1780; whether with or without Franklin's approval is not known (Aldridge, *Franklin and His French Contemporaries*, p. 164). In view of the circumstances surrounding its composition, I find it difficult to accept the suggestion of F. B. Adams, Jr., *Yale Univ. Lib. Gaz.*, XXX (1956), 137, that this is one of the bagatelles which were "propaganda of the subtlest sort."

[35]*Franklin's Wit and Folly*, ed. Richard E. Amacher (New Brunswick, 1953), p. 59.

beings destined to be happy *together are obliged* to part company."[36] From Le Havre and again from Southampton he bid her farewell. "When we meet in Paradise, as I trust we shall," he tells her three years later, "the Pleasure of that Place will be augmented by our Recollection of all the Circumstances of our Acquaintance here below."[37] Often in my dreams "I am dining with you, sitting by your side on one of your thousand sofas, or strolling with you in your beautiful garden."[38] She, writing in her "friendly affectionate *griffonage,* as she is pleased to call it,"[39] hopes that though they may never see each other again in this world, they will in the next; there "we shall meet again, with all we have loved, I a husband and you a wife—but I believe that you who have been a rogue will find more than one."[40]

III

"You combine with the best heart, when you wish," writes Mme Brillon, praising Franklin's letters, "the soundest moral teaching, a lively imagination, and that droll roguishness which shows that the wisest of men allows his wisdom to be perpetually broken against the rocks of femininity."[41] Franklin in turn always found her letters a delightful contrast to the written requests that endlessly beset him at the American Embassy.[42] Between 1777 and 1789 they exchanged over 150 letters and several bagatelles

[36]Smyth, IX, 364.   [37]*Ibid.,* IX, 647.   [38]*Ibid.,* IX, 678.
[39]*Ibid.,* IX, 690.   [40]*Ibid.,* X, 443.

[41]Brillon to Franklin, Dec. 25, [1781], Smyth, X, 436. More than half of their correspondence, all but a few pieces of which are to be found at the American Philosophical Society, remains unpublished.

[42]Franklin to Brillon, Jan. 6, 1782, Franklin Papers, Amer. Philos. Soc., B F85.194, Film 54–60, Frame 93.

and poems, all of them in French except his final letter, in which pieces (one hastens to add) he demonstrated a wit, tact, and sympathy that equalled hers. The vitality of this correspondence between the sage American more than seventy and the beautiful French woman not yet forty lies in its special intimacy; its charm seems at times too fragile, as if gazing too long would dispel it altogether. An eavesdropper is persuaded that these two human beings, for all their difference in age, background, and temperament, were so nearly attuned that there sometimes occurred that almost unconscious transference of mind to mind which Doctor Johnson calls the supreme skill in letter writing.[43]

Madame d'Hardancourt Brillon de Jouy was thirty-six when Franklin met her in 1777. Her marriage to a treasury official twenty-four years her senior, judging by the tone of her letters, was one of convenience. "I know," she confides, "that the man to whom fate has bound me is a worthy person; I respect him as I should and as he deserves; perhaps my capacity for affection is too great for his heart to respond to." Then concerned for the happiness of her daughters, she adds: "We marry a young girl whose heart overflows with youth and its burning desires, to a man in whom all such feelings are extinct. We demand of this woman a perfect propriety. My friend, that is my story and that of how many others!"[44] She admitted to an "excessive

[43]*The Letters of Samuel Johnson,* ed. R. W. Chapman (Oxford, 1952), II, 228, quoted in Irving, *Providence of Wit,* pp. 289–290.

[44]Brillon to Franklin, June 4, [1779?], Franklin Papers, XLIII, 25 (as calendared in Hays); printed in A. H. Smyth, "Franklin's Social Life in France," *Putnam's Monthly and The Critic,* I (1906–1907), 172. All of the letters in this series of articles appear in English translation.

sensitiveness" that makes her "often the victim of a too tender soul and a too lively imagination."[45] Her physical condition, "which a mere whiff of air upsets,"[46] kept her to her bed for long periods, and because of it she frequently went to the country. One year she wintered at Nice, an "eternal springtime" where her health and spirits revived.[47] But she was most at home amidst the social round at Passy: tea, music, chess, visiting and receiving friends. And now there was Franklin.

Having lost her own father early in life,[48] she begs him, "Never call me anything but 'my daughter.'"[49] He in his lonely widower's existence three thousand miles from home and family accepted the role with great pleasure.[50] Whenever, as sometimes happened, he abandoned it to pursue a tactful but aggressive courtship under the not-jealous eye of her husband, she checked him. He tells the following story to demonstrate the force of his love. "A Beggar asked a rich Bishop for a Louis as Alms.—You are mad. One does not give Louis to beggars—A crown then—No, it is too much—Then a farthing—or your blessing—My blessing! Yes, I will give it to you.—No, I will not accept it, for if

[45]Brillon to Franklin, Jan. 22, [1779?], Franklin Papers, XLIII, 13; *Putnam's*, I, 169.

[46]Brillon to Franklin, June 4, [1779?], Franklin Papers, XLIII, 25; *Putnam's*, I, 172.

[47]Brillon to Franklin, Jan. 8, 1782, Franklin Papers, XLIII, 46.

[48]Brillon to Franklin, n. d., Franklin Papers, XLIII, 73; printed in W. C. Ford, "One of Franklin's Friendships," *Harper's Monthly Magazine*, CXIII (1906), 627. All of the letters in this article appear in English translation.

[49]Brillon to Franklin, May 11, 1779, Smyth, X, 412.

[50]Franklin to Brillon, [May 1779?], Franklin Papers, B F85.br. Film 54–60, Frame 121.

it were worth a farthing you would not give it to me."
"That," he urges, "is your charity to a poor unfortunate,
who formerly enjoyed affluence and who is unhappily reduced to beg Alms of you."[51] "You adopted me as your
daughter," she chides, "I chose you for my father: what
do you expect from me? Friendship! well, I love you as a
daughter should love her father. . . . Whatever you may
think or say, no one in this world loves you more than I."[52]

Wednesdays and Saturdays, when the weather was mild
and health permitted, Franklin visited the Brillon home
in the afternoon, where "with her daughters, who sing
prettily, and some friends who play, she kindly entertains
me and my grandson [Temple] with little concerts, a cup
of tea, and a game of chess."[53] In "The Ephemera," one of
the bagatelles addressed to her, he declares that two of the
solid pleasures remaining to him, an "old greyheaded"
fly, are "the sensible Conversation of a few good Lady-
Ephemeres, and now and then a kind Smile and a Tune
from the ever-amiable BRILLANTE."[54] Their affection was
mutual and abiding. She maintains that her loving him
tenderly is better than his loving her furiously and too
much.[55] And he, late in his sojourn abroad, confesses that
since he must one day leave for America with no hope of
seeing her again, he has thought of severing with her
gradually by seeing her less and less often; but finding that

[51]Franklin to Brillon, [c. 1778], Franklin Papers, XLVI (i), 52;
Putnam's, I, 315–316.
[52]Brillon to Franklin, July 1, [1778?], Smyth, X, 424.
[53]Smyth, VIII, 100.
[54]"The Ephemera," Sept. 20, 1778, Cornell MS; printed in Chinard,
Proc. APS, CIII (1959), 744.
[55]Brillon to Franklin, [c. 1778], Franklin Papers, XLIII, 86.

this augments rather than diminishes the desire to be in her company, he would come see her tonight.[56] Well she knew, though, that she must share his heart with other women, especially with her "amiable and formidable rival" Mme Helvétius,[57] who claimed his Saturdays the winter she spent at Nice.[58]

In 1781, anxious to strengthen the bond of friendship, anxious too for a real home, Franklin proposed a marriage between Mme Brillon's eldest daughter Cunegonde and his grandson Temple.[59] Both she and her husband realized there were differences in religion and circumstance that could not be overcome, though she adds tactfully, "What it has cost us to refuse it, should assure you forever of our affection."[60] This rejection did not alter the affection between the two families. Two years later Cunegonde married a Monsieur Paris,[61] and when their first child was born, Franklin shared in Mme Brillon's happiness. "I remember having one day met at your house four generations of your family, when your children were very young, and that I then said that I hoped to live to see the fifth. Now my prophetic wish is realized."[62] "Your letter, my

[56]Franklin to Brillon, [c. 1784?], Franklin Papers, B F85.br, Frame 119.

[57]Brillon to Franklin, Nov. 12, [1781], Franklin Papers, XLIII, 42.

[58]Franklin to Brillon, Oct. 12, [1781], Franklin Papers, B F85.br, Frame 118.

[59]Franklin to Brillon, [Apr. 1781?], Smyth, X, 417–418.

[60]Brillon to Franklin, Apr. 20, 1781, Smyth, X, 420.

[61]The Brillons to Franklin, [Oct. 1783], Franklin Papers, XLIII, 6. A notation, presumably by Franklin, reads, "They were married Monday Oct. 20, 1783."

[62]Franklin to Brillon, Nov. 29, 1784, Franklin Papers, XLIII, 6a; *Putnam's,* I, 36–37.

kind Papa, has given me great pleasure," she graciously
replies; "but if you would give me a greater, remain in
France until you see my sixth generation. I only ask you
for fifteen or sixteen years: my granddaughter will be
marriageable early; she is fine and strong."[63]

At his request Mme Brillon obligingly corrected his mis-
takes, but did so sparingly;[64] in her eyes what he called
"beaucoup de très mauvais français"[65] only enhanced his
epistolary style.[66] It angered her to see how another, either
Morellet or La Roche, had revised his "Dialogue between
Franklin and the Gout."[67] "Believe me," she advises him,
"leave your works as they are, use words that say things,
and laugh at grammarians, who, by their purity, weaken all
your sentences."[68] The wonder is that with the constant
official demands on his time he was able to address as many
as thirty letters to her and five bagatelles: "The Ephemera," "The Morals of Chess," "The Whistle," "Dialogue
between Franklin and the Gout," and "The Handsome
and Deformed Leg." She, having more time at her disposal, sent him more than 120 letters and three original
poems. She sensed the danger in revising her own work
too much. "I have corrected some faults in the fable," she

[63]Brillon to Franklin, Dec. 2, 1784, Franklin Papers, XLIII, 7;
Putnam's, I, 37.

[64]Franklin to Brillon, [Fall 1779?], Franklin Papers, B F85.br,
Frame 123; *Proc. APS*, XL, 109–110.

[65]Franklin to Brillon, [May 1779], Smyth, X, 414.

[66]Brillon to Franklin, [Nov.?] 16, [1779?], Franklin Papers, XLIII,
34; *Proc. APS*, XL, 106–107.

[67]The French text of the Dialogue, with the corrections, is printed
in *Proc. APS*, XL, 98–103.

[68]Brillon to Franklin, Nov. 18, 1780, Smyth, X, 416.

says of one of her poems; "there are many more yet to be corrected. But I fear that I might resemble the sculptor who, finding the nose on a fancied face a little too large, took away so much that no nose remained."[69] Grammatical roughness, an urbane tone, and frequent wit mark both sides of the correspondence, but his is decidedly the more didactic.

Let us now eavesdrop, first as they exchange thoughts on the gout. Since Franklin and later her husband suffered violent attacks, this was no theoretical subject like some they chose to discuss. During a severe attack in October 1780, she sent him *"Le Sage et la Goutte,"* which helped inspire his famous Dialogue and which he eventually had printed on his private press.[70] When the Gout of this poem charges that the Sage eats too much, covets the ladies, no longer walks abroad, and spends his time playing chess and with the ladies, the Sage protests that true wisdom lies in enjoying the good things heaven has given us: a little punch, a pretty lady, sometimes two or three or four, and so forth. Franklin praises her poem but adds:

> One of the personages of your fable, Gout, seems to me to reason pretty well, with the exception of the supposition that mistresses have had a share in producing this painful malady. I believe the contrary, and this is my argument. When I was a young man and enjoyed more of the favors of the sex than I do at present, I had no gout. So if the ladies of Passy had had more of that kind of Christian charity that I have so often in vain recommended to you,

[69]Brillon to Franklin, [Nov. 1780?], Franklin Papers, XLIII, 58: *Harper's,* CXIII, 629.

[70]A copy of the printed poem is located in the bound volume of Passy bagatelles in the Mason-Franklin Collection at Yale.

I should not have had the gout at all. This seems to me good logic.[71]

She is quick to retaliate that there is no logical connection between a man's moral condition and natural events: "THEN you could have had the gout without having deserved it, and you could have well deserved it, as I believe, and not have had it."[72] Several years later she asks him, heretic though he is, to pray for her gout-ridden husband.[73] "I am vexed with Madame Gout for afflicting our friend," he replies. Then, alluding to his Dialogue: "You know that she formerly gave me some good advice. But, unhappily lacking the energy to profit by it, I can do no more, it seems to me, than send it to our friend, to whom it might perhaps be useful." Roguishly he concludes, "If God loves you as much as I love you, my prayers will be useless and superfluous. And heretic as I am, I do not doubt that He loves such Catholics as you."[74]

If they could banter about the gout, it was otherwise when her sensitive nature was hurt. What caused her perhaps the greatest pain was the knowledge in 1779 that her husband was having an affair with their daughters' governess, Mlle Jupin. In agitation she writes Franklin: "*My* life, my friend, is made of fine and thin stuff, that

[71]Franklin to Brillon, Nov. 17, 1780, Franklin Papers, B F85.br, Frame 106; *Putnam's,* I, 312. Hale, *Franklin in France,* II, 314n, detects a play on words in this letter, taking *"goutte"* to mean both "gout" and "wine."

[72]Brillon to Franklin, Nov. 18, 1780, Smyth, X, 415.

[73]Brillon to Franklin, Mar. 4, [1784?], Franklin Papers, XLIII, 18; *Putnam's,* I, 170.

[74]Franklin to Brillon, Apr. 8, 1784, Franklin Papers, XLV, 181; *Autobiographical Writings,* p. 602.

grief tears cruelly. . . . Cure me, or pity me, if you can do
one and the other."[75] "To be sensible of our own faults
is good," comes his wise reply, "for it leads us to avoid
them in future; but to be too sensitive to, and afflicted by,
the faults of other people is not good."[76] When in a more
prudential mood still he suggests that "we might all draw
more good from [this world] than we do and suffer less
evil, if we would only take care *not to give too much for
our whistles,*"[77] she replies—and the letter exposes her
overgenerous nature—that she has paid dearly for bad
whistles, with her heart if not with her purse, that (for example) in loving others she has rarely received the value she
gave.[78] In this crisis and in others Franklin's wisdom
strengthened her in her agonized existence and his sympathy made life endurable. Nowhere is this wisdom, which
she never felt she could attain, expressed more gracefully
than in the following letter:

> I think with you, that there are many annoyances in this
> life. But it seems to me that there are many more pleasures.
> That is why I love to live. One must not blame providence
> inconsiderately. Remember how many even of our duties
> she has arranged to be naturally pleasures; and that she
> has had the further kindness to give the name of Sins to
> several, so that we may enjoy them with more relish.[79]

[75]Brillon to Franklin, May 11, 1779, Smyth, X, 412.

[76]Franklin to Brillon, May 1779, Franklin Papers, XLVI (i), 43;
Putnam's, I, 315.

[77]"The Whistle," Nov. 10, 1779, Franklin Papers, XLV, 149 ½;
Proc. APS, XL, 92.

[78]Brillon to Franklin, [Nov.?] 16, [1779?], Franklin Papers, XLIII,
34; *Proc. APS,* XL, 106.

[79]Franklin to Brillon, n. d., Franklin Papers, XLVI (i), 51; *Putnam's,* I, 316.

It is a sanguine answer to one who was melancholy by nature.

What highlights the correspondence, though, is the thrust and parry of verbal courtship which began at once. When he asks her to undertake his conversion, she finds him guilty of only one capital sin—covetousness; but, knowing his frailties, she will show mercy. "Provided he loves God, America and myself above all else, I absolve him from all his sins, present, past and future, and promise him a heaven whither I will lead him along a pathway strewn with roses."[80] In rapture at the prospect of being absolved of the future, he pleads guilty to coveting his neighbor's wife but asks whether his keeping religiously the two additional Commandments he has been taught is not sufficient compensation: "The first was increase & multiply & replenish the earth. The twelfth is,...*that you love one another*."[81] She dare not decide the question "without consulting the neighbor whose wife you covet, because he is a far better casuist than I am; and then, too, as Bonhomme Richard would say: *In weighty matters, two heads are better than one*."[82] During her absence at Nice his thoughts once again turn to the Commandments, only this time he is for total repeal.

I often pass before your house. It appears desolate to me. Formerly I broke the Commandment by coveting it along with my neighbour's wife. Now I do not covet it any more, so I am less a sinner. But as to his wife I always find these

[80]Brillon to Franklin, Mar. 7, [1778?], Franklin Papers, XLIII, 19; *Putnam's*, I, 310.

[81]Franklin to Brillon, Mar. 10, 1778, Smyth, X, 437.

[82]Brillon to Franklin, [Mar.?] 16, [1778?], Franklin Papers, XLIII, 20; *Putnam's*, I, 312.

Commandments inconvenient and I am sorry that they were ever made. If in your travels you happen to see the Holy Father, ask him to repeal them, as things given only to the Jews and too uncomfortable for good Christians.[83]

Marriage in heaven, which she had hinted at, was a prospect so agreeable and theoretical as to call forth all their powers of wit.

In paradise [she writes] we shall be reunited, never to leave each other again! We shall there live on roasted apples only; the music will be composed of Scotch airs; all parties will be given over to chess, so that no one may be disappointed; every one will speak the same language; the English will be neither unjust nor wicked there; the women will not be coquettes, the men will be neither jealous nor too gallant. ... Every day we shall love one another, in order that we may love one another still more the day after; in a word, we shall be completely happy. In the meantime let us get all the good we can out of this poor world of ours.[84]

He is charmed with her description of paradise and her plan of living there,[85] and wonders how they should arrange their affairs in that country.

Probably more than forty years will elapse after my arrival there before you follow me. I am a little afraid that in the course of such a long period you may forget me. I have therefore thought of proposing that you give me your word of honour not to renew there your contract with Mr. B——. I shall at the same time give you mine that I shall wait for

[83]Franklin to Brillon, Dec. 25, 1781, Franklin Papers, B F85.br, Frame 114; *Autobiographical Writings,* p. 512.

[84]Brillon to Franklin, Nov. 1, [1779], Smyth, X, 427–428.

[85]"The Whistle," Nov. 10, 1779, Franklin Papers, XLV, 149 1/2; *Proc. APS,* XL, 92.

you. But that gentleman is so good, so generous towards us, he loves you so much and we love him, that I cannot think of this proposal without some scruples of conscience. And yet the idea of an eternity in which I shall be favoured with no more than permission to kiss your hands, or sometimes your cheeks, and to pass two or three hours in your sweet society on Wednesdays and Saturdays is frightful. . . . I shall have time, during those forty years, to practise on the armonica, and perhaps I shall play well enough to accompany you on your pianoforte. From time to time we shall have little concerts. . . . We shall eat apples of Paradise roasted with butter and nutmeg. And we shall pity those who are not dead.[86]

She assures him that if his "French is not very pure, it is at least very clear!" and promises to become his wife in paradise, "on condition, however, that you will not covet too much the [heavenly] maidens while waiting for me. I want a faithful husband when I take one for eternity. . . . I accept the sort of life you propose for me in paradise— music, friends," except that "among those people you propose to keep me company, there is one woman [Mme Helvétius] I would cross out."[87] This celestial conceit proved so appealing that Franklin, as we have seen, returned to it the following year in his fruitless wooing of Mme Helvétius.

[86]Franklin to Brillon, [Fall 1779?], Franklin Papers, B F85.br, Frame 123; *Autobiographical Writings*, p. 476.

[87]Brillon to Franklin, [Fall 1779?], Franklin Papers, XLIII, 64. Franklin had employed this conceit at least as early as 1757, telling Henry Bouquet, "How happy are the Folks in Heaven, who, 'tis said, have nothing to do, but to talk with one another, except now and then a little Singing—and Drinking of Aqua Vitae" (Labaree, VII, 182).

One of the poems she sent him, *"Les quatre saisons,"* tells the story of a man who, vowing to remain faithful to the maiden he loves, loves a different one each season.[88] Though he compliments her on this pleasing *"conte,"* Franklin has one reservation: "In my opinion there is only one blemish, that of depriving M. F. of almost the only quality of a lover that he has left, his constancy. And this is very unfair, because it is as clear as the clearest theorem in Euclid that he who is faithful to many is more constant than he who is faithful to only one."[89]

The autumn she went south for her health he was anxious to relieve the fatigue the slow journey caused her. "I am vexed that I am not the angel Gabriel with his great wings," he writes; "for if that were so, I could spare you all these hardships by taking you up like my *Chapeau-bras* and in half an hour setting you down gently in your apartment at Nice."[90] "Your proposition to carry me on your wings, if you were the angel Gabriel, made me laugh," she parries; "but I would not accept it, although I am no longer very young nor a virgin. That angel was a sly fellow and your nature united to his would become too dangerous. I would be afraid of miracles happening, and miracles between women and angels might not always bring a redeemer."[91]

In the spring of 1782 peace negotiations got under way at the American Embassy in Paris, and Franklin seems not

[88]*"Les quatre saisons: conte,"* [*c.* 1781], Franklin Papers, LI, 10.

[89]Franklin to Brillon, Feb. 16, 1781, Franklin Papers, B F85.br, Frame 110.

[90]Franklin to Brillon, Oct. 1, 1781, Franklin Papers, B F85.br, Frame 111.

[91]Brillon to Franklin, Oct. 20, [1781], Smyth, X, 425.

to have written Mme Brillon as often as she wished. From Nice came a formal complaint: She implores Justice to weigh in her "dreaded balance the reciprocal treaties between the Ambassador and the lady whom he has abused in a cruel manner," sets forth the facts, and concludes, "The petitioner in this cause requires that the said M. Benjamin Franklin be condemned in her favor for all expense, damage, and interest which you [Justice] shall be pleased to determine upon the stated facts."[92] Previously Franklin had exploited the language of the official world in which he moved so steadily during the final third of his life, parodying the rhetoric of parliamentary statutes and court gazettes. Now, spurred on by this mock-complaint, he replies after the manner of the preliminary peace treaty with England, on which he was even then hard at work. You, who "would engross all my Affection, and permit me none for the other amiable Ladies of your Country," he writes, are unjust "in your Demands, and in the open War you declare against me if I do not comply with them. Indeed it is I that have the most Reason to complain. My poor little Boy [*Amor*], whom you ought methinks to have cherish'd, instead of being fat and Jolly like those in your elegant Drawings, is meagre and starv'd almost to death for want of the substantial Nourishment which you his Mother inhumanly deny him, and yet would now clip his little Wings to prevent his seeking it elsewhere!" He therefore proposes a treaty between them. "I fancy we shall neither of us get any thing by this War, and therefore as feeling my self the Weakest, I will do what indeed ought always to be done by the Wisest, be first in making the Propositions

[92]Brillon to Franklin, Mar. 20, 1782, Franklin Papers, XLIII, 116; *Harper's,* CXIII, 632.

for Peace. That a Peace may be lasting, the Articles of the Treaty should be regulated upon the Principles of the most perfect Equity & Reciprocity." Nine articles follow. "Let me know what you think of these Preliminaries," he asks her. "To me they seem to express the true Meaning and Intention of each Party more plainly than most Treaties.— I shall insist pretty strongly on the eighth Article ['That when he is with her, he will do what he pleases'], tho' without much Hope of your Consent to it; and on the ninth also ['that he will love any other Woman as far as he finds her amiable'], tho I despair of ever finding any other Woman that I could love with equal Tenderness."[93] Not the least remarkable thing about this treaty letter is the unmistakable inference that Franklin knows how to relax in the midst of the heavy press of official business.

One detects in this verbal courtship the influence of the salon. In salon love-making the man respected his adversary just so far as she knew how to parry his every thrust; always it was hoped that the contest would end in a draw. It ended thus for Mme Brillon and Franklin.

The real war between nations was over at last, and Franklin was anxious to have done with ambassadorial duties and go home. In 1785 Congress gave its consent at last. For Mme Brillon, who had invested the larger amount

[93]Franklin to Brillon, July 27, [1782], Franklin Papers, XLVI (i), 47; *Autobiographical Writings*, pp. 584–586. What strengthens the probability that this letter was written in imitation of peace treaties are such diplomatic remarks as the one that occurs in Franklin's letter of Feb. 16, 1782, to David Hartley: "If your ministers really desire peace, methinks they would do well to *empower* some person to make propositions for that purpose. One or other of the parties at war must take the first step. To do this belongs properly to the wisest" (Smyth, VIII, 383).

of emotional stock in their friendship, it was a painful leave-taking: "Every day of my existence, memory reminds me that a great man, a sage, once deigned to be my friend. . . . If it be sweet for you to recall the woman who loved you most dearly, think of me, think of all those members of my family who were and always must be your best friends."[94] She was happy to learn of his safe arrival at Philadelphia in September but feels keenly the distance that now separates them. "At least recall occasionally the one among your friends who loved you best, and write to her a few lines in what you call your wretched French. For my part, I shall keep you informed concerning a family you once held dear!"[95] His only letter to her from America, at least the only one that has survived, was prompted in part by news of the grief she experienced at the death of her husband and oldest grandchild.

I sympathize with you in all your Losses and Afflictions, and hope the rest of your Life will be as tranquil and free from Trouble as it had been for some Years before we parted. . . . Being now in my 83d Year, I do not expect to continue much longer a Sojourner in this World, and begin to promise myself much Gratification of my Curiosity in soon visiting some other.[96]

In the spring of 1789, when revolution was just four months distant, she wrote him for the last time: "I have given thanks to Providence, which, if it be really endowed with that justice one is accustomed to attribute to it, ought

[94]Brillon to Franklin, July 10, [1785], Franklin Papers, XLIII, 113; *Putnam's,* I, 433–434.

[95]Brillon to Franklin, Nov. 5, 1785, Franklin Papers, XLIII, 9; *Putnam's,* I, 434.

[96]Franklin to Brillon, Apr. 19, 1788, Smyth, IX, 643–644.

to leave you here on earth as an example to mankind and as a model of wisdom, at least to as ripe an old age as that of the patriarch Matusalem [sic]." Pray for France at this "critical stage." "I revere you, honor you, love you; not a day passes that my heart does not draw nigh you at least in thought; not one wherein I fail to recall your friendship, so precious to me that nothing can ever rob me of it, and the memory of the days during which I enjoyed it more closely, more intimately, makes one of the bright spots of happiness in my life."[97] After this letter Mme Brillon passes from view; there is no record, apparently, of what happened to her and her daughters from this time. Franklin for his part must have been thinking especially of her when he told Mme Lavoisier he could not "forget Paris, and the nine years' happiness I enjoyed there, in the sweet society of a people whose conversation is instructive, whose manners are highly pleasing, and who, above all the nations of the world, have, in the greatest perfection, the art of making themselves beloved by strangers. And now, even in my sleep, I find, that the scenes of all my pleasant dreams are laid in that city, or in its neighbourhood."[98]

The letters Franklin exchanged with Mmes Helvétius and Brillon are simply the most noteworthy and extensive of many epistolary friendships he formed with French women in the final years of his life. Herein he is always posing. Many Americans, however, unaware of this fact, unaware too of the conventions of the salon, misconstrued the meaning of these letters, as they did his behavior in the presence of the ladies and certain of his reported con-

[97]Brillon to Franklin, Mar. 6, 1789, Franklin Papers, XLIII, 12; Putnam's, I, 436–437.

[98]Smyth, IX, 668.

versations in France, and thus encouraged the growth of the image of Franklin the philanderer. "Franklin's relations to women," writes Willis Steell, "were quite simple and had been so all his life—rather more than friendship, a little less than love. . . . He played the game of love without consequences with an ingenuity which he guarded to the end of his life. . . . The worst that may be said truthfully of him is that he liked to *'badiner'* with love. . . . It never hurt Franklin nor his fellow triflers."[99] Franklin's familiar letters are living witness to the truth of such a statement.

[99]*Benjamin Franklin of Paris,* pp. 202, 203, 212.

VII

The Bagatelle

NOWHERE are the moral teaching, lively imagination, and droll roguishness which Mme Brillon praised in Franklin more subtly combined than in that elusive type, the bagatelle. The lightness of tone traditionally associated with it depends in large part on an admixture of wit and morality and on the special audience of like minds for whose delight and instruction it is composed. These most sophisticated of Franklin's writings are addressed to groups as dissimilar as members of the Junto with whom he was convivial in parlor and tavern, Polly Hewson and the Shipley girls and their immediate friends, and those French ladies, clerics, and philosophes in whose intimate life he shared. Among all his private writings he is here most clearly posing, presenting various exaggerated aspects of himself—to his fellows at the Junto, that of one experienced in the ways of love and marriage; to Polly, the American boarder presiding magisterially in Craven Street; to Mme Helvétius, a widower aggressively and wittily urging his suit; to Mme Brillon, a father whose affection for his daughter threatens to become more than paternal. A clear measure of the intimate nature of these bagatelles is the fact that, save in "The Speech of Miss Polly Baker," "To the Royal Academy of Brussels," and "An Economical Project," Franklin does not employ a persona; the persona, possessing a dramatic identity distinct from its creator as emphatically as the pose does not, is reserved rather for those public occasions when he thought it necessary to go disguised.

In his bagatelles Franklin does not confine himself to a single genre; some are cast as familiar letters, others as essays or such species of the essay as dialogue, fable, anecdote, and oriental tale. Whenever his purpose is satirical— and this is often—he is apt to employ burlesque. In such instances he achieves the necessary incongruity between manner and matter by imitating, parodying, or "modernizing" traditional forms like the Bible, Book of Common Prayer, court gazette, epitaph, petition, sermon, and speech. Two of these burlesques, "The Speech of Miss Polly Baker" and the "Proposed New Version of the Bible," actually deceived Abbé Raynal and Matthew Arnold, who might have been expected to see the jest.[1]

He characterized his bagatelles as "my little Scribblings,"[2] *"mes Plaisanteries serieuses, ou sourdes,"*[3] statements which suggest that in his view this type of writing should be short and lighthearted. Abbé Morellet, attesting to Franklin's genius for imaginatively combining wit and morality, described certain of his own productions he was sending him from Auteuil as "in your own vein of pleasantry, and somewhat, I conceive, in that of Swift, with

[1]*The Writings of Thomas Jefferson,* ed. A. E. Bergh (Washington, D. C., 1904–1905), XVIII, 171–172; Matthew Arnold, "Sweetness and Light," in *Culture and Anarchy* (New York, 1924), pp. 34–35.

[2]Smyth, VIII, 369.   [3]*Ibid.,* IX, 191.

rather less of his dark misanthropy.... At any rate, Dr. Jonathan and Dr. Benjamin are the models on whom I fixed my eyes; and perhaps Nature herself has given me something of the turn of both in the art of speaking the truth in a jesting way, or without seeming to speak it."[4] And in 1790 another admiring Frenchman praised the high degree of invention to be met with in Franklin's *"opuscules moraux"*:

It is the naïve cleverness of La Fontaine, it is the profundity and elevation of the Holy Scriptures and the oriental moralists, it is the concealed irony of Socrates without the prolix subtlety of Plato. Finally, it is especially the superior and indulgent spirit of a sage, who has judged man both in the rural frankness of the pioneer and in the artificial refinements of French politeness.[5]

William Temple Franklin published as a group the seventeen pieces his grandfather had endorsed as bagatelles, explaining that they had been written "for the amusement of his intimate society in London and Paris."[6] It seems

[4]Morellet to Franklin, July 31, 1787, *The Works of Benjamin Franklin,* ed. John Bigelow (Fed. ed.; New York and London, 1904), XI, 344–345; referred to hereafter as Bigelow.

[5]M. Grouvelle in *Journal de la Société de 1789,* VIII (July 24, 1790), 8; reprinted in Aldridge, *Am. Lit.,* XXVIII (1956), 24.

[6]*The Posthumous and Other Writings of Benjamin Franklin* (3d ed.; London, 1819), I, 216–298. These pieces, bearing William Temple Franklin's titles, are: "The Levée," "Proposed New Version of the Bible: Part of the first chapter of Job, modernised," "Apologue," "Poems addressed to Miss Georgiana Shipley, on the Loss of her American Squirrel," "The Art of procuring Pleasing Dreams," "The Ephemera, an emblem of Human Life," "The Whistle," "A Petition to those who have the Superintendence of Education," "The handsome and deformed Leg," "Morals of Chess," *"Conte,* and

certain, however, that the grandfather would have admitted ten others into the canon: "Old Mistresses Apologue," "The Speech of Miss Polly Baker," "The Craven-street Gazette," "The Lord's Prayer," "A Parable on Brotherly Love," the treaty letter to Mme Brillon, and four other of the Passy imprints, "A Parable against Persecution," "To the Royal Academy of Brussels," "M. Franklin to Mme La Freté," and "The Flies."[7] All twenty-seven of these pieces mingle wit and morality in varying proportions, all are short, their immediate purpose is social, and the majority (which may well have been Franklin's intention for all of them) were published in his own lifetime.

I

By the 1740's Franklin the printer had gained a sufficient competence to begin enjoying those pleasures enumerated in a favorite song of his ("The Old Man's Wish"): "A warm House in a country Town, an easy Horse, some good old authors, ingenious and cheerful Companions, a Pudding on Sundays, with stout Ale, and a bottle of Burgundy, &c. &c."[8] The period surrounding 1745, aptly described by Carl Van Doren as his "salty year,"[9] constitutes a brief

---

Translation," "An Arabian Tale," "Dialogue between Franklin and the Gout," "Letters to Madame Helvetius," "Letter to the Abbé de la Roche, with a Song," "On Wine, addressed to the Abbé Morellet," and "An Economical Project."

[7]Although Amacher includes them in his volume, *Franklin's Wit and Folly,* I do not regard "Information to Those Who Would Remove to America" and "Remarks Concerning the Savages of North America" as bagatelles.

[8]Smyth, IX, 332–333.

[9]*Benjamin Franklin,* p. 154.

social interlude in the life of this man of province business,
one in which he wrote his first two bagatelles for the enter-
tainment of his "intimate Pot Companions" at the Junto,
"who have heard me say a 1000 silly Things in Conversations."[10] Both pieces are a sophisticated outgrowth of
earlier newspaper and almanac writings on the conventional battle of the sexes, like the following essay, wherein
Franklin takes to task the author of some verses in the
Pennsylvania Gazette advising men to remain single. "So
ill-natur'd a Thing," he declares, "must have been written,
either by some forlorn old Batchelor, or some cast-away
Widower, that has got the Knack of drowning all his softer
Inclinations in his Bowl or his Bottle. I am grown old
and have made abundance of Observations, and I have had
three Wives my self; so that from both Experience and
Observation I can say, that this Advice is wrong and untrue
in every Particular." Having refuted the versifier's advice
clause by clause, Franklin concludes:

> His Case is like that of many other old He-Maids I have
> heard of.... Having in some of their first Attempts upon
> the kinder Sort of the Fair Sex, come off with Shame and
> Disgrace, they persuade themselves that they are, (and per-
> haps they are) really Impotent: And so durst not marry,
> for fear of those dishonourable Decorations of the Head,
> which they think it the inevitable Fate of a Fumbler to wear.
> Then, like the Fox who could not use his Tail, (but the
> Fox had really lost it) they set up for *Advisers,* as the
> Gentleman I have been dealing with; and would fain per-
> suade others, that the Use of their own Tails is more
> mischievous than beneficial.[11]

[10]Labaree, I, 264.

[11]*Pennsylvania Gazette,* Mar. 4, 1735; reprinted in Labaree, II,
22, 24.

On June 25, 1745, perhaps recalling "that hard-to-be-govern'd Passion of Youth" which had prompted him to take Deborah Read to wife, Franklin, in what purports to be a letter to a young man, declares that marriage "is the most natural State of Man," a single man resembling "the odd Half of a Pair of Scissars." "But if you will not take this Counsel, and persist in thinking a Commerce with the Sex inevitable," then I advise "that in all your Amours you should *prefer old Women to young ones*." Conversation with them "is more improving and more lastingly agreable," and "they supply the Diminution of Beauty by an Augmentation of Utility." There is "no hazard of Children," and "they are more prudent and discreet in conducting an Intrigue to prevent Suspicion."

> In every Animal that walks upright, the Deficiency of the Fluids that fill the Muscles appears first in the highest Part: The Face first grows lank and wrinkled; then the Neck; then the Breast and Arms; the lower Parts continuing to the Last as plump as ever: So that covering all above with a Basket, and regarding only what is below the Girdle, it is impossible of two Women to know an old from a young one. And as in the dark all Cats are grey, the Pleasure of corporal Enjoyment with an old Woman is at least equal, and frequently superior, every Knack being by Practice capable of Improvement.

"The debauching a Virgin may be her Ruin, and make her for Life unhappy.... The having made a young Girl *miserable* may give you frequent bitter Reflections; none of which can attend the making an old Woman *happy*." Lastly, old women "are *so grateful!!*"[12]

---

[12]"Old Mistresses Apologue," Labaree, III, 30–31; known familiarly as "Advice to a Young Man on the Choice of a Mistress." Else-

The pseudological reasoning conceals momentarily the mock-seriousness of this advice to a young man who would diminish his "violent natural Inclinations" but will not marry. The arguments advanced for preferring old women to young ones seem plausible until the last is reached. With the words "They are *so grateful!!*" the logic stands exposed. Franklin, who in fact preferred his own "prudent healthy Wife" to mistresses old or young, here poses as a worldly philosopher, whose practical suggestions sound like those of an experienced rake. The fact that no nineteenth-century editor or biographer dared print this piece suggests an inability, or at least an unwillingness, to see through the pose. What undoubtedly gave members of the Junto the greatest delight must have offended Victorian sensibility most deeply, the climactic observation that "regarding only what is below the Girdle, it is impossible of two Women to know an old from a young one."

Polly Baker, one of Franklin's most memorable American characters and the protagonist of his first important hoax after that on Titan Leeds, furnishes an example of a virgin debauched. Dragged "before a Court of Judicature, at Connecticut near Boston" to be prosecuted for having borne her fifth bastard, she pleads for clemency. "Twice I have paid heavy Fines, and twice have been brought to Publick Punishment, for want of Money to pay those Fines." What is the nature of my offence? "Can it be a Crime (in the Nature of Things I mean) to add to the Number of the King's Subjects, in a new Country that really wants People?" I would remind the court that "I readily consented to the only Proposal of Marriage that

where Franklin compared the married state to a pair of scissors— see Smyth, V, 158; IX, 14, 583.

ever was made me, which was when I was a Virgin; but too easily confiding in the Person's Sincerity that made it, I unhappily lost my own Honour, by trusting to his; for he got me with Child, and then forsook me." Because the law bears unjustly on such as myself, I urge you, Gentlemen, to "take into your wise Consideration, the great and growing Number of Batchelors in the Country, many of whom from the mean Fear of the Expences of a Family, have never sincerely and honourably courted a Woman in their Lives; and by their Manner of Living, leave unproduced (which is little better than Murder) Hundreds of their Posterity to the Thousandth Generation." Compel them "either to Marriage, or to pay double the Fine of Fornication every Year." Instead of suffering fines and whipping for performing "the first and great Command of Nature, and of Nature's God, *Encrease and Multiply,*" I should "have a Statue erected to my Memory."[13] This hoax is built on the incongruity between the law's view of illegitimacy and Polly's conviction that she has only been obeying nature's first law. Her naïve sincerity at once wins the reader over. What is more ironical, though, it wins over the court; for one of the judges, perhaps conscience-stricken by the recollection that he who first debauched Polly "is now become a Magistrate of this Country," marries her the next day.

[13]"The SPEECH of Miss POLLY BAKER," *General Advertiser* (London), Apr. 15, 1747; reprinted in Labaree, III, 123–125. According to Max Hall, who traces the publication history of this bagatelle in *Benjamin Franklin and Polly Baker* (Chapel Hill, 1960), the first known American printing was that in the *Boston Weekly Post-Boy,* July 20, 1747.

II

"For my own Part," wrote Franklin the colonial agent in 1761, "I find I love Company, Chat, a Laugh, a Glass, and even a Song, as well as ever."[14] In place of the Junto there was now "the club of honest whigs" at the London coffeehouse,[15] whose "honest, sensible & intelligent Society [as he recalled in 1780] did me so long the Honour of admitting me to share in their instructive Conversations."[16] It was in such an atmosphere that he wrote several bagatelles during the busy years of his agency in England. Of three Biblical imitations he had the most fun with "A Parable against Persecution," a fifty-first chapter to the Book of Genesis, which he had bound up "as a leaf in his Bible, the better to impose" upon those "Scripturians" to whom he read it.[17] "I found there was no such chapter," noted Strahan in his printing of this hoax, "and that the whole was a well meant invention of my friend, whose sallies of humour...have always an unusual and benevolent tendency."[18] Two other bagatelles of this period, an ironic modernization of the Lord's Prayer and verses from the first chapter of Job, were in actuality a defense of the plain direct style Franklin ever admired and most often practiced.

At a time when Mrs. Stevenson was away on a trip to Rochester in 1770, her American boarder, posing as "the *great* Person (so called from his enormous Size) of a

[14]Smyth, IV, 96.   [15]*Ibid.*, VI, 430.   [16]*Ibid.*, VIII, 8.

[17]*Ibid.*, I, 181; X, 53. While this bagatelle is now known to have been written at least as early as the summer of 1755, it was in England that Franklin had the most fun with it. See Labaree, VI, 114–122, for the complicated history of its publication.

[18]*London Chronicle,* Apr. 17, 1764.

certain Family in a certain Street," composed a daily series of "we hears," in parody of contemporary court gossip sheets like the long-established *London Gazette*.

We have good Authority to assure our Readers, [he writes on Saturday] that a Cabinet Council was held this Afternoon at Tea; the Subject of which was a Proposal for the Reformation of Manners, and a more strict Observation of the Lord's Day. The Result was, an unanimous Resolution that no Meat should be dress'd to-morrow; whereby the Cook and the first Minister [Polly and her husband] will both be at Liberty to go to Church, the one having nothing to do, and the other no Roast to rule. It seems the cold Shoulder of Mutton, and the Applepye, were thought sufficient for Sunday's Dinner. All pious People applaud this Measure, & 'tis thought the new Ministry will soon become popular. . . .

It is now found by sad Experience, [he continues on Sunday] that good Resolutions are easier made than executed. Notwithstanding yesterday's solemn Order of Council, no body went to Church today. It seems the *great* Person's broad-built-bulk lay so long abed, that Breakfast was not over till it was too late to dress. At least this is the Excuse. In fine, it seems a vain thing to hope Reformation from the Example of our great Folks.—The Cook and the Minister, however, both took Advantage of the Order so far, as to save themselves all Trouble, and the Clause of *cold Dinner* was enforc'd, tho' the *going to Church* was dispens'd with; just as the common working People observe the Commandment;—*the seventh Day thou shalt rest,* they think a sacred Injunction; but the other *Six Days shalt thou labour* is deem'd a mere Piece of Advice which they may practice when they want Bread & are out of Credit at the Alehouse, and may neglect whenever they have Money in their Pockets.

Ever amorous, and momentarily envious of Polly's recent marriage, Franklin relates that James Hutton, the bookseller, came to call.

> He then imparted to the big Man a Piece of Intelligence important to them both, which he had just received from Lady Hawkesworth, viz. That [that?] amiable & excellent Companion Miss Dorothea Blount had made a Vow to marry absolutely him of the two, whose Wife should first depart this Life. . . . They parted at length with Professions and outward Appearances indeed of ever-during Friendship; but it was shrewdly suspected that each of them sincerely wished Health and long Life to the other's Wife; and that however long either of these Friends might like to live himself, the other would be very well pleas'd to survive him.

Professing extreme displeasure that the remains of Saturday's mutton which were served him for dinner on Tuesday had "very little Flesh, or rather none at all (Puss having din'd on it yesterday after Nanny)," Franklin resorts to fictitious controversy. Over the signature "Indignation" he charges:

> A certain great *Person* has been half-starved on the bare Blade-bone, *of a Sheep* (I cannot call it *of Mutton* because none was on it) by a Set of the most careless, thoughtless, inconsiderate, corrupt, ignorant, blundering, foolish, crafty, & Knavish Ministers that ever got into a House and pretended to govern a Family & provide a Dinner. Alas, for the poor Old England of Craven Street! If these nefarious Wretches continue in Power another Week, the Nation will be ruined.—Undone!—totally undone, if the Queen [Mrs. Stevenson] does not return; or (which is better) turn them all out and appoint me & my Friends to succeed them.

Then, writing as "A Hater of Scandal," he counters:

Your Correspondent *Indignation* has made a fine Story in your Paper against our excellent Cravenstreet Ministry, as if they meant to starve his Highness, giving him only a bare Blade Bone for his Dinner, while they riot upon roast Venison, &c. The Wickedness of Writers in this Age is truly amazing! I believe we never had since the Foundation of our State, a more faithful, upright, worthy, careful, considerate, incorrupt, discreet, wise, prudent & beneficent Ministry than the present. But if even the Angel Gabriel would condescend to be our Minister and provide our Dinners, he could scarcely escape Newspaper Defamation from a Gang of hungry, ever-restless, discontented and malicious Scribblers.—It is, Sir, a piece of Justice you owe our righteous Administration to undeceive the Publick on this [Occas]ion, by assuring them [of?] the Fact, which is, that there was provided, and actually smoking on the Table under his Royal Nose at the same Instant, as fine a Piece of Ribs of Beef, roasted, as ever Knife was put into; with Potatoes, Horse radish, pickled Walnuts, &c.[19]

The studied casualness of this domestic gossip sheet, written in the manner of the then popular court gazette, must certainly have delighted such knowing readers as Polly Hewson and her husband, the more so since they themselves were "the new Family Administration" that took place on Queen Margaret's departure for Rochester. Though he situates himself at the center of this parody, Franklin avoids a show of vanity by picturing himself as the most absurd personality at this court; thus he writes, "Dr Fatsides made 469 Turns in his Dining Room as the

[19]"The Cravenstreet Gazette," Sept. 22–26, 1770, Bradford Collection, Amer. Philos. Soc. Smyth, V, 272–280, reproduces a foul text, one that differs from the Bradford manuscript in diction, pointing, italicizing, and capitalization.

exact Distance of a Visit to the lovely Lady Barwell, whom he did not find at home, so there was no Struggle for and against a Kiss, and he sat down to dream in the Easy Chair that he had it without any Trouble." The intimate and homely routine of this genteel boardinghouse world—dressing, taking meat and drink, shopping, paying and receiving visits, gaming—is couched in so appropriate a species of official language as to make this bagatelle one of the most effective burlesques he ever wrote and one of his gentlest satires. Like the treaty letter to Mme Brillon, it was composed at intervals stolen from the business of the day.

Franklin, it will be recalled, entered actively into the life of the Shipley girls in 1771. When Georgiana's squirrel died the next year, he composed a mock-epitaph "in the monumental style and measure, which, being neither prose nor verse, is perhaps the properest for grief; since to use common language would look as if we were not affected, and to make rhymes would seem trifling in sorrow."

> Alas! poor MUNGO!
> Happy wert thou, hadst thou known
> Thy own felicity.
> Remote from the fierce bald eagle,
> Tyrant of thy native woods,
> Thou hadst nought to fear from his piercing talons,
> Nor from the murdering gun
> Of the thoughtless sportsman.
> Safe in thy wired castle,
> GRIMALKIN never could annoy thee.
> Daily wert thou fed with the choicest viands,
> By the fair hand of an indulgent mistress;
> But, discontented,
> Thou wouldst have more freedom.

Too soon, alas! didst thou obtain it;
And wandering,
Thou are fallen by the fangs of wanton, cruel RANGER!

Learn hence,
Ye who blindly seek more liberty,
Whether subjects, sons, squirrels or daughters,
That apparent restraint may be real protection;
Yielding peace and plenty
With security.

"You see, my dear Miss," he concludes, "how much more decent and proper this broken style is, than if we were to say, by way of epitaph,

> Here SKUGG
> Lies snug,
> As a bug
> In a rug.

and yet, perhaps, there are people in the world of so little feeling as to think that this would be a good-enough epitaph for poor Mungo."[20] This performance is a clear example of the badinage Georgiana later recalled acquiring a taste for from him.

Home after the war, Franklin complied with Catherine Shipley's request and set down rules for procuring pleasant dreams: If you get sufficient exercise and eat sparingly afterwards (he writes), sleep "will be natural and undisturbed; while indolence, with full feeding, occasions night-

[20]Franklin to Georgiana Shipley, Sept. 26, 1772, Smyth, V, 438–439. Franklin sent his wife a copy "to amuse you a little, and nobody out of your own House," explaining, "Skugg, you must know, is a common Name by which all Squirrels are called here as all cats are called *Puss*" (Smyth, VI, 16–17).

mares and horrors inexpressible; we fall from precipices, are assaulted by wild beasts, murderers, and demons, and experience every variety of distress." Have "a constant supply of fresh air in your bed-chamber."

> It is recorded of Methusalem, who, being the longest liver, may be supposed to have best preserved his health, that he slept always in the open air; for, when he had lived five hundred years, an angel said to him; "Arise, Methusalem, and build thee an house, for thou shalt live yet five hundred years longer." But Methusalem answered, and said, "If I am to live but five hundred years longer, it is not worth while to build me an house; I will sleep in the air, as I have been used to do."

(Kitty searched her Bible in vain for this passage.) "These are the rules of the art. But, though they will generally prove effectual in producing the end intended, there is a case in which the most punctual observance of them will be totally fruitless. I need not mention the case to you, my dear friend, but my account of the art would be imperfect without it. The case is, when the person who desires to have pleasant dreams has not taken care to preserve, what is necessary above all things, A GOOD CONSCIENCE."[21] Even though this is one of the most didactic of his bagatelles, Franklin here speaks to the woman who as a child had been his stagecoach companion on the journey to London with more whimsy than Poor Richard, who had soberly observed that "a good Conscience is a continual Christmas" (Dec., 1741).

[21]"The Art of Procuring Pleasant Dreams," enclosed in a letter of May 2, 1786. First printed in the *Columbian Magazine* (Philadelphia), I (Oct., 1786), 64–67; reprinted in Smyth, X, 131–137.

195

III

The bagatelles Franklin wrote while in France are inter-woven with his friendships at Passy and Auteuil. Several of them take the form of familiar letters to Mmes Brillon and Helvétius and the Abbés Morellet and La Roche; all are a product of the atmosphere of the salon, which both stimulated and responded to his excursions into this literary type. We have seen how Mme Brillon's *"Le Sage et la Goutte"* furnished inspiration for the "Dialogue be-tween Franklin and the Gout" and how Mme Helvétius' rejection of his proposal provoked the Elysian Fields letter. Conversely, when he moralized somewhat too strenuously, "Life is a kind of Chess," in that by playing the game "we may learn, *Foresight...Circumspection...Caution*" and "the habit of not being discouraged by present appearances in the state of our affairs,"[22] his friend Dubourg tactfully countered:

> Do not chess lovers delude themselves too much in imagin-ing their favored game as the image of human life, and in deceiving themselves that the former will teach them to know better and to fulfill better the duties of the latter?... No game is made to teach us the business of life; their sole usefulness is limited to filling innocently life's few empty moments; and the most fortunate of all mortals is the one to whom the fewest remain.[23]

Morellet informed Franklin, after his return to Phila-delphia, that the cats, "now eighteen and will soon be thirty," were overrunning Mme Helvétius' house: "A cunning sophist [Morellet himself]...has undertaken the defense of the cats, and has composed a *Petition* for them,

[22]Smyth, VII, 358–359.
[23]*Franklin's Wit and Folly,* pp. 114, 115.

that may serve as a companion-piece to the *Thanks* that
you made for the flies of your rooms, after the destruction
of the spiders ordered by *Our Lady*."[24] In this *"plaisanterie
de société,"*[25] which Morellet enclosed with his letter, Mme
Helvétius' cats, sentenced "to be seized, put into a cask,
rolled down to the river, and abandoned to the mercy of
the waters," ask her to let them speak in their own defense.
"Alas!" they exclaim, "what are the crimes that we have
committed! We are accused...of eating your chickens
while they are still young, of making depredations from
time to time upon your pigeons, of watching your canary-
birds incessantly, and seizing any that come near enough
to the lattice of your aviary, and of suffering the mice to
infest your house unmolested." The cats, having cleverly
countered these accusations, conclude their petition: "Ah,
most illustrious Lady! let the memory of the cat you so
much loved, inspire you at least with some compassion
towards us. We are not indeed of his race, since he was
devoted to *chastity* from his youth; but we are of his
species. His manes, still wandering about this spot, call
upon you to revoke the sanguinary order which menaces
our days; and all those which you preserve to us shall be
consecrated to mewing forth our lasting gratitude, while
the beneficent act shall be handed down by us to our
children's children."[26] Franklin confessed to La Roche,

[24]Morellet to Franklin, [Oct. 30, 1785?], *Mémoires,* I, 301, quoted
in Parton, *Franklin,* II, 561. The *"Thanks"* is a reference to "The
Flies," a bagatelle considered on page 162.

[25]*Mémoires,* I, 307.

[26]*"Lettre à Franklin en lui envoyant la requête des chats,"* [1785–
1786?], *Mémoires,* I, 307–313; translated in *Franklin's Wit and Folly,*
pp. 121–129.

another member of Mme Helvétius' circle, "Their Requêté is admirably well written; but their continually Increasing in Number will in time make their Cause insupportable: Their Friends should, therefore, advise them to submit voluntarily either to Transportation or to Castration."[27]

In salon talk, as Morellet later recalled, Franklin approximated the ideal described by Rousseau:

> His conversation was exquisite—a perfect good nature, a simplicity of manners, an uprightness of mind that made itself felt in the smallest things, an extreme gentleness, and, above all, a sweet serenity that easily became gayety; such was the society of this great man, who has placed his country among the number of independent States, and made one of the most important discoveries of the age.
>
> He seldom spoke long, except in composing tales—a talent in which he excelled, and which he greatly liked in others. His tales always had a philosophical aim; many had the form of apologues, which he himself invented, and he applied those which he had not made with infinite justice.[28]

In the bagatelles Franklin gives full play to the habitual urge to tell a story. Through anecdote he achieves unity in "The Ephemera," "An Arabian Tale," "Dialogue between Franklin and the Gout," "The Elysian Fields," "Apologue," "The Flies," and *"Conte"* and imparts force and gives point to "The Whistle" and "The Handsome and Deformed Leg," thus turning the conversational talent Morellet admired to literary advantage.

At Passy Franklin found his audience ready and even eager for the *jeux d'esprit* he now composed and, in some

[27]Smyth, IX, 505.

[28]*Mémoires,* I, 299–300; Parton, *Franklin,* II, 424, reprints William Duane's translation, which is given here.

cases, had printed "by means of a small set of types and a press he had in his house."[29] These bagatelles, whose reckless Frencl disturbed Mmes Brillon and Helvétius far less than it did such purists as Morellet and La Roche, approach the ideal balance between wit and morality more often than those he wrote in Philadelphia and England. They are also more urbane, even the scatological "To the Royal Academy of Brussels." In 1795 Renouard, the Paris publisher who made the first collection of his bagatelles, said of such pieces as "The Whistle," "The Ephemera," and "Dialogue between Franklin and the Gout":

> Written without any pretension and as bagatelles of society, they were formerly printed only to the number of fifteen or twenty copies and in order to be distributed solely among those who made up Franklin's select society.... One would like to see Franklin as he was in that private society; at all times the naïve and profound philosopher, always accompanying his advice and reflections with some trait of humor and in an easy manner that rendered them agreeable even to those who were the object of them.[30]

The earliest of Franklin's French bagatelles, and one of his most delicately balanced, is "The Ephemera," addressed to Mme Brillon: "You may remember," it begins, alluding to a small island in the Seine, "that when we lately spent that happy Day in the delightful Garden and sweet Society of the Moulin Joli," we were shown "numberless Skeletons of a kind of little Fly, called an Ephemere all whose successive Generations we were told were bred and expired

---

[29]*Memoirs of the Life and Writings of Benjamin Franklin,* ed. W. T. Franklin (Philadelphia, 1818), I, 337, cited in *Proc. APS,* XL, 122.

[30]Luther S. Livingston, *Franklin and His Press at Passy* (New York, 1914), p. 13, reprints the French text of this advertisement.

within the Day. I happen'd to see a living Company of
them on a Leaf, who appear'd to be engag'd in Conversation." I stopped to listen to their chatter and found "by
some broken Expressions that I caught now & then, they
were disputing warmly the Merit of two foreign Musicians,
one a *Cousin,* the other a *Musketo;* in which Dispute they
spent their time seemingly as regardless of the Shortness
of Life, as if they had been Sure of living a Month." "I
turned from them to an old greyheaded one [Franklin him-
self]," whose soliloquy amused me so that "I have put it
down in writing in hopes it will likewise amuse her to
whom I am So much indebted for the most pleasing of
all Amusements, her delicious Company and her heavenly
Harmony."

"It was, says he, the Opinion of learned Philosophers of
our Race, who lived and flourished long before my time, that
this vast World, the *Moulin Joli,* could not itself subsist
more than 18 Hours.... I have lived seven of these Hours;
a great Age; being no less than 420 minutes of Time. How
very few of us continue So long.... By the Course of
Nature, tho' still in Health, I cannot expect to live above
7 or 8 Minutes Longer. What now avails...the political
Struggles I have been engag'd in for the Good of my Com-
patriotes, Inhabitants of this Bush, or my philosophical
Studies for the Benefit of our Race in general!"

After a busy life (the venerable fly concludes) "no solid
Pleasures now remain, but the Reflection of a long Life
spent in meaning well, the sensible Conversation of a
few good Lady-Ephemeres, and now and then a kind
Smile and a Tune from the ever-amiable BRILLANTE."[31]

[31]"The Ephemera," Sept. 20, 1778, printed in *Proc. APS,* CIII,
741–744; first published in French on the Passy press, probably not

Franklin here avoids the danger of didactic dullness by constructing a delicate allegory in which the world is shrunk to the size of an island and human history to the space of eighteen hours. He conducts us swiftly but gracefully from the human world to the ephemeral and, under the double guise of a fly philosopher, discourses whimsically on the vanity of political debate, scientific investigation, and life itself. When we are returned to the human world at the end, we realize that she for whom this bagatelle was written has never really been absent from his thoughts. It stands forth finally as an enduring compliment to the French woman he loved above all others.

Two years later he sent her the "Dialogue between Franklin and the Gout," wherein Madam Gout appears in his chamber at midnight and lectures him on his sedentary life, administering "wholesome twinges" to drive her points home:

> Instead of gaining an appetite for breakfast by salutary exercise, you amuse yourself with books, pamphlets, or newspapers, which commonly are not worth the reading. Yet you eat an inordinate breakfast, four dishes of tea with

before 1782 (Livingston, *Franklin and His Press,* p. 30). Franklin sent a copy of this bagatelle to William Carmichael on June 17, 1780, explaining, "The thought was partly taken from a little piece of some unknown writer, which I met with fifty years since in a newspaper, and which the sight of the Ephemera brought to my recollection" (Smyth, VIII, 100). Aldridge, *New Eng. Quar.,* XXVII (1954), 390–391, suggests that this "little piece" is not the essay in the *Pennsylvania Gazette,* Dec. 11, 1735, on the venerable insect vainglorious of his great age, usually cited as the source, but another *Gazette* essay (Oct. 21, 1731), wherein the antediluvian Pulgah warns his daughter Shual of the brevity of life. Neither piece, as Aldridge demonstrates, was written by Franklin.

cream, and one or two buttered toasts, with slices of hung beef, which I fancy are not things the most easily digested. Immediately afterwards you sit down to write at your desk, or converse with persons who apply to you on business. Thus the time passes till one, without any kind of bodily exercise.... What is your practice after dinner?... To be fixed down to chess, where you are found engaged for two or three hours!... What can be expected from such a course of living but a body replete with stagnant humours, ready to fall a prey to all kinds of dangerous maladies, if I, the Gout, did not occasionally bring you relief by agitating those humours, and so purifying or dissipating them?... The same taste prevails with you in Passy, Auteuil, Mont-martre, or Sanoy, places where there are the finest gardens and walks, a pure air, beautiful women, and most agreeable and instructive conversation: all which you might enjoy by frequenting the walks. But these are rejected for this abominable game of chess.

You content yourself with dining out and returning in your carriage, the motion of which "of all imaginable exercises, is the most slight and insignificant." Why not burn it? Better still, let your coachman convey "to their smoky huts" each night "four or five old men and women, bent and perhaps crippled by weight of years, and too long and too great labour." "This is an act that will be good for your soul; and, at the same time, after your visit to the Brillons, if you return on foot, that will be good for your body." When finally Franklin promises "faithfully never more to play at chess, but to take exercise daily, and live temperately," Madam Gout coolly replies: "I know you too well. You promise fair; but, after a few months of good health, you will return to your old habits;

your fine promises will be forgotten like the forms of the last year's clouds."[32]

Even though Franklin is only posing as a sedentary, gout-ridden diplomat, this bagatelle is thoroughly dramatic in conception and execution. Mindful of Poor Richard's aphorism,

> Be temperate in wine, in eating, girls, and sloth;
> Or the Gout will seize you and plague you both,
> [Feb., 1734]

he conceives a dialogue to give objectivity and immediacy to a physical condition he now knew all too well. In his midnight agony he is made to endure the double affliction of gouty twinges and an uneasy conscience. What finally ensures the triumph of this dialogue, a rhetorical convention he had sometimes employed with indifferent success, is the three-dimensional scene that unfolds, satirically to be sure and for this reason more vividly, of his life at Passy.

Just as skillfully balanced as these two bagatelles but written in a grosser vein is "To the Royal Academy of Brussels," wherein Franklin assumes a spectator mask: Since you gentlemen (he writes) "esteem *Utility* an essential Point in your Enquiries... permit me then humbly to propose one of that sort for your consideration, and through you, if you approve it, for the serious Enquiry of learned Physicians, Chemists, &c. of this enlightened Age." It is, *"To discover some Drug wholesome & not disagreable,*

---

[32]*"Dialogue entre la goutte et M. Franklin,"* dated Oct. 22, 1780; however, a Passy imprint of this bagatelle was probably struck off "early in 1780" (Livingston, *Franklin and His Press*, p. 22). The English version herein quoted appears in *Autobiographical Writings*, pp. 484–489.

to be mix'd with our common Food, or Sauces, that shall render the Natural Discharges, of Wind from our Bodies, not only inoffensive, but agreable as Perfumes. . . . A few Stems of Asparagus eaten, shall give our Urine a disagreable Odour; and a Pill of Turpentine no bigger than a Pea, shall bestow on it the pleasing Smell of Violets. And why should it be thought more impossible in Nature, to find Means of making a Perfume of our *Wind* than of our *Water?*" In contrast to such inquiries as this, how unimportant the recent discoveries in science appear!

> What Comfort can the Vortices of Descartes give to a Man who has Whirlwinds in his Bowels! The Knowledge of Newton's mutual *Attraction* of the Particles of Matter, can it afford Ease to him who is rack'd by their mutual *Repulsion,* and the cruel Distensions it occasions? The Pleasure arising to a few Philosophers, from seeing, a few Times in their Life, the Threads of Light untwisted, and separated by the Newtonian Prism into seven Colours, can it be compared with the Ease and Comfort every Man living might feel seven times a Day, by discharging freely the Wind from his Bowels? Especially if it be converted into a Perfume: For the Pleasures of one Sense being little inferior to those of another, instead of pleasing the *Sight* he might delight the *Smell* of those about him, & make Numbers happy, which to a benevolent Mind must afford infinite Satisfaction.

"In short, this Invention, if compleated, would be, as *Bacon* expresses it, *bringing Philosophy home to Mens Business and Bosoms.* And I cannot but conclude, that in Comparison therewith, for universal and continual UTILITY, the Science of the Philosophers abovementioned . . . are, all together, scarcely worth a FART-HING."[33]

[33]"To the Royal Academy of*****," a Passy imprint written

A comparison between this bagatelle and Part III of *Gulliver's Travels* suggests itself. Both Swift and Franklin, mindful of the important scientific advances being made in their day, devise ironic masks, the one that of an unimaginative sailor now retired, the other that of a modest proposer, in an effort to expose and exploit impractical scientific projectors. Both heighten the irony by introducing scatological matter. Franklin further intensifies his by employing puns: "to avoid the Report," "give Vent to his Griefs," *"Ex-pressing* one's *Scent-iments,"* "scarcely worth a FART-HING." If early editors of Franklin's works, shocked by such obscenities and accepting at face value his mock-earnest judgment that this piece "has too much *grossièreté* to be borne by the polite Readers of these Nations,"[34] chose to suppress it, it is refreshing to learn that two of the "honest whigs," Price and Priestley, were "entertained with the pleasantry of it, and the ridicule it contains."[35]

Again masking as a modest proposer, Franklin asks the editors of a Paris journal to communicate to the public a useful discovery he recently made: "I was the other evening in a grand company," the proposer explains, "where the new lamp of Messrs. Quinquet and Lange was introduced, and much admired for its splendour," though no one knew "whether the oil it consumed was...in proportion to the light it afforded, in which case there would be no saving in the use of it." Retiring "three or four

---

before 1782; reprinted in *Franklin's Wit and Folly,* pp. 66–69, wherein Amacher explains that "Brusselles" is written after the title in the original MS.

[34]Smyth, VIII, 369.

[35]*Ibid.,* IX, 100n.

hours after midnight, with my head full of the subject," I was accidentally awakened at six and surprised to find my room filled with light. "Your readers, who with me have never seen any signs of sunshine before noon, and seldom regard the astronomical part of the almanac, will be as much astonished as I was, when they hear of his rising so early; and especially when I assure them, *that he gives light as soon as he rises.*" Others do not believe me. "One, indeed, who is a learned natural philosopher, has assured me that I must certainly be mistaken.... It being well known...that there could be no light abroad at that hour, it follows that none could enter from without; and that of consequence, my windows being accidentally left open, instead of letting in the light, had only served to let out the darkness." I have calculated what an immense sum "the city of Paris might save every year, by the economy of using sunshine instead of candles." For those who persist, even after learning of my discovery, in the old custom of rising at noon, I propose the following regulations:

First. Let a tax be laid of a louis per window, on every window that is provided with shutters to keep out the light of the sun.

Second. Let the same salutary operation of police be made use of, to prevent our burning candles, that inclined us last winter to be more economical in burning wood; that is, let guards be placed in the shops of the wax and tallow chandlers, and no family be permitted to be supplied with more than one pound of candles per week.

Third. Let guards also be posted to stop all the coaches, &c. that would pass the streets after sun-set, except those of physicians, surgeons, and midwives.

Fourth. Every morning, as soon as the sun rises, let all the

bells in every church be set ringing; and if that is not
sufficient, let cannon be fired in every street, to wake the
sluggards effectually, and make them open their eyes to see
their true interest.

As for the great benefit deriving from my discovery that
the sun *"gives light as soon as he rises,"* "I demand neither
place, pension, exclusive privilege, nor any other reward
whatever. I expect only to have the honour of it." It was
certainly unknown by the Parisians, who like myself
profess to be lovers of economy. "I say it is impossible that
so sensible a people, under such circumstances, should
have lived so long by the smoky, unwholesome, and
enormously expensive light of candles, if they had really
known, that they might have had as much pure light of
the sun for nothing."[36] This piece, written in what Morellet
called Franklin's "vein of pleasantry," may be compared
with *A Modest Proposal*. Franklin's modest proposer, like
Swift's, is bent on economy and efficiency and is innocently
eager to see his plan put into effect at once, but whereas
the one plan is terrifyingly inhumane the other requires
only that sluggards retire and rise at an earlier hour.

Wide-ranging imaginative energy, a sense of leisure, and
the presence of a sophisticated audience are conditions
essential to the creation of the bagatelle. Franklin's imagination was vigorous from the first—witness Silence Dogood and the world in which she moves—but it would be
many years before he mastered a range of rhetorical forms
through which it might play at will. Always busy whether at

[36] *Journal de Paris,* Apr. 26, 1784; reprinted under its usual English title, "An Economical Project," in Smyth, IX, 183–189. See
Par. Text Ed., pp. 320–322, for serious observations on the same
subject.

home or abroad, he early learned how to relax, and from at least 1748, the year he gave up the management of the *Pennsylvania Gazette,* he was freer to do so than he had been before. At Philadelphia, in England, in France, he sought and found audiences to stimulate and be stimulated by him. The audience largely controlled the tone of the particular bagatelle; it would have been equally inappropriate, for example, to have addressed "The Speech of Miss Polly Baker" to the Shipley girls and the mock-epitaph on Mungo to members of the Junto. At Passy he felt less restrained since his audience was so enlightened that it could at once enjoy the delicacy of "The Ephemera" and the coarseness of "To the Royal Academy of Brussels." The distance separating Franklin's usually direct plain manner as essayist and philomath from the burlesque and irony that mark most of the bagatelles is dramatic proof that over the years he became master of many styles.

VIII

Autobiography

BIOGRAPHY—including autobiography—has this in common with the epic, the history play, and the historical novel, that its author "moves between the poles of poetry and history."[1] The "poetry" present in biography takes the form of informal incidents, through which the writer breathes life into the subject known to history. In Plutarch's "Life of Alexander" there occurs this passage, one that Boswell saw fit to cite near the beginning of his *Life of Samuel Johnson:* "Nor is it always in the most distinguished achievements that men's virtues or vices may be best discerned; but very often an action of small note, a short saying, or a jest, shall distinguish a person's real character more than the greatest sieges, or the most important battles." What finally elevates the *Autobiography* of Benjamin Franklin to this Plutarchian ideal are such seemingly insignificant actions as going about the streets of Boston hawking his ballads of the *Light House Tragedy* and *Teach,* saving the drunken Dutchman from

[1]Donald A. Stauffer, *The Art of Biography in Eighteenth-Century England* (Princeton, 1941), p. 11.

drowning, a wet copy of *Pilgrim's Progress* in his pocket, and his visit with a Catholic maiden lady of seventy living out her frugal existence in a London garret. The British critic who complained that the *Autobiography* contained "too many trifling details and anecdotes of obscure individuals"[2] either failed to grasp Franklin's method or simply chose to ignore it.

The eighteenth century, moving away from the medieval and Renaissance view that biography should be objective and typical, believed that, although "all men are essentially one," there are as many lives to be written as there are men who have lived.[3] Men differ more in their private than in their public character, and even when the biographer writes from a clearly defined moral or spiritual motive, it is possible for him to differentiate the particular life by including actions of small note. Autobiographical writing in colonial America, to narrow the field of vision at once, tended from the beginning toward rounded portraiture. Thomas Shepard's *Autobiography,* the earliest known example in New England, a work dedicated "To my deare son...with whom I leave these records of gods great kindnes to him not knowing that I shall live to tell them my selfe with my own mouth, that so he may learne to know & love the great & most high god: the god of his father,"[4] achieves an individuality that serves to distinguish this autobiographer from others who followed. Although Franklin never abandoned the classical stance of his youth, in respect to its greater insistence on the unique-

[2]*Edinburgh Review,* VIII (July, 1806), 344.
[3]Stauffer, *Art of Biography,* pp. 255, 166–167.
[4]*Pub. Col. Soc. Mass.,* XXVII (1930), 352.

ness of the individual the *Autobiography* is a more nearly romantic work than, say, the *Dogood* papers.

"In no branch of literature," writes Donald Stauffer, "is moral judgment more important than in biography, dealing as it must with the actions of actual men." The eighteenth century accepted "the time-honored statement that biography is of use to the reader in helping him to imitate virtue and avoid vice."[5] While "such professional didacticism seems to have grown out of the *Spectator* and the *Rambler* papers,"[6] a tradition long familiar to Franklin, another key to understanding his *Autobiography* is the much older tradition of the conduct book, more especially that species in the seventeenth and eighteenth centuries which offered parental advice. Such advice, as John Mason observes, "is entirely practical in character, and is based, not upon any academic theorizing about life, but upon a real appreciation of its actual difficulties and problems."[7] Caleb Trenchfield counsels his son, a London apprentice, in the following manner: "Green Heads are apt to think themselves the wisest.... You have this advantage then, to have that stock which hath been traded for by elder years, and those too exercised not in a few concerns: add these unto your own, and you may be as wise as if you had already lived some more years";[8] and exhorts him to cultivate such virtues as piety, veracity, fidelity, temperance, taciturnity, affability, frugality, and industry. And John Barnard prefaces his parental advice thus: "Recollecting,

[5]*Art of Biography,* pp. 309, 310.

[6]*Ibid.,* p. 314.

[7]*Gentlefolk in the Making* (Philadelphia, 1935), pp. 111–112.

[8]*A Cap of Gray Hairs for a Green Head: or, the Father's Counsel to His Son, an Apprentice in London* (4th ed.; London, 1688), p. 4.

therefore, that life is a scene of care, and prudence, generally, the child of experience and calamity, I have thought
it advisable to make you the heir of what knowledge I
am possessed of, as well as my estate; that you may be
guarded against all the snares to which youth is obnoxious
and that you may be as well provided with advice in all
exigencies, as when under my wing; or as if you had already
suffered all I would teach you to avoid."[9] It is no accident
that bound together with the 1805 edition of Barnard's
work were two essays by Franklin, "HINTS for those that
would be Rich" (1737) and "Advice to a Young Tradesman" (1748); after all, in the pages of the *Gazette* and
Almanack he had long offered Philadelphia tradesmen advice on how to conduct themselves and their affairs. He
must surely have been aware of the tradition when he began the *Autobiography* as a letter to his son, that son being
then forty and his apprenticeship ended long since; aware
of it, too, when thirteen years later he broadened his sights
and told young men in general how he had early striven
to gain moral perfection. Indeed, the *Autobiography* is
Poor Richard's Almanack writ large, this not only with
respect to the audience for whom it was finally written but
also in its frequently aphoristic expression.

The year following the publication of *The Way to
Wealth* there appeared a "Letter from Father Abraham to
His Beloved Son"; if, as seems probable, Franklin was the
author, it serves as a material link between the almanacs
and the *Autobiography*. Herein Abraham advises Isaac:

> Set apart a Portion of every Day for the Purpose of *Self-
> Examination.* . . . Observing this Course steadily for some

[9]*A Present for an Apprentice* (3rd ed.; London, 1807), pp. 9–10.

Time, you will find (through God's Grace assisting) that your Faults are continually diminishing, and your Stock of Virtue encreasing.

Then, to illustrate the maxim, "Be *really* good, if you would *appear* so," Abraham coarsely declares:

If you have a *Sir-Reverence* in your Breeches, what signifies it if you *appear* to Others neat and clean and genteel, when you *know* and *feel* yourself to be b – – – – – – – t.... Never flatter yourself with *Concealment;* 'tis impossible to last long. One Man may be too cunning for another Man, but not for *all Men:* Some Body or other will smell you out, or some Accident will discover you; and who can be sure that he shall never be heard to talk in his Sleep, or be delirious in a Fever, when the working Mind usually throws out Hints of what has inwardly affected it?[10]

I

The *Autobiography* is an unfinished work in two respects: Franklin brought his story down only to 1760, when he stood on the threshold of political greatness; and he did not live to revise even this long fragment, composed at four intervals during the last nineteen years of his life, to his final satisfaction. The bulk of the work, comprising 84 per cent, was written rapidly—Part I probably in the portions of not more than thirteen days at his disposal while a house guest in the country and Part III during the final two months of a long public career just coming to a close. For all this confident dispatch, so different were his

[10]*New-England Magazine* (Boston), I (Aug., 1758), 20–28. Jack C. Barnes, *New Eng. Quar.*, XXX (1957), 73–84, presents a convincing case for including this essay in the Franklin canon and reprints the text.

circumstances and his attitude toward the work on these two widely separated occasions that the one part reads spontaneously and the other so matter-of-factly as to sound at times like a different man writing.

It was at the home of his good friend Bishop Jonathan Shipley in late July 1771 that Franklin, "expecting a Weeks uninterrupted Leisure in my present Country Retirement," began to reminisce about the circumstances by which he rose "from the Poverty & Obscurity in which I was born & bred, to a State of Affluence & some Degree of Reputation in the World."[11] He wrote eighty-seven pages in this sunny mood before having to break off. So congenial did he find the undertaking that later, when weighed down by public duties in revolutionary Philadelphia, he told the Bishop, "How happy I was in the sweet retirement of Twyford, where my only business was a little scribbling in the garden study, and my pleasure your conversation, with that of your family!"[12]

For thirteen years Franklin had neither the time nor, apparently, the inclination to resume work on his memoirs. Then at Passy in 1784, encouraged by recent letters from Abel James, an American Quaker who then had the holo-

[11]*Par. Text. Ed.*, p. 2. In the present chapter page references to this edition will often appear in the body of the text. Jack C. Barnes, "Benjamin Franklin and His Memoirs" (unpublished dissertation, Univ. of Maryland, 1954), p. 58, explains the change in wording, from "a Weeks uninterrupted Leisure in my present Country Retirement" in the original manuscript to "a few weeks' uninterrupted leisure" in the Temple Franklin edition, by the conjecture "that Franklin did not write all of Part I at the Bishop's, but continued it while on his vacation into Scotland and Ireland that autumn."

[12]Franklin to Jonathan Shipley, Sept. 13, 1775, printed in J. L. Peyton, *Rambling Reminiscences of a Residence Abroad* (Staunton, Va., 1880), p. 288.

graph of Part I in his possession, and Benjamin Vaughan, an English friend of Franklin's who edited his political writings in 1779, Franklin returned to the work, writing another seventeen pages at this time; as he explains it, "having just now a little Leisure, I will endeavour to recollect & write what I can; If I live to get home, it may there be corrected and improv'd" (p. 198). It is clear that he did not wish his story to be made public at this time. When Mathew Carey sought permission in 1786 to publish an account of his life in the *Columbian Magazine,* making use of materials in Part I, Franklin dissuaded him: "The Memoirs you mention would be of little or no Use to your Scheme, as they contain only some Notes of my early Life, and finish in 1730. They were written to my Son, and intended only as Information to my Family. I have in hand a full Acc^t of my Life which I propose to leave behind me; in the meantime I wish nothing of the kind may be published, and shall be much oblig'd to the Proprietors of the Columbian Magazine if they will drop that Intention, for the present."[13]

Although Franklin's pen was not idle during the voyage to America in 1785, he did not work on his memoirs at that time. Nor did he find time back home, being elected

[13]Franklin to Carey, Aug. 10, 1786, Smyth, IX, 533–534. After Franklin's death Carey received Temple's permission to make extracts from the holograph of the *Autobiography.* The "authentic sketches of the life of dr. Franklin," which Carey published in the *American Museum,* VIII (July, 1790), 12–20, constitutes a synopsis that omits most of the actions of small note and proportions the narrative more evenly than Franklin himself had seen fit to do. A briefer sketch in the November, 1790, issue continues Franklin's story from 1760 (where Part IV breaks off) down to the time of his death.

President of Pennsylvania three years in succession and serving as delegate to the Constitutional Convention. He was able to return to it only in August 1788. Now in possession of the holograph of Part I again, he went forward with the writing so rapidly that by October he had come as far as his fiftieth year. "I expect to have it finished in about two months," he informs Le Veillard, "if illness or some unforeseen interruption does not prevent. I do not therefore send a part at this time, thinking it better to retain the whole till I can view it all together, and make the proper corrections."[14] The text of Part III, totaling 108½ pages, makes it clear that he was then confident of carrying the story well beyond this point in his life.[15] But severe and prolonged illness lay ahead, a fact he records in a despairing letter to Le Veillard the following September: "I have a long time been afflicted with almost constant and grievous Pain, to combat which I have been obliged to have recourse to Opium, which indeed has afforded me some Ease from time to time, but then it has taken away my Appetite and so impeded my Digestion that I am become totally emaciated, and little remains of me but a Skeleton covered with a Skin. In this Situation I have not been able to continue my Memoirs, and

[14]Smyth, IX, 673.

[15]For example, alluding to his appointment in 1753 as Deputy Postmaster General, Franklin writes, "But it soon after began to repay us, and before I was displac'd, by a Freak of the Minister's, of which I shall speak hereafter, we had brought it to yield *three times* as much clear Revenue to the Crown as the Post-Office of Ireland" (p. 324). He was, of course, dismissed from this office on Jan. 31, 1774, fourteen years after the date at which the narrative of his life breaks off in Part IV.

now I suppose I shall never finish them."[16] With his grand-son Benny Bache serving as amanuensis, he managed dur-ing 1789 to prepare the "fair copies" long promised to Le Veillard and Vaughan, embodying in them the changes he had made in Parts I–III.[17] These copies went off to France and England early in November, and with them a request that they—Le Veillard and La Rochefoucauld in France, Vaughan and Price in England—read and criticize the copies, suggest alterations, and pronounce the work fit for publication or not. "I shall rely upon your opinions," he confesses to Vaughan, "for I am now grown so old and feeble in mind, as well as body, that I cannot place any confidence in my own judgment."[18] During the five months of life still left to him Franklin added seven and one-half pages, constituting Part IV, to his memoirs and further revised what he had written to date.[19]

[16]Smyth, X, 35.

[17]It is difficult to accept Donald Mugridge's charge, in *Wm. and Mary Quar.*, ser. 3, VI (1949), 653–654, that Benny Bache, as he prepared the Le Veillard fair copy, reworked the original manu-script without his grandfather's knowledge. In view of the importance Franklin attached to the preparation of these copies, it is unlikely that he would have passed them on unread to Vaughan and Le Veillard.

[18]Smyth, X, 50.

[19]A careful examination of the original manuscript reveals that more than a dozen of the insertions made in Parts I–III and noted by Farrand are in the trembling hand that characterizes Part IV: "considerable" (p. 2), "hot" (p. 88), "23ᵈ" and "11th" (p. 128), "under the Title of the Busy Body" (p. 160), "Months" (p. 160), "In-sert these Remarks in a Note" (p. 160), "in a few Years" (p. 160), "at Philadelphia" (p. 174), "by me" (p. 180), "or thought I knew" (p. 210), "my remaining" (p. 216), "exactly" (p. 226), and "a while" (p. 276).

The original manuscript, totaling 220 pages, survives and is now located at the Huntington Library; the fair copies, which seem to have incorporated further revisions not made in the holograph, are lost. Consequently we cannot be certain what Franklin's final intention was. An attempt in 1949 to "restore" the fair-copy text proved unsuccessful.[20]

II

"To instruct and to amuse are the two grand objects intended by authors," declared Henry Stüber in the Preface to his "History of the life and character of Dr. Franklin." "Writings, which combine the useful with the pleasing, are, therefore, the most acceptable, and the most beneficial. It is, perhaps, for this reason, that Biography has been a favourite species of writing in all ages, and in all countries. The life of most men affords something to amuse; and the history of their vices and their virtues, and the consequences of them, will excite us to avoid the one, and to imitate the other."[21] This characteristically eighteenth-century statement of the purpose of biography helps explain the interest in Franklin's *Autobiography*

[20]See *The Autobiography of Benjamin Franklin: A Restoration of a "Fair Copy,"* ed. Max Farrand (San Marino, California, 1949). Farrand, who died in 1945, was responsible only for Part I, and the edition was completed at the Huntington Library under the supervision of Godfrey Davies; in a searching review-article in *Mod. Phil.*, XLVII (1949), 127–134, Verner Crane discusses what he finds to be its most serious shortcomings.

[21]*Universal Asylum and Columbian Magazine* (Philadelphia), IV (May, 1790), 268. Barnes, "Memoirs," p. 123, conjectures that Stüber had access to Part I of the original manuscript while it "was in the hands of Abel James, the Quaker merchant, between 1782 and 1785."

even during his lifetime and the rush after his death to bring out French, English, and American editions of this work and other accounts of his life.

Franklin the autobiographer thought of himself first as a moralist. Convinced that posterity may wish to know how he, God willing, rose from poverty and obscurity to affluence and reputation, he selects episodes in his early life which point a moral. Thus, as one of several boys apprehended for building a wharf with stones intended for a new house, he argues the usefulness of the work until convinced by his father that "nothing was useful which was not honest" (p. 22). Mindful of the subsequent conduct of the strumpets against whom a Quaker matron had warned him on the voyage from Newport to New York, he concludes, "So tho' we had escap'd a sunken Rock which we scrap'd upon in the Passage, I thought this Escape of rather more Importance to me" (p. 80). When finally disabused of Keith's show of good faith, he observes, "But what shall we think of a Governor's playing such pitiful Tricks, & imposing so grossly on a poor ignorant Boy!" (p. 106). He underscores the description of his busy life at Keimer's print shop thus: "I mentioned this Industry the more particularly and the more freely, tho' it seems to be talking in my own Praise, that those of my Posterity who shall read it, may know the Use of that Virtue, when they see its Effects in my Favor throughout this Relation" (p. 158). In other words, although ostensibly Franklin is writing for his son William, before he is very far into his story it is evident that he also wishes to instruct both young men now living and those not yet born in the art of virtue.

This fact is confirmed by the two letters that Franklin asked be inserted between Parts I and II. Abel James, having come into possession of the holograph of Part I during the Revolution ("about 23 Sheets in thy own hand-writing"), finds it "a Work which would be useful & entertaining not only to a few, but to millions," and hopes that it will be published. "I know of no Character living nor many of them put together," he declares, mentioning several of the virtues Franklin had stressed, "who has so much in his Power as Thyself to promote a greater Spirit of Industry & early Attention to Business, Frugality and Temperance with the American Youth." Benjamin Vaughan, too, though he had seen only James's letter and the outline Franklin drew up in 1771, had such confidence in the usefulness of the work that he urged Franklin to carry it forward. He assures Franklin that other reasons are insignificant,

> compared with the chance which your life will give for the forming of future great men; and...of improving the features of private character, and consequently of aiding all happiness both public and domestic.... The nearest thing to having experience of one's own, is to have other people's affairs brought before us in a shape that is interesting; this is sure to happen from your pen.

Vaughan then alludes to the state of contemporary biographical writing:

> This style of writing seems a little gone out of vogue, and yet it is a very useful one; and your specimen of it may be particularly serviceable, as it will make a subject of comparison with the lives of various public cut-throats and intriguers, and with absurd monastic self-tormentors, or vain literary triflers. If it encourages more writings of the same kind with your own, and induces more men to spend

lives fit to be written; it will be worth all Plutarch's Lives put together.

He therefore exhorts Franklin:

> Extend your views even further; do not stop at those who speak the English tongue, but after having settled so many points in nature and politics, think of bettering the whole race of men.

Franklin's passionate pursuit of the art of virtue now spurred by such enthusiastic encouragement, small wonder that when he resumed work on his memoirs in 1784 he was more explicitly the moralist than before. Having early had his attention turned "to what was good, just, & prudent in the Conduct of Life" (p. 24), he now describes "the bold and arduous Project of arriving at moral Perfection" he conceived as a youth (p. 210), in the hope "that some of my Descendants may follow the Example & reap the Benefit" (p. 230).

Learning from Le Veillard that the *Autobiography* would be finished shortly, La Rochefoucauld wrote Franklin on July 12, 1788: "What a precious monument this memoir must be.... It will be a gift most dear to your friends, who will always pray that the last chapter of a life so valuable to humanity may have the longest possible extent."[22] Franklin replied that he had completed the work down to his fiftieth year; then, in a statement that relates the *Autobiography* to the tradition of the conduct book, he adds, "It seems to me that what is done will be of more general Use to young Readers; as exemplifying strongly the Effects of prudent and imprudent Conduct in the Commencement of a Life of Business."[23] In a letter of October

[22]Bigelow, XI, 435–436.   [23]Smyth, IX, 665.

24, 1788, Franklin tells Vaughan his criterion for decid-
ing what material to include in Part III, on which he
was then hard at work:

> To shorten the work, as well as for other reasons, I omit all
> facts and transactions, that may not have a tendency to
> benefit the young reader, by showing him from my example,
> and my success in emerging from poverty, and acquiring
> some degree of wealth, power, and reputation, the advantages
> of certain modes of conduct which I observed, and of avoid-
> ing the errors which were prejudicial to me. If a writer
> can judge properly of his own work, I fancy, on reading
> over what is already done, that the book will be found en-
> tertaining, interesting, and useful, more so than I ex-
> pected when I began it.

Previously Franklin had outlined his course for system-
atically cultivating thirteen virtues. Continuing in this
vein, he now urges young printers to preserve a free press
(p. 246), recommends to young women the value of "the
Knowledge of Accompts" in the event that they are
widowed (p. 248), advises that young men "always render
Accounts & make Remittances with Great Clearness and
Punctuality" (p. 260), and warns all those who would enter
into partnerships to have set down in writing "every thing
to be done by or expected from each Partner" (p. 276).
Even so, he is here writing less didactically than he had
in 1784. The plain fact is that the account of his early struggle to transcend the poverty and obscurity in which he was
born was the most instructive part of his story, especially
to young men bent on making their mark in the world.

In addition to such didactic elements there is much in
the *Autobiography* to amuse, though quite properly the
humor is never so witty nor so vulgar as it is elsewhere in

his writings. Sometimes the humor is situational, as when he calls the Quaker meetinghouse he entered that first Sunday morning "the first House I was in or slept in, in Philadelphia" (p. 64); or when he charges that his friend Osborne, now dead, defaulted on their agreement that "the one who happen'd first to die, should if possible make a friendly Visit to the other, and acquaint him how he found things in that Separate State" (p. 98). More often, though, it is verbal. Thus, having broken his "Resolution of not eating animal Food" by dining heartily upon cod, he recollects that "when the Fish were opened, I saw smaller Fish taken out of their Stomachs: Then thought I, if you eat one another, I don't see why we mayn't eat you." "So convenient a thing it is," he adds, "to be a *reasonable Creature,* since it enables one to find or make a Reason for every thing one has a mind to do" (p.88). At Watts's printing house in London, Franklin drank only water whereas the other workmen drank beer. "On occasion I carried up & down Stairs a large Form of Types in each hand, when others carried but one in both Hands. They wonder'd to see from this & several Instances, that the water-American as they call'd me was *stronger* than themselves who drank *strong* Beer" (p. 114). Franklin describes how the equivocal Quakers in the Pennsylvania Assembly so far reconciled their inbred pacifism with the necessity for colonial defense in 1745 as to vote Governor Thomas £3000 "for the Purchasing of Bread, Flour, Wheat, *or other Grain,*" it being clearly understood by all parties that *"other Grain"* meant gunpowder. Slyly he remarks, "It was in Allusion to this Fact, that when in our Fire Company we feared the Success of our Proposal in favour of the Lottery, & I had said to my Friend Mr Syng, one of

our Members, if we fail, let us move the Purchase of a Fire
Engine with the Money; the Quakers can have no Objection to that: and then if you nominate me, and I you,
as a Committee for that purpose, we will buy a great Gun,
which is certainly a *Fire-Engine*" (p. 290).

Nevertheless, readers of the *Autobiography*, drawn to it
by the example of Franklin's life, admired the work first of
all for the instruction it contained. In the 1790's Dr.
Cabanis, who as a member of Mme Helvétius' immediate
circle had heard Franklin relate boyhood experiences like
the story of the whistle, wrote a biographical sketch of his
American friend, of which the underlying theme is, *"Sa
personne valait bien mieux encore que sa gloire."*[24] Even
if, as Aldridge thinks, Cabanis "sees essentially what Franklin had taught him to look for,"[25] still his sketch throws
light on the *Autobiography*. It explains why, for example,
Franklin gave so full an account of his first London visit.

No period in his life [writes Cabanis] is more decisive for
the happiness of the rest. One cannot dwell too much on
the dangers which encompass him, even in a generally prudent and reasonable system of conduct; and nothing is more
instructive than that which shows clearly the road to follow
in order not to go astray. . . . He was conscious of his errors
and resolved to make amends for them. Therefore, he
leaves London and returns to Philadelphia. From this
moment one can date the philosophy of life from which
he never afterwards departed; from this moment he stops
groping like a young man. He sees clearly the purpose and
the way and never turns aside from it for a single moment.[26]

[24]*Oeuvres posthumes de Cabanis*, V, 221.
[25]*Franklin and His French Contemporaries*, p. 203.
[26]*Oeuvres posthumes de Cabanis*, V, 228, 230. In the same vein

If the reader is inclined to question the validity of Cabanis' inference, let it be recalled that, by Franklin's own account, not long after the appearance of his *Dissertation on Liberty and Necessity,* wherein "Vice & Virtue were empty Distinctions," "I grew convinc'd that *Truth, Sincerity & Integrity* in Dealings between Man & Man, were of the utmost Importance to the Felicity of Life," and thanked God for having "preserved me (thro' this dangerous Time of Youth & the hazardous Situations I was sometimes in among Strangers, remote from the Eye & Advice of my Father)" (pp. 146–148).

III

Franklin seems clearly to have conceived of the *Autobiography* as lying at the center of a longer, perhaps much longer, autobiographical work, which was to encompass at least four other writings: "Journal of occurrences in my voyage to Philadelphia on board the Berkshire, Henry Clark Master, from London," July 22–October 11, 1726, to which the reader is referred (p. 128); "Articles of Belief and Acts of Religion," November 20, 1728 (alluded to on p. 210); "An Account of Negotiations in London for Effecting a Reconciliation between Great Britain and the American Colonies," written on board ship March 22, 1775, as a letter to his son;[27] and "The Art of Virtue," a project first mentioned in 1726 and many times there-

---

Parton, *Franklin,* II, 642, writes, "From the manifold perils of his London life, his inherited good sense and his early good habits barely sufficed to deliver him."

[27]Smyth, VI, 318–399. In his Outline, Franklin calls it "Negociation to prevent the War," *Par. Text Ed.,* p. 422.

after but never written. Although "the *Plan*... for regulating my future Conduct in Life," mentioned in the *Autobiography* as being part of the "Journal" of 1726 (p. 128), does not appear in the surviving holograph, this is clearly a reference to the oft-mentioned "Art of Virtue." All that survive, unless one regards his account of the plan for arriving at moral perfection as the germ of this projected book, are "the preamble and heads."[28] Vaughan referred to it as a work that might profitably be published with the *Autobiography*.[29] Franklin's most precise description of it there occurs in a passage following his discussion of the thirteen virtues: "I purposed writing a little Comment on each Virtue, in which I would have shown the Advantages of possessing it, & the Mischiefs attending its opposite Vice; and I should have called my Book the ART *of Virtue*."[30] The fact that Franklin considered these four fragments integral parts of a larger autobiography emphasizes anew how unfinished and fragmentary a work his most ambitious literary undertaking is.[31]

[28]Labaree, I, 99–100.

[29]See his letter of Jan. 31, 1783, in *Par. Text Ed.,* p. 188, and that of Mar. 4, 1789, printed in Bigelow, XII, 69.

[30]*Par. Text Ed.,* p. 232. For a more detailed description, see his letter of May 3, 1760, to Kames, in Smyth, IV, 12–14.

[31]Still other fragmentary journals, which Franklin kept in the final years of his life, have been regarded by some scholars, Barnes for one, as parts of the longer autobiography he did not live to complete, notably those for Dec. 13, 1778 (an extract); Oct. 4, 1778–Jan. 16, 1780 (notes on his health); Feb. 14–24, 1779 (a political journal); Dec. 18, 1780–Jan. 29, 1781 (the same); June 26–July 27, 1784 (the same); July 12–Sept. 14, 1785 (a record of a voyage). These texts appear in *Autobiographical Writings,* pp. 460–461, 455–457, 462–463, 494–500, 605–612, 650–654.

And yet, as Verner Crane rightly observes, "In its main character and, indeed, in most of its content, Franklin's history of his life had been planned from the beginning."[32] The Morgan copy of the Outline, the one Franklin had in all probability "written right through during the holiday at Twyford" down to the topic "Hutchinson's Letters,"[33] enumerates the important episodes in nearly the order they are taken up in the *Autobiography*, though understandably enough it fails to list many of the actions of small note that impart individuality to the work, especially in Part I. It seems reasonable to assume, therefore, that had Franklin continued well enough to carry his history beyond 1760, he would have been guided at all important points by his outline and would eventually have attempted to assemble and integrate all the fragments of his projected autobiography.

In contrast to the tighter, more logical organization Franklin imposed on the letter to the press and the bagatelle, his method here is loose and discursive. "By my rambling Digressions," he remarks, having interrupted the account of his early boyhood to characterize his father and mother, "I perceive my self to be grown old. I us'd to write more methodically. But one does not dress for private Company as for a publick Ball. 'Tis perhaps only Negligence" (p. 26). The *Autobiography* is essentially a private writing, and the reader accepts negligence here that he would not in more public writings like the letter to the press. This is not to say that Franklin neglected method in

[32] *Mod. Phil.*, XLVII, 129.

[33] *Loc. cit.* The Morgan copy of the Outline appears in *Par. Text Ed.*, pp. 419–422.

this instance; after all, before commencing to write he took time to set down short hints, just as he would later urge Vaughan to do. While the *Autobiography* is unfinished, its formal components, down to syntactical arrangement, observe a logical though loose order.

A central problem in all literary undertakings, and one that the biographer has special difficulty in surmounting, is how to bring order and unity out of the chaos of human events. Beyond being guided throughout by a topical and roughly chronological outline Franklin succeeds in structuring only the first part of the *Autobiography* at all tightly. "That Felicity, when I reflected on it," he announces in the opening paragraph, "has induc'd me sometimes to say, that were it offer'd to my Choice, I should have no Objection to a Repetition of the same Life from its Beginning, only asking the Advantages Authors have in a second Edition to correct some Faults of the first." The erratum trope, introduced at this point though not yet named, must have suggested itself naturally to one who always thought of himself as a printer; it was not the first time he had employed it, nor was it to be the last.[34] He describes five episodes in Part I as errata—running out on the secret indenture his brother James had drawn up with him, breaking into Vernon's money, writing Deborah only once from London, printing *A Dissertation on Liberty and Necessity,* and attempting familiarities with Ralph's milliner friend—but fails to carry the trope beyond this point, except to remark how he made amends for all but the last of these faults.[35]

[34]See *Almanack* verses for Dec., 1737; Smyth, IX, 334; X, 4.
[35]See *Par. Text Ed.,* pp. 50, 86, 108, 112, 146, 164, 180, 254.

Franklin, as has been said, did not live to view the *Autobiography* "all together, and make the proper corrections." It seems probable that among surviving texts the one that comes closest to representing his final intention is that edited by William Temple Franklin, supplemented by Part IV of the original manuscript (see the Appendix). A comparison of the Temple Franklin version with the original manuscript for Parts I–III reveals many instances in which Benjamin Franklin made deletions and additions, reshaped the syntax, and altered diction; the great majority of these changes occur in Part I, which he revised extensively after 1785. He deletes some expressions that later seemed to him redundant or obvious: "I was employed to carry the papers [thro' the Streets] to the customers"; or unnecessarily explicit: "There was a [Saw] mill near, round which were left several pine boards."[36] On occasion he deletes qualifying statements, details, and general observations.[37] Elsewhere he makes additions in the interest of being more explicit: "I was suspected to be some runaway *indentured* servant" (pp. 56–58); and of intensifying statements: "From my infancy [a Child] I was *passionately* fond of reading" (p. 28). At least once he supplies a conclusion based on earlier evidence. Having described how his brother James lorded it over him at the *Courant* office, he added at a later date, "Perhaps this harsh and tyrannical treatment of me, might be a means of impressing me with the aversion to arbitrary power, that has stuck to me through my whole life" (p. 48). It is more than likely

[36]*Par. Text Ed.,* pp. 46, 366. Words he deleted are placed in brackets; those he added appear between asterisks.

[37]See *Par. Text Ed.,* pp. 38, 40, 42, 46, 62, 78, 80, 96, 160, 166, 266, 408.

that the discourtesies he suffered under the North Ministry during the final years of his agency and his diplomatic struggles in the cause of American independence, culminating in the peace negotiations of 1782–1783, brought home to him all the more forcefully the meaning of tyranny and prompted this afterthought, which he added with a different wording in the margin of the original manuscript. No definite conclusions can be drawn from these and like examples, but it can be said that in general a concern for greater perspicuity prompted such deletions and additions.

Although Franklin frequently reshaped the original syntax, the changes do not always mark an improvement. For example:

Original MS	*William Temple Franklin*
In 1751. Dr Thomas Bond, a particular Friend of mine, conceiv'd the Idea of establishing a Hospital in Philadelphia, for the Reception and Cure of poor sick Persons, whether Inhabitants of the Province or Strangers. A very beneficent Design, which has been ascrib'd to me, but was originally his.	In 1751, Dr. Thomas Bond, a particular friend of mine, conceived the idea of establishing a hospital in Philadelphia, (a very beneficent design, which has been ascribed to me, but was originally and truly his) for the reception and cure of poor sick persons, whether inhabitants of the province or strangers. [p. 306]

In the Temple Franklin version the fragment emphasizing the beneficence of the plan for the Pennsylvania Hospital is clumsily imbedded in the sentence as a parenthetical insertion. In defense of this change, however, it can be said that, though the elimination of the fragment seems clearly a bowing to the ideal of syntactical completeness, the resulting shift of emphasis helps direct attention at the outset to what is after all the topic of the paragraph, Bond's effort to implement his proposal. Elsewhere the revision of a passage describing Peter Folger's *Looking Glass for the Times* involves a sacrifice.

Original MS	*WTF*
It was written in 1675, in the homespun Verse of that Time & People, and address'd to those then concern'd in the Government there. It was in favour of Liberty of Conscience, & in behalf of the Baptists, Quakers, & other Sectaries, that had been under Persecution; ascribing the Indian Wars & other Distresses, that had befallen the Country to that Persecution, as so many Judgments of God, to punish so heinous an Offence; and exhorting a Repeal of those uncharitable Laws.	It was written in 1675. It was in familiar verse, according to the taste of the times and people; and addressed to the government there. It asserts the liberty of conscience, in behalf of the Anabaptists, the Quakers, and other sectaries, that had been persecuted. He attributes to this persecution, the Indian wars, and other calamities that had befallen the country: regarding them as so many judgments of God to punish so heinous an offence, and exhorting the repeal of those laws, so contrary to charity, [pp. 16–18]

Breaking two sentences into four results in a choppy, less natural movement. If such revision were carried to its logical conclusion, "exhorting" would have to be made a finite verb too, though to do this would produce a still choppier effect.

In most cases, though, Franklin improved the syntax in revising it, being guided by his early conviction that "a too frequent Use of Phrases...[makes] the Meaning obscure to a great number of English Readers."[38] In the following two passages he revises in the direction of better ordered sentence construction.

Original MS	*WTF*
From these Notes I learnt that the Family had liv'd in the same Village, Ecton in Northamptonshire, for 300 Years, & how much longer he knew not (perhaps from the Time when the Name *Franklin* that before was the Name of an Order of People, was assum'd by them for a Surname, when others took Surnames all over the Kingdom.—(Here a Note) on a Freehold of about 30 Acres, aided by the Smith's Business which had continued in the Family till his Time, the eldest Son being always bred to that Business. A Custom which he & my Father both followed as to their eldest Sons.	From these notes I learnt that they lived in the same village, Ecton in Northamptonshire, on a freehold of about thirty acres, for at least three hundred years, and how much longer could not be ascertained. This small estate would not have sufficed for their maintenance without the business of a smith, which had continued in the family down to my uncle's time, the eldest son being always brought up to that employment: a custom which he and my father followed with regard to their eldest sons. [p. 6]

The first sentence in the original straggles to a close, and there is no compelling reason why the idea in the second

[38]Labaree, I, 329.

should be emphasized. In the Temple Franklin version the parts are more logically ordered: the break between the sentences, emphasized by starting a new paragraph, comes at a logical point, and balance between the sentences is achieved. The second passage reads:

Original MS	WTF
But my Father in the mean time, from a View of the Expence of a College Education which, having so large a Family, he could not well afford, and the mean Living many so educated were afterwards able to obtain, Reasons that he gave to his Friends in my Hearing, altered his first Intention, took me from the Grammar School, and sent me to a School for Writing & Arithmetic kept by a then famous Man, Mr Geo. Brownell, very successful in his Profession generally, and that by mild encouraging Methods.	But my father, burdened with a numerous family, was unable without inconvenience to support the expense of a college education: considering moreover, as he said to one of his friends in my presence, the little encouragement that line of life afforded to those educated for it; he gave up his first intentions, took me from the grammar-school, and sent me to a school for writing and arithmetic, kept by a then famous man, Mr. George Brownwell [sic]. He was a skilful master, and successful in his profession, employing the mildest and most encouraging methods. [pp. 18–20]

The original version, consisting of a single loose sentence, makes use of a long, interrupting substantive construction ("and the mean Living. . . in my Hearing") and rambles to an unemphatic close. In the Temple Franklin version the first sentence moves forward more naturally and clearly, and a second is formed to set off and point up Brownell's abilities as a schoolmaster.

Another passage, describing young Franklin's first entry into Philadelphia, achieves proper emphasis in its revised form.

Original MS	*WTF*
I was dirty from my Journey; my Pockets were stuff'd out with Shirts & Stockings; I knew no Soul, nor where to look for Lodging. I was fatigued with Travelling, Rowing & Want of Rest. I was very hungry, and my whole Stock of Cash consisted of a Dutch Dollar and about a Shilling in Copper. The latter I gave the People of the Boat for my Passage, who at first refus'd it on Acc^t of my Rowing; but I insisted on their taking it, a Man being sometimes more generous when he has but a little Money than when he has plenty, perhaps thro' Fear of being thought to have but little.	I was dirty from my being so long in the boat: my pockets were stuffed out with shirts and stockings, and I knew no one nor where to look for lodging. Fatigued with walking, rowing, and the want of sleep, I was very hungry, and my whole stock of cash consisted in a single dollar, and about a shilling in copper coin which I gave to the boatmen, for my passage. At first they refused it, on account of my having rowed, but I insisted on their taking it. Man is sometimes more generous when he has little money, than when he has plenty, perhaps to prevent his being thought to have but little. [pp. 60–62]

In the original version the first three sentences are quite short and begin monotonously "I was." In the Temple Franklin version the second sentence successfully combines

sentences two and three of the original, and, what is more
effective still, the fourth sentence sets off the aphorism
about man and generosity. Although again the evidence is
inconclusive, generally speaking Franklin undertook syntactical revision in an effort to achieve complete sentence
forms, logical movement, and proper emphasis.

Assenting to the majority opinion in eighteenth-century
England, Franklin increasingly preferred language which,
in the words of George Campbell, is "reputable, national,
and present." An inspection of the revisions in the original
manuscript noted by Farrand makes it clear that Franklin
came to favor the more reputable expression over the more
colloquial: "a very (mighty) little"; "Stephen (Steve)
Potts"; "Oeconomist (Manager)"; "you will soon work
(worm) this Man out of his Business"; "conceiv'd
(thought)"; "I said (Then says I)"; "she prov'd a good &
faithful Helpmate, assisted me much (a good wife, helped
me much)"; "in [most] other Countries"; "Discourse (Conversation)"; "Explications (our attempts to explain)";
"Communicating Instructions (spreading useful Knowledge among)"; "acknowledg'd (own'd)"; "reduc't it to Mud
[or Slush]"; "din'd (supp'd)"; "a Ship is form'd, fitted for
the Sea (is built, and rigg)."[39] Similarly the changes in the
Temple Franklin version frequently result in a less colloquial expression: "[most] probably a very bad" poet;
"I made (cut) so miserable a figure"; "Keimer stared with
astonishment (like a Pig poison'd)"; Collins "had acquired
a habit of drinking of brandy (Sotting with Brandy)"; the

[39]*Par. Text Ed.*, pp. 120, 132, 136, 144, 170, 176, 180, 202, 208, 244,
250, 316, 332, 406. The original wording here and in subsequent
examples appears in parentheses; words deleted are placed in
brackets.

workmen at Watts's "were great drinkers (Guzzlers) of beer"; Keimer, receiving a large sum for some job printing at Burlington, "was enabled thereby to keep himself longer from ruin (to keep his Head much longer above Water)"; Keimer "was an odd creature (Fish)"; "I went on prosperously (swimmingly)."[40] Still other changes in the Temple Franklin version produce euphemism: "had an intrigue with a girl of bad character (got a naughty Girl with Child)"; "I clapt my hand under his thighs (Crutch), and rising, pitched him head foremost into the river."[41] An examination of the Temple Franklin version side by side with the original manuscript reveals, moreover, the substitution of current words for archaic, notably "dollar" for "Piece of Eight,"[42] and the excision of provincialisms: "boats (Canoes)"; "provisions (Victuals)"; "Our supper was only half an anchovy each, on a very little slice (Strip) of bread and butter"; reading a book "was seldom, was private (snug), and gave no scandal"; "twelve hundred signatures (Hands)"; the merchants were uneasy about the orders they had given "for autumnal (Fall) goods"; "theatre (Play-house)."[43] Such revisions in diction have the effect of "purifying" the initial wording of the *Autobiography* and cast serious doubt on McMaster's assertion, "It is impossible to believe that Franklin, who formed his style by a study of the Spectator, ever hesitated to use plain English."[44]

[40]*Par. Text Ed.,* pp. 32, 56, 72, 82, 114, 142, 174.

[41]*Par. Text Ed.,* pp. 52, 84.

[42]*Par. Text Ed.,* p. 76. On July 6, 1785, Congress formally adopted the dollar.

[43]*Par. Text. Ed.,* pp. 56, 90, 120, 172, 278, 396, 410.

[44]*Franklin as a Man of Letters,* p. 268.

As in the case of the syntax, so with the diction many of the changes in the Temple Franklin version were undertaken in the interest of greater perspicuity. Benjamin Franklin strives to be more precise: "some trifling (little) jobs"; "So we dropped anchor, and swung out our cable (swung round) towards the shore"; Collins, who was drunk every day, "behaved himself in a very extravagant manner (very oddly)"; an idea "originating (arising) in each of" the Clubs.[45] And more explicit: Collins "undertook to manage my flight (a little for me)"; "Italian, and Latin (Italian &c.)"; Dr. Spence came "to lecture in Philadelphia (here)."[46] Had he been able to press ahead with his memoirs it seems certain that he would have continued to revise the work and brought it still more nearly into conformity with his understanding of neoclassic ideals.

In calling the *Autobiography* "an American Pilgrim's Progress," Charles Sanford misrepresents the author's purpose.[47] Although Franklin had read Bunyan's work and admired it, he was instinctively suspicious of the allegorical method Sanford professes to find operating (consciously or unconsciously) in the *Autobiography*. The analogy Sanford draws between the "confessed *errata*" and "Christian's bundle of sins" is basically unsound, and one has the uncomfortable feeling that an interpretation is being imposed on Franklin's private history that seriously distorts its form and meaning. When all is said and done, the *Autobiography* remains a discursive, unfinished personal narrative; didactic, yes, but one whose parts were never, like *Pilgrim's Progress,* ordered to the author's final satis-

[45]*Par. Text Ed.,* pp. 28, 54–56, 82, 262.
[46]*Par. Text Ed.,* pp. 52, 254, 300.
[47]*Am. Quar.,* VI (Winter, 1955), 297–310.

faction. A fairer judgment on the work than Sanford's is the one La Rochefoucauld pronounced shortly after Franklin's death: "In it, he speaks of himself as he would have spoken of another. He traces his thoughts, his actions, and even his errors and his faults. He portrays the development of his genius and of his talents with the sentiment of a clear conscience which has never had to reproach itself."[48]

[48]"*Hommage rendu par le voeu unanime de la société de 1789 à Benjamin Franklin, objet de l'admiration et des regrets des amies de la liberté,*" *Journal de la Société de 1789*, VIII (June 19, 1790), quoted in Aldridge, *Franklin and His French Contemporaries*, p. 158.

IX

Conclusion

BENJAMIN FRANKLIN, while sharing the colonial attitude that *utile* is more important than *dulce,* was wise and humane enough to sweeten and even conceal his utilitarian purpose so that his prose might entertain the reader at the same time that it educated him. He employs such a strategy openly in the familiar letters and the bagatelles, of course, but he is likely to color even his more artless work, the *Autobiography* for a notable example, with trope, aphorism, anecdote, dialogue, and verbal and situational humor and make it more pleasing than if his purpose had been only to point a moral. The reader who fails to recognize that Franklin usually adorned his writings is likely to miss the point of them; if, for example, he equates Richard Saunders' morality with Franklin's, he will never see that the developing characters of Richard and Bridget and the running battle between them invigorates what would otherwise have been pedestrian if highly moral prose. Granted that Franklin late in life declared, "Prose Writing...was a principal Means of my Advancement," a surer index of his greatness as a writer is this desire and ability to disguise the end he has in view.

From the outset of his literary career Franklin cultivated types of prose that were readily publishable in issues of the eighteenth-century press. He was following a fashion to which his reading and apprenticeship led him when he undertook the *Dogood* papers in his brother's newspaper at Boston, and because the periodical essay continued to enjoy a vogue he was soon favoring Philadelphians with more such productions. The fact that the matter and manner of the essay had already been fixed by English convention proved fortunate, for it enabled him to begin to control and mature his literary expression while working within a well-defined tradition. He did not hesitate to venture beyond conventional limits, however, when it suited his purpose to do so—witness the colloquial American flavor of Silence Dogood's speech and the Busy-Body's reflections on those who search for imaginary hidden treasure.

Another kind of press issue in colonial times, one just as clearly defined as the essay and second only to the Bible in popularity, was the almanac. To enliven its pages and also to promote sales, Franklin created and sustained the character of Poor Richard, ridiculed astrology, and reshaped the sayings he had mined in proverb collections. His almanacs, like his essays, are social in emphasis; well he knew that these types of writing were traditionally too light to be put to political, religious, or philosophical use. But because he sometimes chose to engage in such weighty discourse, he may be seen in the Philadelphia years (1723–1757) wearing two hats, as it were, composing essays and almanacs in a sunny, nonpartisan mood while engaging in polemic in editorials and pamphlets.

During the years of his London agency (1757–1762,

1764–1775) the vehicle that best served his impulse to write was again the newspaper; this time, however, because the fate of the colonies, not merely provincial manners and morality, was at stake, he employed a polemic style. In a succession of letters to the English press the persona, which in his essays and almanacs at Boston and Philadelphia had been confined to such domestic types as the widow and artisan, assumed the darker color of impartial historian and modest proposer. Franklin was well acquainted with the temper of both England and America and strove resourcefully and eloquently, but finally in vain, to heal the breach between them before it became permanent.

While Franklin's official correspondence and those State Papers in which he had a hand have been judged to lie outside the scope of this study, it should be remarked here that whereas his diplomatic missions in England ended in failure, he was successful at home and in France. A command of intricate detail, an understanding of men and affairs broad enough to transcend regional and even national differences of opinion, and unfailing perspicuity of expression were talents he brought into full play as the revolutionary documents of the Second Continental Congress, the American Embassy in Paris, and the Constitutional Convention took shape. In these final years in public office (1775–1788) he put the various skills gained through half a century of journalism to work in the cause of independence and confederation.

At the center of Franklin's private writings stands the letter, a type of prose more highly regarded in the eighteenth century than it is today. Although letter writing was a lifelong pursuit, he engaged in it more steadily and heavily from the middle years of his life, bringing to what was often a congenial pastime a relaxed conversational tone, aptness of rhetorical figure and trope, and copiousness of subject. The number and variety of his personal letters to men and women of widely differing temperament and taste and the eagerness with which they responded suggest how nearly he mastered the epistolary art. The familiar letter is a more demanding type than the personal because its studied manner requires artifice; in it spontaneity gives way to self-consciousness and metaphor is teased into conceit. The bagatelle, often epistolary in form, is a more self-conscious production still, one usually meant for publication; its rhetorical strategy is more indirect, frequently tending toward burlesque and irony. Of course, the individual familiar letters and bagatelles addressed to such correspondents as Mmes Brillon and Helvétius ought finally to be viewed as epistolary gambits in a larger literary strategy.

In those works that are immediately autobiographical Franklin writes a largely unself-conscious prose. Like the personal letter, autobiography is colloquial and spontaneous. At least the first part of the *Autobiography* is spontaneous; thereafter Franklin, encouraged by James's and Vaughan's letters, is writing consciously for a larger public. Even so, the rhetorical figures he employs are less intricate than those in, say, the letter to the press or the bagatelle, and the tropes are seldom conceited. Although it may seem at first glance that he is here returning to the plainer manner of his early years, inevitably this late and most ambitious of his writings sometimes exhibits the polemical and epistolary styles he had cultivated in the meantime.

Although the chapter organization of this study might

suggest that Franklin maintained a sharp distinction at all times between public and private utterance, in actual fact he moved back and forth between them instinctively and with ease, letting them interact in ways that vitalize his literary expression. For example, on the same day that he composed the treaty letter for Mme Brillon, he was presumably working on one of the many drafts of the preliminary peace treaty with England; for another, since he regarded Polly Stevenson as both pupil and friend, sometimes scientific explanations, which would have been of general interest, are followed in the same letter by gossip, which could have interested no one but Polly and her closest friends. Such vigorous movement between and within his writings saves them from sinking into the stereotypes inherent in too unimaginative an exercise of neoclassical theory.

The stylistic ideals John Hughes set forth in his neoclassic manifesto of 1698 anticipated Franklin's literary theory and expression. A concern for propriety led him to suit his writings, the bagatelles for example, to a wide range of audiences; instinctively he found his way to the style or styles—anecdotal, aphoristic, bawdy, conceited, polemical—that the occasion demanded. As time went on he esteemed purity of language more and more highly, refining his diction away from colloquial, archaic, and provincial English toward one more reputable, current, and national. In the interest of perspicuity he often revised his syntax and diction, and he sharpened the meaning of his proverbial borrowings. Recognizing the value of elegance, he nevertheless confined himself to those tropes the response to which he could most easily control. Cadence he achieved through the skillful management of rhetorical figures like repetition, exclamation, parallelism, and balance. His native instinct toward plain prose underlay such neoclassic observance, however, and was never wholly submerged by it. So it happens that the *Dogood* and *Busy-Body* papers, because they are addressed to Boston and Philadelphia artisans, not coffeehouse wits, are plainer than the *Tatler* and *Spectator* and clearly American in manner and matter. While respectful of neoclassic precept, Franklin was no more a slave to it than were Addison and Swift; as each of them evolved an effective English idiom which made for a vigorous and individual style, so he his very different American idiom.

From his youth onward Franklin possessed powers of literary invention. His imagination, let it be emphasized, was not romantic but classic, the sort that could devise metaphysical conceits for intimate friends and ironic modes of expression for political audiences at home and abroad. Nowhere is this imaginative energy more forcefully displayed and better sustained than in the range and vitality of the personae he created. Honest, unsophisticated, inquisitive, his American characters are more authentic than such later examples as Diedrich Knickerbocker and Hosea Biglow in that they are composed by an insider and lie closer to the folk. Passed through the alembic of their author's imagination, the scandalmonger and the tradesman of colonial times emerge as the comic creations, Alice Addertongue and Anthony Afterwit. The personae conceived before 1757 wear a comic mask, Richard Saunders' hoax on Titan Leeds marking this early mood at its most playful. The later personae, notably the situational masks in "The Sale of the Hessians" and "On the Slave Trade," are frequently delineated in ironic terms. Coincident with this darker manner, the matter grows more serious. Except for Silence Dogood, and then only overtly in the eighth and ninth papers, the early characters confine themselves to social observations; after 1757, when Franklin was so heavily engaged in affairs of state, the emphasis is political. The rich variety of personae he presented in the American and European press over the space of nearly seventy years is one of the clearest proofs that Benjamin Franklin was indeed an important American man of letters.

APPENDIX, BIBLIOGRAPHICAL

NOTE, AND INDEX

Appendix

AMONG "the residue and remainder of all [the] books, manuscripts, and papers" that William Temple Franklin inherited from his grandfather in 1790 was the holograph of the *Autobiography*. Temple did not publish his version of the *Autobiography* until 1818, and then apparently he based this the first official English edition on the Le Veillard fair copy of Parts I–III. Since the Le Veillard and Vaughan copies may now be presumed lost, it is impossible to reconstruct the fair-copy text. However, the existence of the Buisson translation (*Mémoires de la vie privée de Benjamin Franklin* [Paris, 1791]) and that of Le Veillard (which survives in manuscript at the Library of Congress) makes it possible to speculate with a measure of certainty about Franklin's final intention, though it must be added that in view of his advanced age and steadily declining health he began to distrust his own judgment in the final months of his life and was not always certain what the final wording should be.

In 1949 the Parallel Text Edition appeared, comprising the texts of the original manuscript, the Buisson and Le Veillard versions, and that edited by Temple. Having granted that (1) the original manuscript is the most important of the four texts, Max Farrand assigns the following priority to the other three:

> The fair copies embodied changes which, it must be assumed, were made with Franklin's tacit or expressed approval. . . . One of them was probably used by Franklin's grandson for printer's copy, and (2) the Temple Franklin text is, therefore, the best obtainable. Next in importance is (3) the French translation of Part I, published by Buisson in 1791, which must have been derived from a fair copy and may be used to support or refute the Temple Franklin text. . . . Finally, there is (4) Le Veillard's translation, made at least in part from a fair copy but revised from the original manuscript. This translation must carry great weight when supporting the wording of a fair copy, for it means that Le Veillard thought Franklin wished it to read in that way (p. xxxvii).

In the Preface to the *Autobiography of Benjamin Franklin* (Philadelphia, 1868), the first edition to be based on the original manuscript and the one which superseded the Temple Franklin version to become the generally accepted edition, John Bigelow charged that Temple had mutilated his grandfather's manuscript. The appearance of the Parallel Text Edition affords us the first clear opportunity to test the validity of this charge.

Jack C. Barnes, in his unpublished dissertation "Benjaman Franklin and His Memoirs," makes use of the Parallel Text Edition to exonerate Temple. Examining the Buisson text side by side with the original manuscript and the Temple Franklin version, he advances the hypothesis that the revisions in the Temple Franklin Edition, generally attributed to him, must in fact have been the work of his grandfather. Barnes thinks it "safe to conclude that Temple was a fair, honest editor who carefully followed the copy before him. It is true, of course, that he was responsible for modernizing a few spellings, altering some punctuation, and abandoning the earlier practice of capitalizing nouns, to which Franklin held tenaciously; but such liberties seem unimportant" (p. 70). It is his contention that probably the closest we can come to an authentic text is that of the Temple Franklin version, supplemented by Part IV of the original manuscript—a contention voiced long ago by Richard M. Bache, in the *Pennsylvania Magazine of History and Biography* (XXIV [1900], 195–199).

I am strongly inclined to support this view. Confining my examination to Part I, I matched the Buisson reading against that of the original manuscript and of the Temple Franklin version to discover where it tipped the balance toward the one or the other. Out of 111 points at which the diction of these two texts differ, Buisson supports Temple in 59 cases and the original manuscript in only 36, while failing to tip the balance either way in the remaining 16. While Buisson supports only 8 of 23 deletions from the original made in the Temple Franklin version, it supports 10 out of 12 additions made in Temple Franklin. Finally, Buisson supports 7 out of 9 important syntactical changes made by Temple. The weight of this evidence, though certainly not decisive, seemed to me sufficiently impressive to warrant the analysis of certain syntactical and verbal changes undertaken on pages 229–237.

Bibliographical Note

WHEN completed some years hence, *The Papers of Benjamin Franklin,* ed. Leonard W. Labaree and Others (New Haven, 1959———), will supersede all existing editions; seven volumes, covering the period down to March 31, 1758, have been published to date. For the period following this date, *The Writings of Benjamin Franklin,* ed. Albert H. Smyth (10 vols.; New York and London, 1905–1907), remains the most nearly definitive edition; but since Smyth failed to include a good many documents now known to be by Franklin and included bowdlerized versions of others, I have frequently turned to the manuscripts and to printed sources more reliable than Smyth in an effort to ground this study in what is currently thought to be the full and textually accurate canon of Franklin's writings. In preparing Chapter I, I made use of drafts of the letters from Anthony Afterwit, Celia Single, and Alice Addertongue and "On the Providence of God in the Government of the World" in a Commonplace Book [1731–1732?] at the Historical Society of Pennsylvania and a draft of "Remarks Concerning the Savages of North America" at the Library of Congress. In succeeding chapters I have quoted from manuscripts located at the American Philosophical Society Library: in Chapter IV, the fragment "Courage, Britains!"; in Chapter V, the Franklin-Stevenson-Hewson correspondence; in Chapter VI, the Franklin-Brillon correspondence; in Chapter VII, "The Cravenstreet Gazette." In preparing Chapter VIII I consulted a photostatic copy of the Huntington MS of the *Autobiography*. Other than the Labaree and Smyth editions, the following printed sources have been drawn upon: in Chapter II, a photostatic copy of the *New-England Courant* (Massachusetts Historical Society: Boston, 1924–1925) and a microfilm of the *Pennsylvania Gazette* (Historical Society of Pennsylvania: Philadelphia, 1941); in Chapter IV, *Benjamin Franklin's Letters to the Press, 1758–1775,* ed. Verner W. Crane (Chapel Hill, 1950); in Chapter V, *Benjamin Franklin's Autobiographical Writings,* ed. Carl Van Doren (New York, 1945), *Benjamin Franklin and Catharine Ray Greene: Their Correspondence, 1755–1790,* ed. William G. Roelker (Philadelphia, 1949), *The Letters of Benjamin Franklin and Jane Mecom,* ed. Carl Van Doren (Princeton, 1950), and Whitfield J. Bell, Jr., "'All Clear Sunshine': New Letters of Franklin and Mary Stevenson Hewson," *Proc. APS,* C (1956), 521–536; in Chapter VI, A.H. Smyth, "Franklin's Social Life in France," *Putnam's Monthly and The Critic,* I (1906–1907), 30–41, 167–173, 310–316, 431–438, and W. C. Ford, "One of Franklin's Friendships," *Harper's Monthly Magazine,* CXIII (1906), 626–633—articles which contain English translations of letters in the Franklin-Brillon correspondence; in Chapter VII, *Franklin's Wit and Folly,* ed. Richard E. Amacher (New Brunswick, 1953), J. G. Rosengarten, "Franklin's Bagatelles," *Proc. APS,* XL (1901), 87–135, Gilbert Chinard, "Random Notes on Two 'Bagatelles,'" *Proc. APS,* CIII (1959), 727–760, and Max Hall, *Benjamin Franklin and Polly Baker* (Chapel Hill, 1960); and in Chapter VIII, *Benjamin Franklin's Memoirs. Parallel Text Edition,* ed. Max Farrand (Berkeley and Los Angeles, 1949).

Two bibliographical aids proved invaluable: Paul Leicester Ford, *Franklin Bibliography: A List of Books Written by, or Relating to Benjamin Franklin* (Brooklyn, 1889) and I. Minis Hays, *Calendar of the Papers of Benjamin Franklin in the Library of the American Philosophical Society* (6 vols.; Philadelphia, 1908). The most useful biographical studies were James Parton, *Life and Times of Benjamin Franklin* (2 vols.; Boston and New York, 1864); Carl Van Doren, *Benjamin Franklin* (New York, 1938); and Alfred Owen Aldridge, *Franklin and His French Contemporaries* (New York, 1957). Finally I am indebted to two unpublished doctoral dissertations completed at the University of Maryland: Robert Howard Newcomb, "The Sources of Benjamin Franklin's Sayings of Poor Richard" (1957) and Jack C. Barnes, "Benjamin Franklin and His Memoirs" (1954).

A complete entry for these and all other primary and secondary sources is given in the footnotes the first time each is cited.

Index

INDEX